Freud and the Culture of Psychoanalysis

of Psychoanalysis

*Studies in the Transition from
Victorian Humanism to Modernity*

Steven Marcus

W · W · NORTON & COMPANY
New York · London

To my son, John

First published as a Norton paperback 1987 by arrangement with
George Allen & Unwin (Publishers) Ltd,
40 Museum Street, London WC1A 1LU, UK

Published simultaneously in Canada by Penguin Books Canada Ltd,
2801 John Street, Markham, Ontario L3R 1B4.

ISBN 0-393-30410-8

W. W. Norton & Company, Inc., 500 Fifth Avenue, New York, N.Y. 10110
W. W. Norton & Company Ltd., 37 Great Russell Street, London WC1B 3NU

1 2 3 4 5 6 7 8 9 0

Contents

Acknowledgements

I should like to thank the Rockefeller Foundation for a Fellowship in the Humanities, and I should like to thank the National Humanities Center for a Fellowship as well. These grants, and the free time they made possible, enabled me to finish this book. At the National Humanities Center, I should like in particular to thank Karen Carroll and Jan Paton for their unflagging and cheerful help with typing and other problems that a manuscript of any length inevitably entails. Parts of this book have previously appeared elsewhere in *Partisan Review* and *Grand Street*.

Introduction

As the twentieth century moves through its last two decades, it becomes increasingly evident that the figure of Sigmund Freud remains as one of a very small handfull of intellectual presences who have presided over the complex courses that Western thought and culture have taken throughout the entire epoch. His reputation and place in the history of the modern world have never stood higher or enjoyed a firmer security than they do today. That this extraordinary position of intellectual pre-eminence in modern life should be occupied by a Victorian physician from Vienna is only one among many of the odd circumstances about the extremely odd world we have come to both occupy and not adequately understand.

Although Freud's pre-eminence is, for the moment, assured, the locus that such distinction occupies is by no means to be pointed to with equal certitude. Freud remains a figure around whom considerable controversy still revolves – though he is, of course, no longer an object of notoriety. It is difficult to imagine how the matter could be otherwise. To begin with, Freud's contributions range across an immense variety of disciplinary and professional intellectual activities. Some of them remain located in various domains of the natural, physical and biological sciences and are pertinent to research recently done and currently being carried on in the study of sleep and dreaming, in infantile and childhood development and in human sexuality. Some of them remain pertinent to both current research and practice in medicine, in particular in psychiatry, and in the endlessly proliferating non-medical branches of psychotherapy as well. Some of his contributions have been long since internalized in a number of the social sciences. And others have found enduring salience in the humanities. This distribution has never been and is not today a stable one; and one of the more interesting debates in current philosophical writings entails a long-continuing, but recently heated-up, dispute about the epistemological character or status of Freud's writings themselves and of psychoanalysis as a whole. I am in no position to do more than observe this argument and to comment upon its general interest; any pronouncement or judgement on such matters would be, on my part, entirely an impertinence. For the purposes of the present volume, however, Freud's writings and the psychoanalytic discipline of which they are the foundations are considered as part of the cultural sciences, as a cultural science themselves, or as an interpretative discipline.

To put it in other terms, in this volume of studies Freud is regarded as a writer or cultural figure. What I mean by this remark requires clarification. I do not discuss Freud as a stylist or writer of German prose. I discuss him as a writer in the sense that he addresses parts of experience through creating structures in written language that purport to represent, analyze and make sustained coherence out of those experiences by means of their translation or transposition into such constructions of exposition, narrative, analysis, argument, or case history as he finds appropriate. Moreover, and more specifically, I have undertaken to present a Freud who, beginning as a Victorian physician, early neuro-scientist, late-nineteenth-century minister of therapies to the neurotically afflicted, writer and humanist, becomes in the course of his development one of the paramount figures in the impulsion behind and movement of the Western world into its decisive phase of twentieth-century modernity. The essays in this volume are, I hope, contributions to our understanding of how certain of these momentous – indeed revolutionary – changes were in some important part negotiated.

The first chapter is accordingly a re-examination of Freud's most important set of letters, his early correspondence with his friend and colleague, Wilhelm Fliess. In this one-sided flow of communications (Fliess's letters did not survive the dissolution of their association) one can see with an unexampled perspicuousness the intellectual and emotional urgings, forces and conflicts that were at work in the youthfully mature Freud, as the first original insights and discoveries that constituted the inception of psychoanalysis as a theory, discipline of inquiry, and new kind of therapy, came suddenly, often unexpectedly and without being bidden, upon him.

This essay is followed by a discussion of Freud's early, small masterpiece, *Three Essays on the Theory of Sexuality*. Together with the much more frequently examined *The Interpretation of Dreams*, this work forms the central segment of Freud's first general theoretical scheme or paradigm; and I have undertaken a critical analysis of its structure, argument, and significance. I have tried to demonstrate how this speculative and theoretical triad of essays generates the most exceptional consequences upon our conceptions of personal life, of childhood, and of human development. In my view, no work of its kind or scope is more important for the understanding of how modernity – or the generally recognized modern point of view – came into being or was brought about. As one reads it, one can almost see certain vital parts of modernity in the very processes of disclosure, formation and construction.

Chapters 3 and 4 are the longest sections of the book and consist of literary critical analyses of two of Freud's great case histories. The first of these, which deals with the case of Dora, focuses mainly, though not exclusively, on the central role of narrative in Freud's view of the human world, on his early methods and insights and on some of his mistakes (as well as on some of his most dazzling moments), especially when it came to the understanding of women and the phenomenon of what has come to be known as the transference. The second has to do with the immensely more complex case of the Rat Man, an intricately psychological analysis of an entirely psychological neurosis – an obsessional neurosis can exist without the physical conversion symptoms that generally characterize hysteria – which does not reduce itself to coherent narrative form or structure. It deals hence, and perforce, with what strategies of understanding, therapy, and writing Freud took to when he was confronted with a case or a case history that did not easily, naturally, inevitably, or eventually turn itself out as or into a story. This analysis has, in addition, some further bearings on literary theory in an era – such as the present – in which the great authority that narrative once asserted historically in our culture has for the time being been suspended.

There follow two chapters on psychoanalytic theory and cultural change. The first of these concentrates on the development of Freud's theory of the super-ego, and on how that intrapsychic and largely unconscious institution, being the last of the major agencies of the unconscious mind to come into developmental being, is the most accessible to influence by the enveloping medium of culture; it goes on to suggest, and I hope to demonstrate, that the current epidemic of narcissistic or super-ego-deficient neurotic disorders may be understood as a function of changes in the social culture, and adduces as well certain innovations and formulations in recent psychoanalytic theory that move towards an explanation of such alterations in the dominant presenting symptomatology. The second of this pair of studies has to do with certain developments in English cultural and intellectual history in the mid-nineteenth century which I have read or interpreted as precursors in a number of senses of the changes that were discussed in the immediately foregoing chapter. They are also regarded as a commentary upon such changes, and the chapter itself has an additional sub-theme, which is the phenomenon of cultural change as a field of humanistic inquiry in itself.

The last full chapter in the book is about Freud and biography. In no region of cultural activity has Freud exerted a more profound and lasting influence on modern consciousness. He has affected our notions of biography itself as a genre, as the structured, written form taken by or given to a human life; because he has changed our notions of what constitutes the centers of significance in each human existence, he has also changed our conceptions of the significance of each such existence as a whole. Moreover, he is himself one of the most arresting of biographical subjects – and is an exemplary figure in the contemporary evolution of the biographical genre, including many of its problems and problematics. The chapter is divided into four sections. The first and last of these sections deal with Freud himself as a subject of revisionist biography; and such topics as the transference effect that Freud has on those who study him biographically are touched upon, as are more recent developments, such as the increasing interest in the external facts of Freud's life, the searching among students of biography for hidden or unsavory biographical episodes or events that concern Freud, and the continuing interest in the early history of the psychoanalytic movement, a movement that is itself inseparable from Freud's life story – after a certain point the movement may be said in fact to have become the most important part of that story. The second and third parts of this chapter are discussions of biographies of figures who are related to Freud – first, his English contemporary, the student of sexual behavior, Havelock Ellis; and second, the dissident American psychiatrist and psychoanalyst, Harry Stack Sullivan. The biographies of these figures are regarded within the context of how biographical studies have themselves been changed by the work of Freud.

The book ends with a short postscript, which consists in the main of some moderately gloomy reflections on the state of the institution of psychoanalysis today. Yet such animadversions and reservations serve largely as well to throw into still sharper relief the permanent significance of Freud the writer and thinker. That significance has never been more perceptible or more striking than it is today, almost 100 years after his central life's work began. It is the purpose of the following volume of studies to cast some new light on certain sides of that work and to understand it as part of a series of changes that our culture has both created and passed through. These changes have by no means come to an end.

New York City
November, 1982

Note on References

All references to the writings of Freud, unless otherwise indicated, are to *The Standard Edition of the Complete Psychological Works of Sigmund Freud*, translated from the German under the General

Editorship of James Strachey, in collaboration with Anna Freud, assisted by Alix Strachey and Alan Tyson, XXIV vols., London, 1953-1974.

When for purposes of clarity, meaning or literary nuance, the translations had to be checked against the German originals, the following edition was referred to: *Sigmund Freud: Gesammelte Werke*, edited by Anna Freud with the collaboration of Marie Bonaparte (and others), XVIII vols., London and Frankfurt am Main, 1940-1968.

1 The Origins of Psycho-analysis Revisited

Although such large and general topics as "The Relation of Psychoanalysis to Morals" or "The Influence of Psychoanalysis on Moral Values" are of the greatest interest and of enduring pertinence, I find that discussion of such matters is most usefully conducted when it is confined within a more modest and manageable scope. In this connection I should like to examine some of the scientific, medical, cultural, and personal circumstances out of which this new discipline arose. And I should like to sketch briefly how it arose out of them. That this nexus was highly charged with moral or ethical implications and that what emerged from them has bearings upon our large or general conceptions of what constitutes moral life is, I should suggest, not a matter for argument.

Since I am a literary critic, I have chosen to focus my attention on a text. That text consists of the letters, notes, and drafts that Freud wrote and sent to Wilhelm Fliess between 1887 and 1902. It is an incomplete text because of the 284 surviving documents only 168 were published in *The Origins of Psychoanalysis*, which first appeared in German in 1950 and in English in 1954.[1] It is further incomplete in the sense that significant parts of some of the 168 published documents have been edited out – some of these parts can be recovered in Ernest Jones's biography and in Max Schur's *Freud: Living and Dying*. And it is incomplete as well in the sense that no parts of Fliess's side of this intense correspondence and lengthy relationship in writing seem to have survived. Nevertheless, most texts are incomplete in one sense or another. All texts are constructions, and the student of literature soon becomes accustomed to the awareness that one of the central problematics of his discipline has to do with what it is that constitutes a text. Once one has put aside the accepted conventions about what a text is, a theoretical snake-pit opens up. I will not at this point enter such a snake-pit, but will content myself with observing that just as there is hardly a text worth considering that does not present us with problems – and problems about its own theoretical status – so too there is nothing to deter us from treating a set of letters and related documents, even an edited set, as a text as well. As long as we preserve the integrity of such a text as we have (and here I am departing from certain currents of advanced contemporary critical practice) we are no more constrained than we are when we deal with a play by Shakespeare, a novel by Dickens, an autobiography by, say, John Stuart Mill or Thomas Carlyle, or a journal by Gerard Manley Hopkins. So I think that without more ado we can turn to the text in question.

The letters that Sigmund Freud wrote to Wilhelm Fliess between 1887 and 1902, along with the notes, drafts, and other material that Freud included with those letters, make up an extraordinary account. They constitute a singular record of creative discovery in Western thought, and are indispensable to our understanding of how psychoanalysis – itself a unique development of Western civilization – was brought into being. That development may be appropriately regarded as a culmination of the particular tradition of introspection which began with the adjuration of the oracle at Delphi to "Know thyself." This rationally governed method of self-examination takes as its principal objects of scrutiny everything within us that is not rational – our affects, our instinctual strivings, our fears, fancies, dreams and nightmares, our guilts, our endless reproachfulness, our sexual obsessions, our uncontrollable aggressions.[2] And it is more than a fortunate accident that this most highly developed form of Western secular introspection should have returned at one of its moments of climactic breaking-through to its cultural origins. When Freud in October 1897 writes that "I have found love of the mother and jealousy of the father in my own case too, and now believe it to be a general phenomenon of early childhood," and then goes on at once to discuss *Oedipus Rex*, one senses reverberations of profound historical depth. An organic line of cultural evolution is being brought to a decisive moment of conclusion. That conclusion represents the attainment of a new degree of consciousness in Western civilization. Yet this new or higher degree of consciousness resumes what has gone before, incorporates and reintegrates its past and intervening history, and by thus returning to its original point of departure simultaneously moves forward into a future that has been significantly altered.[3]

The Freud we meet in these documents is the person within whom this historical drama of development first occurred. At the outset he was certainly not consciously prepared for the direction in which such a development would lead him. He was a young neurologist or neuropathologist with a generous range of interests and high ambitions. He had already published scientific papers on a variety of topics – including the use of cocaine – and had in Paris come under the influence of Charcot, whose notions about hysteria and sexuality he had accepted. He was also interested in the new discoveries that were taking place in the study of the anatomy of the brain and the nervous system, and in such related pathologies as aphasia and the battery of afflictions that accompanied syphilis in its advanced states. One large connection between these pathologies and the neuroses, in particular hysteria, was that they tended to mimic each other. Hysterically distorted speech or hysterical loss of speech functions often was indistinguishable from the reduced or deformed speech functions of persons who had, from one cause or another, incurred damage of the brain. And vice versa. The blindnesses, paralyses, tics, lamenesses, spasms, pains, and phantom sensations of hysteria were all produced as well by syphilis in its tertiary phase. Indeed the nineteenth-century epidemics of venereal disease and hysteria were connected in a number of intimate ways. Not only was their symptomatology often convertible and interchangeable, but they often tended as well to occur coincidentally or in tandem, and in the same persons. The cultural and moral history of these entities still remains to be written.

The other conditions with which neurologists largely occupied themselves – apart from what today are regarded as actual neurological illnesses – were obsessions, phobias, depressions of certain magnitudes, paranoia in its milder forms, and a variety of symptoms that were bundled together to form the syndromes of neurasthenia and anxiety neurosis. These conditions had a number of attributes in common – apart from the circumstance that no one understood them. One such attribute was essentially negative: they were all in some sense residua, left behind or overlooked by German psychiatry, which at that time and point in its historical development was almost exclusively concerned with psychoses and the other more florid and spectacular conditions of mental disorder. Such conditions all seemed, in addition, sooner or later to have something to do with sexuality, but this common feature too was understood, if that is the right word, in a primitive and unformed sense. The store of therapeutic measures that was available to the young Freud was equally rudimentary. The traditional pharmacopia was of very limited use. Other current resources or treatments of choice were electrogalvanic sessions, hydropathic or water cures, and rest cures of differing descriptions. Hypnotism was relied on by some, and Freud experimented with it, as he did with just about everything else. In addition to hypnotism accompanied by suggestion, there was also therapy by suggestion alone, and Freud seemed at the outset to rely on these two procedures as much as on any others. As he wryly observes to Fliess in one of the early letters, "Talking people into and out of things ... is what my work consists of." Occasionally some of these methods worked, but no one knew why. More often they failed to make any difference, but again it was generally beyond anyone's power of explanation to say why a particular treatment didn't work in particular cases. As Freud's remark suggests, it was by no means a satisfactory state of affairs – neither therapeutically nor theoretically.

It was by no means a satisfactory state of affairs culturally either. Situated as he was, Freud could not help but observe and be struck by what appears to have been the plague that had settled upon the sexual lives of the middle classes in the latter part of the nineteenth century. The early letters to Fliess, like other medical writings about sexuality of the same period, and like much contemporary literature – such as the novels of Hardy and Gissing or the plays of Ibsen – all refract the same sexual climate of gloom, frustration, fear, muted despair, and moral uncertainty and bafflement. For example, quite early on, Freud connects neurasthenic impotence in men with a history of masturbation, and then connects in turn hysteria in women with neurasthenic sexual inadequacy in men: if worn-out men excite but cannot satisfy women, hysteria is the result. It is not quite to the point to say that Freud was mistaken; the value of these early formulations lies in what they suggest to us about the material that Freud was observing. In a similar way Freud was at first concerned with the adverse effects that *coitus interruptus* seemed to have on both middle-class men and women, and collaterally the even wider adverse effects that the absence of any innocuous form of contraception seemed to threaten. "In the absence of such a solution," he wrote at the beginning of 1893, "society seems doomed to fall a victim to incurable neuroses which reduce the enjoyment of life to a minimum, destroy the marriage relation and bring hereditary ruin on the whole coming generation." And in the same document he declares that even though neuroses can be prevented, they are at the same time "completely incurable." He was soon to change his mind on this matter; nevertheless, from the very beginning Freud made and continued to make a firm connection between his patients' range of distresses and states of distress in their sexuality.[4] Although he was at first able to explain very little about either the etiology or the dynamics of his patients' unhappy circumstances, he was also unable to overlook what he had observed or had strongly inferred: namely, that the neuroses in all their differences were all connected in some profound but as yet undisclosed way by disturbances of sexuality. Having made this observation and inference he clung to the connections they pointed to with what would later prove to be characteristic tenacity. Others at the time had made similar connections. Yet, the question remained: what could result from these connections; to what did they lead; how was one to proceed?

Freud begins by trying to describe and classify the various afflicted states that come before his attention, and tries at first to find a simple, physical causal explanation for the various neuroses. For example, in

1893 he tried to explain anxiety attacks as a direct result of sexual experience, adducing the case "of a gay old bachelor, who denies himself nothing." This patient, Freud continued, produced "a classic attack after allowing his 30-year-old mistress to induce him to have coitus three times. I have come to the opinion that anxiety is to be connected, not with a mental, but with a physical consequence of sexual abuse." And indeed Freud's first psychological explanation of anxiety as either dammed-up libido or as a transformation of it may be properly regarded as a derivative of this still-earlier view. These physical or physiological theories had to do with notions of stimulus, excitation, building up of hydraulic pressures or electrical charges or sexual substances, and with such other notions as discharge, equilibrium, homeostasis, constancy, and the like. One sees Freud in these letters and drafts beginning again and again with such ideas and being led inexorably away from them by the complexity of the psychic states that he encountered accompanying them. This is to say that the physiological theories that were available to Freud were simply and finally inadequate to deal with the richness of the psychic material produced by his patients. Freud did not move willingly towards the establishment of an independent psychology. He moved slowly and reluctantly, and one of the outstanding achievements of this early period, his long-unpublished "Project for a Scientific Psychology" of 1895, is clearly a work of genius. It is an effort to construct a unified systematic theory of the mind, rising in an unbroken set of connected stages from neurones to complex psychic states; it is not less than an effort to solve or transcend the mind-body duality, and it was, of course, abandoned. Nevertheless, after having given up this heroic undertaking and turned toward the slow and laborious construction of an autonomous psychology, Freud never forgot that the mind was in fact in the body; furthermore, by making questions of sexuality central to his psychology he made it certain that his chances of ever transcending this overriding duality remained minimal. And indeed one can say that in no other psychology is the mind-body relation so inclusively and centrally a presence as in Freud's.

Since its first publication in 1950, the "Project" has come in for a good deal of comment and considerable praise from such students of modern neuro-science as Pribram, and perhaps a further word on it might at this point be appropriate. The theory is based on the neurones, which had been discovered in 1891, and the model it follows is taken from neuroanatomy. It posits at first two systems of neurones, permeable and impermeable, and a series of "contact barriers" that separate and join them (the synapse had not yet been described). It has to do with such notions as energy, inertia, and homeostasis, and in particular focuses upon Q, or the electrical energy that builds up in and innervates the nervous system. Hence Freud's later notion of "psychic energy" has a clear physicalist base or origin. The energy in question is biological, or electrical energy as it exists in a biological organism. It is not directly mechanical or Newtonian energy. And indeed the not quite unambiguous use to which Freud puts this notion of energy permits him to avoid the crude dualism of conceiving of the human body on the one hand as mere mechanism or machinery and the human mind or person on the other as conscious, willing, and goal-directed.

Yet when Freud abandons the "Project" he does not return to some simple Cartesian dualism either – to a dualism, say, of psychology and neurology. What he does is to retain the neuro-physiological "hydraulic" model of energy, resistance, discharge, inertia, storage and so on – but what he gives up is the *neuroanatomical* model, and the concomitant effort to locate such physiological processes in determinate anatomical positions in the central nervous system. Instead of that he substitutes a virtually or conceptually spatial "psychic apparatus" which acts as a kind of functional isomorph of the abandoned neuroanatomical model; this "psychic apparatus" provided him with a means of making functional localizations of psychic processes without committing him to discovering specific parts of the brain wherein this apparatus was localized. Yet he never at the same time gave up on the primary model except, as he said, "for the present." He believed that some day – in the neuro-science of the twenty-third century perhaps – the systems of his psychic apparatus would in fact, in some as yet unimagined way, be localized.

I have always found something quite moving in this complex set of strategic maneuvers managed by Freud. He remained a materialist without going over to some kind of positivism or systematic reductionism. He developed an autonomous psychology without committing himself either to idealism or to some form of Cartesian dualism. He remained loyal to the idea of science – even as the science of the late nineteenth century thought of itself – and his loyalty has, I believe, been rewarded. If I ask myself why I am so moved by these complex and sometimes obscure conceptual shiftings-about, I am prompted to reply that Freud's intellectual commitment and adherence to the idea of science has a profoundly moral component to it.

This vexed and difficult set of passages may be momentarily summed up as follows. Freud did not, on the one hand, make a reduction of the mental to the physical; and he did not, on the other hand, use these physical motives simply and solely as convenient explanatory models for mental functions. Nor did he merely trim his sails and settle for some compromise in between. It was the inadequacy of the physiological theories then available to Freud that moved him towards the creation of an autonomous psychology; he would never have taken the position that all physiological accounts of mental functioning were by definition bound to be inadequate. His belief in science was far too strong for that. At the same time, even though "the mind was in fact in the body," Freud did not describe the mind as a physical system, though he did use "energic" terms to describe the workings of the psychic apparatus.

If I may be permitted to use an analogy from literature, Freud seems to me, in this very large and general connection, to have demonstrated his powers of what Keats describes as "negative capability." "Brown and Rilke walked with me and back from the Christmas pantomime. I had not a dispute but disquisition, with Rilke on various subjects; several things dovetailed in my mind, and at once it struck me what quality went to form a Man of Achievement, especially in Literature, and which Shakespeare possessed so enormously – I mean *Negative Capability*, that is, when a man is capable of being in uncertainties, mysteries, doubts, without any irritable reaching after facts and reason – Coleridge, for instance, would let go by a fine verisimilitude caught from the penetralia of mystery, from being incapable of remaining content with half-knowledge."[5]

Freud's correspondent and interlocutor was admirably qualified to be the witness of such a complex journey of discovery. Wilhelm Fliess was also fascinated by the mind–body relation, and made its mysteries the center of all his researches and theories. With his hypotheses of nasal reflex neuroses and of the arithmetical periodicities that governed the course of all human – and even non-human – existence, Fliess was precisely the right kind of person on whom Freud could securely try out his new insights, theoretical flights and systematic wild hunches. The careful reader of the documents I have been discussing can hardly escape the realization that for many of the years covered by these documents, Freud was something of a scientific wild man, a "conquistador or adventurer" as he described his own temperament. Great creative geniuses often are, and it was a necessity of Freud's nature that he needed a male companion to accompany him on his forays into the darker regions of mental existence. His friendship and professional alliance with Josef Breuer had come to an end on just these grounds; Breuer was unable to go along with Freud's embarrassing insistence upon the central importance of sexuality. Fliess took Breuer's place as Freud's confidant and *alter ego*. He was much younger than Breuer and two years younger than Freud. He was quite unembarrassed by considerations of sexuality; in fact he led Freud to place the notion of the bisexuality of all human beings close to the center of his theoretical system. Fliess was a scientific wild man as well; he was not, however, a genius, and his theories were not transmuted under the influence of new insight and experience, as Freud's were, and thereby made to conform more adequately to the differentially relative requirements of science, medicine, or psychology. Fliess's theories remained wild, were elaborated in ever more flamboyant displays of explanatory epicycles, and ended up as a kind of monomania. The occasion that provided the impetus for the final break-up of this most important friendship of Freud's life was, appropriately, a profound theoretical difference, which in this instance, as in others, had certain moral bearings; Fliess insisted upon believing that the arithmetical and numerological laws of periodicity governed everything, including psychopathology. Such a belief was clearly incompatible with Freud's developing notions of psychic determinism – notions that asserted whatever might *ultimately* be true about the physical laws that govern all phenomena, in our present state of knowledge mental existence has certain autonomous functions, and most mental activities can be traced no farther than to antecedent determinations that are themselves psychic.[6] When Fliess remarked accusingly of Freud (and to him) that "the thought-reader [Freud] reads only his own thoughts in those of others," the time to break had come. It was an appropriate pretext to end a relation that had been going downhill for some time. Freud parted company with Fliess when his friend was no longer able adequately to sustain the mind–body duality, and when he insisted upon depriving one side of that relation of its due importance and complexity.

Freud's friendship with Fliess was close, intense, richly personal as well as intellectual and deeply intimate. Though the two men met at irregular intervals, at what Freud liked to call "congresses," the relation was sustained in large measure through their correspondence. Of the 284 letters written by Freud to Fliess that have survived, all but 40 were written in the years 1893–1900, the period of highest intensity in their friendship. Looking back upon that friendship from the perspective that Freud's own discoveries has enabled us to achieve, we can perceive that it was in the main constituted out of transference-like characteristics. Freud overvalued and idealized the intelligence, originality, and powers of judgement of his friend. He consulted Fliess about his own health and submitted to Fliess's medical advice as if his ear-nose-and-throat friend in Berlin were Aesculapius himself. He kept his own critical faculties in abeyance as far as Fliess was concerned. He looked to him for approval, and he dreamed about him – some of the dreams are included in *The Interpretation of Dreams*. Naturally and unavoidably certain neurotic processes were involved in this relationship, and among the many things these letters permit us to observe are the points of connection between such processes and Freud's creativity during this period. As they also allow us to observe the gradual disentanglement of the two. Freud's relation with Fliess was an essential and enabling part of that creativity. His resolution of that relation brings this major phase of his career to a close. With the publication in 1900 of *The Interpretation of Dreams*, Freud had reached a new plateau, an intellectual elevation from which he could regard large parts of the human world afresh.

The path he followed to reach that goal was not direct but circuitous, as these documents amply demonstrate. Freud was only gradually to be convinced of the primary independence of psychic reality. He began with materialist views and physicalist assumptions, and he was in no hurry to abandon them. The first stage in that evolution, as we have already seen, was represented by the "Project" of 1895 – and by the fact that Freud gave it up. The second, and more dramatic, stage occurred in 1897. In working with his neurotic patients, Freud kept continually coming across accounts produced by them that pointed to certain sexual experiences in childhood, in particular among his female patients with accounts that pointed to experiences of seduction perpetrated upon them by their fathers. Freud took these accounts at face value, and proceeded thereupon to construct a theory of neuroses which had at its genetic center the actual experience of sexual seduction in childhood; at one of its dynamic centers was the idea that such patients were unable adequately to react to, or "abreact," the traumatic excitement of those experiences. This incapacity somehow to achieve a "discharge" of such highly stimulated states, even though such states remained behind as mental representations, such as memories, fantasies, and dreams, was itself based on a physical model, and indeed the same states in question converted themselves into the bodily symptoms of hysteria. In September 1897 Freud wrote to Fliess that he had been compelled to give up his theory that he had been building up for some years. The letter merits quoting at length:

> Let me tell you straight away the great secret . . . I no longer believe in my *neurotica*. That is hardly intelligible without an explanation; you yourself found what I told you credible. So I shall start at the beginning and tell you the whole story of how the reasons for rejecting it arose. The first group of factors were the continual

disappointment of my attempts to bring my analyses to a real conclusion, the running away of people who for a time had seemed my most favourably inclined patients, the lack of the complete success on which I had counted, and the possibility of explaining my partial successes in other familiar ways. Then there was the astonishing thing that in every case ... blame was laid on perverse acts by the father, and realization of the unexpected frequency of hysteria, in every case of which the same thing applied, though it was hardly credible that perverted acts against children were so general. ... Thirdly, there was the definite realization that there is no "indication of reality" in the unconscious, so that it is impossible to distinguish between truth and emotionally-charged fiction. (This leaves open the possible explanation that sexual phantasy regularly makes use of the theme of the parents.)

Freud's response to this reversal, to the overthrow of a theory to which he had given so much of himself and on which he had placed such weight, is as remarkable as the reversal itself. Were I depressed, jaded, unclear in my mind," he writes, "such doubts might be taken for signs of weakness. But as I am in just the opposite state, I must acknowledge them to be the result of honest and effective intellectual labor, and I am proud that after penetrating so far I am still capable of such criticism. Can these doubts be only an episode on the way to further knowledge?" And towards the end of the letter, he adds, "In the general collapse only the psychology has retained its value. ... It is a pity one cannot live on dream-interpretation."

It is characteristic of Freud's personal and intellectual courage – as well as of the ethical aspect of that courage – that he should have regarded such a defeat as a partial victory and that he should appear altogether undeterred by it. As almost any reader of these documents will soon perceive, the years 1893–1900 are the *anni mirabili* of Freud's life and career. During this period, living in relative isolation, Freud was literally a man possessed and driven. He had found, he wrote, what he needed in order to live – "a consuming passion – in Schiller's words a tyrant. I have found my tyrant, and in his service I know no limits. My tyrant is psychology; it has always been my distant, beckoning goal and now, since I have hit on the neuroses, it has come so much the nearer." The Freud of these years is possessed by a creative demon. He describes the demands he is making on his own mind as "superhuman," and speaks of psychology as "an incubus." When he writes to Fliess in December 1895 that "we cannot do without men with the courage to think new things before they can prove them," he is describing himself. Ideas, insights, partial theories were coming to Freud faster than he could handle them, set them down, or reflect upon them. Several months after he had written the "Project" he could write to Fliess that "I no longer understand the state of mind in which I concocted the psychology." There is no reason to doubt the candor or truthfulness of this observation. For a large part of this period, Freud appears to have inhabited states of creative possession; his ambitions were of a magnitude that, fortunately for him, bore some plausible correspondence with the extent of his powers. On New Year's Day, 1897, he writes: "Give me another ten years and I shall finish the neuroses and the new psychology. ... When I am not afraid I can take on all the devils in hell."

The documents that make up the text I have been discussing are the first-hand record of how Freud took on those devils, most of which arose from the hell that was within himself as well as his patients. In May 1897 he says: "No matter what I start with, I always find myself back again with the neuroses and the psychical apparatus. It is not because of indifference to personal or other matters that I never write about anything else. Inside me there is a seething ferment, and I am only waiting for the next surge forward." He speaks regularly of things "fermenting" in him and of the "turbulence of my thoughts and feelings." Like a great poet, he had during this period exceptional access to his own unconscious, and parts of the turbulence he refers to have to do with the unremitting efforts he had to make to bring structure, organization, and meaning to this mysterious, dark, and threatening material. When he turns to the composition of *The Interpretation of Dreams*, he enters a state of creative transport and withdrawal. Having worked over a draft of one section, he writes to Fliess, "it is nearly finished, was written as if in a dream, and certainly not in a form fit for publication." Three weeks later, having finished work upon another section of the book, he sent it to Fliess with the following comments:

> It was all written by the unconscious, on the principle of Itzig, the Sunday horseman. "Itzig, where are you going?" "Don't ask me, ask the horse!" At the beginning of a paragraph I never knew where I should end up. It was not written to be read, of course – any attempt at style was abandoned after the first two pages. In spite of all that I of course believe in the results. I have not the slightest idea yet what form the contents will finally take.

And Freud's son, Ernst, later recalled how during this period his father used to come in to meals, from the place where he had been writing, "as if he were sleepwalking." Freud's own comments on this material – almost certainly the great seventh chapter, "On the

Psychology of the Dream-Processes" – including his slightly benumbed incomprehension, suggest something of the depths at which he had been seized. Even after *The Interpretation of Dreams* had been finished and published, he still could write: "The big problems are still unsettled. It is an intellectual hell, layer upon layer of it, with everything fitfully gleaming and pulsating; and the outline of Lucifer-Amor coming into sight at the darkest centre." If we are led in the context created by such illusions to think of Dante, Milton, Goethe, and Blake, we are not bringing in material that is irrelevant. The creative discoveries of Freud during these years were indeed of the highest order.

Those discoveries were legion. There is scarcely a notion that Freud was to elaborate upon in the course of his long subsequent career that is not touched upon, hinted at, presented in abbreviated, elliptical or nuclear form in these letters and drafts. The writing itself is on occasion obscure and even incomprehensible, for Freud is moving about in darkness. Nevertheless, the main features of the mental terrain that he is exploring gradually come into focus and clarity. With an increasingly sure sense of intellectual priorities Freud concentrates his attention upon areas of major discovery: first, the meaning of dreams and the construction of a psychology of unconscious mental functioning; second, the occurrence and development of infantile and childhood sexuality; and third, the central place in that development occupied by the Oedipal experience. The major vehicle through which these discoveries were made was also an unprecedented occurrence. I am referring of course to Freud's self-analysis, a process in which, as I have already suggested, the classical instruction to know thyself was brought into historical and momentous conjunction with *Oedipus Rex*. That this process also fulfilled in part the quizzical injunction, "Physician, heal thyself," is only one further demonstration of the centrality of Freud's discoveries to the history and traditions of Western civilization. It also serves to remind us that the Freud who appears at the end of this correspondence is not entirely the same man who wrote the bulk of it. He is still to be sure a great genius and is on his way to becoming a great man, but he is not the wildly driven, creatively tormented, fitfully inspired, and demonic creature of the largest part of this text. Although Freud is a central figure in the European tradition of Romanticism, and one of its last important legatees, there is a classical side to his achievements and character as well. This side comes into view when we observe that the making of this genius coincided with the maturing of it. He was not afraid that the rational understanding of his own nature would undo the creative energies that had sustained him. And he was equally unafraid that the achievement of personal integration was incompatible with the continuation of a creative and useful life.

The expression "Physician, heal thyself" occurs within and is part of the dominant religious tradition of our civilization. Freud belongs to that group of writers and thinkers who during the last 200 years have undertaken the major task of transforming that tradition by secularizing it. Freud himself was not religious in either temperament or sympathy. Nevertheless, like the other great modern figures he retained one belief, albeit in secular form, that belongs to that tradition. This is the belief in meaning – a belief of extensive moral and cultural consequence. In the instance of Freud it was a belief that all human thought and behavior had a meaning and meanings – that they were understandable, purposeful, had structure and rose to significance.[7] For example, in 1897 he writes: "Perverted actions are always alike, always have a meaning, and are based on a pattern which can be understood." And in the same year, he also states: "Phantasies arise from an unconscious combination of things experienced and heard, constructed for particular purposes. These purposes aim at making inaccessible the memory from which symptoms have been generated." Discussing the distortions that are built into fantasies that masquerade as memories, he remarks: "I am learning the rules which govern the formation of these structures, and reasons why they are stronger than real memories." And he follows his discovery of "Love of the mother and jealousy of the father," with the following observations.

> If that is the case, the gripping power of *Oedipus Rex*, in spite of all the rational objections to the inexorable fate that the story presupposes, becomes intelligible, and one can understand why later fate dramas were such failures. Our feelings rise against any arbitrary, individual fate ... but the Greek myth seizes on a compulsion which everyone recognizes because he has felt traces of it in himself. Every member of the audience was once a budding Oedipus in phantasy, and this dream-fulfillment played out in reality causes everyone to recoil in horror, with the full measure of repression which separates his infantile from his present state.

This deep belief in the meaningfulness of human experience and the equally deep belief in the power of the human mind to effect coherent explanations of that experience acted as general motives in the work of Freud. Without divine sanction and without a theodicy, the story of each human life could yet be rendered into some measure of intelligibility. There might even be moments of surpassing clarity. Such a moment occurred on January 16, 1898, when Freud wrote:

"Happiness is the deferred fulfillment of a prehistoric wish. That is why wealth brings so little happiness; money is not an infantile wish." If there is such a thing as secular wisdom, such a statement, it seems to me, approximates the form it is likely to take. The paths by which such knowledge was attained are imperishably recorded in the text I have been briefly examining.

That last quotation is, it seems to me, a piece of wisdom and belongs in a formal sense to the formal genre known as Wisdom Literature. That genre begins in our tradition with Proverbs and includes such writers familiar to Freud as Epictetus, Marcus Aurelius, Bacon, and Goethe. It is useful to remind ourselves how generously Freud's writings are studded with such remarks and observations. "Wisdom is the principal thing, therefore get wisdom: and with all thy getting get understanding" might easily serve as one of several epigraphs to part of Freud's achievement. What I have been trying to demonstrate is how in the working out of that achievement the scientific and intellectual discoveries made by Freud were inseparable from the moral values that informed such a work of discovery and the moral insights that emerged from it. Whatever one may want to say about other topics – such as the influence of psychoanalysis or our thinking about sexuality or our notions of childhood and child-rearing, or the moral nature of the psychoanalytic situation itself – in the text I have been discussing there is no such thing as an autonomous or detachable ethical sphere.[8]

At various points in his later career Freud went out of his way to deny that he was a genius. What he had achieved in the creation of this discipline, therapy, mode of inquiry, and institution, he insisted, was largely a matter of character. One of the things he meant by this not entirely perspicuous remark is that he was not in the formative years of discovery afraid to confront unpleasant ideas, live in isolation, and stand squarely in "The Opposition" – as he was fond of putting it. But I also think he meant that psychoanalysis did not simply spring, as a system, out of his mind, out of contemplation or pure research. He meant, I think, that much of what he had discovered had been tested in his own life and was the result of his experience. Indeed Freud's writings are on one side properly considered as part of "the literature of experience." Experience goes with great learning, which Freud wore very lightly; it goes as well with shrewdness in the analysis of character; and both are combined with brevity of phrase and irony. Such writing surprises the reader with a sense of its truth and simultaneously leads him to self-examination. And this brings me back to where I began. The notion of self-examination – and the value attached thereto – is surely somewhere close to the center of whatever it is we think psychoanalysis may mean.

Notes

1   Sigmund Freud, *The Origins of Psycho-Analysis*, ed. M. Bonaparte, A. Freud, E. Kris, trans. E. Mosbacher and J. Strachey (New York, 1954); *Aus den Anfängen der Psychoanalyze* (London, 1950).

2   Freud assumed that human existence is intelligible and that a coherent representation of all the psychic forces that are typical of human beings might someday be possible. Within the context of this presumptively rational model, certain behaviors or kinds of mental processes – namely, our affects, our instinctual strivings, etc. – are characterized as irrational.

3   The organic line of cultural evolution I am referring to has to do with the development in Western civilization of a tradition of rationally directed introspection or self-examination. Other cultures have other methods and traditions of introspection, and indeed Western civilization contains within itself alternative introspective traditions as well – *The Spiritual Exercises* of St Ignatius Loyola, for example, are in some measure part of such an alternative tradition. The new or higher degree of consciousness I refer to has to do: (1) with the training of the rationally governed self-examination on the irrational and the unconscious, and (2) with the accompanying awareness, in the instance of Freud, that he was in fact completing work that had, historically, begun with the Greeks.

4   It is my impression that very few patients came to Freud because they were generally "unhappy." The complaints tended to be fairly specific, if not multiple, and included the somatic symptoms of hysteria, the uncontrollable behavior of obsessional neuroses, frigidity, impotence, premature ejaculation, and various forms of perverse sexual gratifications. In the historical context of the period, such distresses all tended to be regarded as medical problems, although there was still a strong cultural component of moral condemnation when it came to perverse sexual behavior. In 1905, when he published *Three Essays on the Theory of Sexuality*, Freud did not include homosexuality among either the perversions or the neuroses. He put homosexuality into the separate category of "inversion" and decisively refused to reprehend it on moral grounds. He had not, by that date, ever had a homosexual as an analytic patient.
    In addition, there was at the time very little positive cultural sanction for someone who had a general complaint of "unhappiness." Happiness was not, in official nineteenth-century culture, a much respected idea. Suffering, labor, affliction were still largely thought of as the common human lot, and complaints about personal unhappiness tended to be discounted, often scornfully. As exemplary in their respective contexts, are the writings of Schopenhauer and Thomas Carlyle.

5   Letter of Sunday, December 21, 1817.
    In a thoughtful and useful essay, "Psychoanalysis, Physics and the Mind-Body Problem," Stephen Toulmin discovers how under the influence of Kant, German scientists and philosophers had "authority, in a way that their colleagues in other countries did not, to justify their ignoring the more rigid dichotomies of *mind* and *matter*." Among those so influenced were such figures as Müller, Helmholtz, Meinert, and Wernicke, all of whom in turn were there to influence, in different degrees, the thinking of the younger Freud.

6   By "psychic determinism" Freud meant a number of things. He could mean, as he did here, that psychic processes constituted an autonomous domain. He could also mean that there are no psychic events without causes, and that when it comes to mental events there are no such things as accidents. He could also mean that there are no mental events without meaning. And he could mean as well that mental events are overdetermined. On occasion he combined several of these meanings, but it is usually not very difficult to tell which meaning he is enlisting by consulting the context in which the usage occurs.

7   Freud did appear to believe that this search for meaning was a kind of functional norm; that it was a valid human function; and that thoughts and behavior are expressions of that functioning.

8   What I mean by this assertion is that the scientific discoveries and the moral insights emerge from a single imagination and bear the marks of their common origin; it is difficult for me to contemplate the one arising without the other. What I also mean is that these particular scientific discoveries entail moral insights and consequences, and possibly vice versa. And what I mean as well is that this extended experience of scientific and intellectual exploration was itself an undertaking in which a formidable moral component can be made out. Whether the connections between the two are either necessary or methodologically strict is a question that I am unable to answer. In the text in question, and throughout Freud's work in general, the two seem to me to be sustained in a single, complex, and heterogeneous matrix.

2 Freud's *Three Essays on the Theory of Sexuality*

In 1905 Freud published three works of major importance. The first of these, "Fragment of an Analysis of a Case of Hysteria," destined to be known as the case of Dora, had been originally drafted in 1901; however, for reasons which still remain unclear, Freud returned it to a drawer. Four years later, he took it up again, revised it and sent it forth into the medical world; it appeared in the *Monatschrift für Psychiatrie und Neurologie* during the autumn. Earlier in the year he published a volume called *Jokes and Their Relation to the Unconscious*, one of the several larger spin-offs, derivatives, or subsidiary consequences that the monumental *The Interpretation of Dreams* had left residually in its wake. The third publication was a small paper-covered book, *Three Essays on the Theory of Sexuality*. Freud had written this work simultaneously with the book on jokes. He kept the two manuscripts on adjoining tables and moved freely back and forth between them according to his mood.[1] Although it took more than four years to sell the thousand copies that were printed of the first edition, it was not very long before the exceptional importance of the *Three Essays* began to be recognized. Today it is by common consent regarded, along with *The Interpretation of Dreams*, as Freud's most fundamental and original work.

Freud himself was aware of this circumstance, and one of his ways of registering that awareness was by returning to this text repeatedly during the next twenty years in order to revise, correct, amend, alter, clarify, and add to its substance. As a result, as the contemporary reader of this work will quickly see, the text of the *Three Essays* is something of a palimpsest. Moreover, it is a peculiar kind of palimpsest. Not only is the visible surface or layer of writing difficult, sometimes obscure and frequently problematical. As we, so to say, peel away the surface and retrieve the hidden earlier layers, versions, or formulations, the difficulty, obscurity and problematicality tend to deepen. Indeed if one consults the first German edition of 1905 or the first English translation made by A. A. Brill in 1910 from the second German edition, it is difficult to know what an original generation of readers could have made out of the formidable darknesses that involve so many parts of this work. Freud was manifestly sensitive to these difficulties. He ends the text with a sentence of complaint that the "unsatisfactory conclusion ... that emerges from these investi-gations ... is that we know far too little ... to be able to construct from our fragmentary information a theory adequate to the understanding alike of normal and of pathological conditions." He returns to this complaint in the preface to the second edition: "the author is under no illusions as to the deficiencies and obscurities of this little work," is the way he characteristically puts it. He is still at it in his preface to the fourth edition of 1920: "that part of the theory," he writes, "which lies on the frontiers of biology and the foundations of which are contained in this little work is still faced with undiminished contradiction." And the reader will have no difficulty in picking up similar remarks throughout the text and in the additions and notes to it made up until 1924.

I am suggesting that what we have before us – as is usual with Freud – is something that cannot be thought of as an innocent text. This suggestion should come as no surprise, since it was Freud as much as anyone else in the history of the modern world who taught us to suspect the claim to, or the appearance of, innocence of any kind.[2] The *Three Essays* are innocent in neither form, substance, nor intention. Indeed from the outset one of the overt aims of this work was to declare the end of a historical innocence. In its disclosure to the world of the universality and normality of infantile and childhood sexuality in all its polymorphously perverse impulsiveness, the *Three Essays* was bringing to a close that epoch of cultural innocence in which infancy and childhood were regarded as themselves innocent, as special preserves of our lives untouched by desires, strivings after selfish pleasure, twinges of demonic perversity, drives towards carnal satisfactions. Some considerable measure of the odium that was attached for years to Freud's name has to be understood in this light. In the name of truth and reality, he undertook to deprive Western culture of one of its sanctified myths. Cultures do not as a rule take kindly to such demythologizings, and it should come as no surprise that of all of Freud's findings those that have to do with infantile and childhood sexuality were resisted with the most persistency.

If we turn to the form of the *Three Essays*, the evidence of Freud's complex intentionality is immediately in view. Each of the essays is divided into a number of sections, each of which is given a title. These sections are in turn further divided into smaller subsections, to each of which another substantive heading is also attached. The work as a whole is composed out of these small juxtaposed blocks of material. If the *Three Essays* resemble a palimpsest in the dimension of historical time, then they resemble a mosaic in either the dimension of printed space or in the dimension of the experiential time that any single reading of them requires. In contrast to the grand expository sweep that we usually associate with Freud's writing, the discourse of the *Three Essays* is made up of these fragments that are both connected and easy to separate, manipulate, revise, or delete. They function as movable parts of a system, and Freud's complex intentionality in this text includes the explicit intentionality of being systematic, of setting forth a coherent, systematic theory. Freud is explicitly conscious of the circumstance that he is on this occasion setting forth a theory that as a *psychology* has to stand up in point of comprehensiveness, depth, systematic integrity, and heuristic value to the demands of what a theory should be.

A second question of form has to do with the large structure of these essays. Why, it may be asked, did Freud begin the way he does? Why did he start out with an essay on "The Sexual Aberrations" and move on from these to essays on "Infantile Sexuality" and "The Transformations of Puberty"? His strategy in this context is not difficult to understand. In starting out with the sexual aberrations he was seeking to deal in the first place with certain forms of adult sexual behavior; in addition, the sexual practices in question were familiar and recognizable to whatever limited audience he might in 1905 think he was addressing. Such behaviors were, moreover, aggregated wholes, and Freud's procedure in the opening essay is to take these aggregated phenomena and arrange them in such a way that they can be disaggregated and decomposed. A further pertinence of this device of working backwards begins to be revealed when we see Freud regarding these adult manifestations of sexual behavior as being on one level integrated forms of sexual activity and at the same time on another level failures of integration, developmental outcomes in which the various component drives of the sexual instinct have not been put together in a fully integrated way. In addition to the relative familiarity of this material, however, a further strategic consideration *vis-à-vis* his audience may have been guiding him. The explosive material of this book is to be found in the second essay; it would have been imprudent in the most elementary sense to begin straightaway with that material. A groundwork in the familiar and paradoxically less inflammatory subject of the sexual aberrations had first to be put down before Freud could proceed to the unsettling question of infantile sexuality.

In this connection, it may be useful to note that in the *Three Essays* Freud is writing with a model somewhere in his mind. That model is Darwin, and the *Three Essays* is Freud's most truly Darwinian work. It occupies the boundary that both separates and connects the biological and the psychological realms of existence, and it touches unavoidably upon the complex relations that obtain between phylogenesis and ontogenesis. It is about "origins" in more ways than one, and is written from a consistently evolutionary point of view. Like Darwin, Freud is concerned with the "variations" in form and structure that the sexual instinct takes, and he is interested in arranging or classifying these "variations" in such a way that both their resemblances and differences be rendered in full account. Thus in enumerating the various kinds of homosexual activities, Freud remarks that though there are certainly distinctions and differences among them, it is nonetheless "impossible to overlook the existence of numerous intermediate examples of every type, so that we are driven to conclude that we are dealing with a connected series." At the same time, he is concerned to discover "the general conditions under which mere variations of the sexual instinct pass over into pathological aberrations." This double interest is clearly analogous to the interest in Darwin of tracing both the relations of variations within a species to one another and discovering the point or points at which variations subtly pass over into new or different species. And just as the principal theme of Darwin's work was the "transmutation" of species, so the fundamental preoccupation of the *Three Essays* is with "the transformation[s] of the sexual instinct." Yet each time that he works out such a transformation, Freud hastens to remind us "that an unbroken chain bridges the gap between the neuroses in all their manifestations and normality." The distinctions between variation and species or the normal and the pathological are never simple, nor are they ever held simply. The purpose of Freud's taxonomy is not merely to create new distinctions and classifications; its purpose is to understand how all the distinctions are related to one another, and how one is created out of the transformation of another.

Freud also reminds us of Darwin in some of his larger statements and speculations. The penultimate paragraph of the section on "Deviations in Respect of the Sexual Object" reads as follows:

> The very remarkable relation which thus holds between sexual variations and the descending scale from health to insanity gives us plenty of material for thought. I am inclined to believe that it may be explained by the fact that the impulses of sexual life are among those which, even normally, are the least controlled by the higher activities of the mind. In my experience anyone who is in any way, whether socially or ethically, abnormal mentally is invariably abnormal also in his sexual life. But many people are abnormal in their sexual life who in every other respect approximate to the average, and have, along with the rest, passed through the process of human cultural development, in which sexuality remains the weak spot.

What Freud is saying in this passage among other things is that in human cultural evolution – which the species as a whole has undergone, and which each individual recapitulates in his own development – sexuality remains the "weak spot." That is to say it is the part of us that is most recalcitrant to civilized constraints and does not undergo evolution smoothly. Hence individual development is precarious, and the achievement of "normal" heterosexual maturity is in fact something that has to be achieved. Nothing about it is assured or inevitable; it is contingent upon almost everything else.[3] In a similar sense, Freud regards the childhood of each person as a "primeval period, which falls within the lifetime of the individual himself," and he goes on to remark of infantile amnesia that it "turns everyone's childhood into something like a prehistoric epoch and conceals from him the beginnings of his own sexual life." Although Freud, like Darwin, was rigorously antiteleological in his formal point of view, there are some moments in this text when the evidence of structure, design, and a coherent and meaningful sequence of developments seems so overwhelming that he (like Darwin again) wrote passages that can only be construed in a teleological way. One of these he later excised.

Darwin mulled over his material for two decades before he sent it into print. (And even then he only did so because Alfred Russell Wallace had in the meantime also discovered the principle of natural selection.) Freud had been dealing with much of the material in the *Three Essays* for almost ten years, and he too, living in his self-styled "splendid isolation," was in no great hurry to publish his theoretical findings. Darwin was a confirmed empiricist who was at the same time capable of pursuing a grand theoretical hypothesis with originality and ingenuity and thus introduce a successful scientific revolution. A similar though not the same assertion may be made about Freud. Freud parts company with Darwin at the point at which empirical evidence on the one hand and speculation and inferential boldness of thought on the other meet. How beforehand in his boldness Freud can be is revealed in two critical footnotes which he almost casually sets down. The first of these is the first footnote in the first essay. In its original form Freud says that the information on homosexuality and the adult perversions on which the first two-thirds of the essay are based is derived from the "well-known writings" of Krafft-Ebing, Havelock Ellis, *et al.* In other words, Freud went through these large volumes of medical and psychiatric case summaries and drew from them the material on which he based his analysis. What goes without saying, and what does not quite get said, is that in 1905 Freud had as yet had no direct psychoanalytic experience of either homosexual patients or adults who practiced some form of perverse sexual behavior.[4] This lack of first-hand empirical evidence appears to have been in no way a deterrent to Freud's theoretical inclinations and energies. A similar circumstance occurs in the second essay on infantile sexuality. In a footnote added in 1910, Freud writes: "When the account which I have given above of infantile sexuality was first published in 1905, it was founded for the most part on the results of psycho-analytic research upon adults. At that time it was impossible to make full use of direct observation on children: only isolated hints and some valuable pieces of confirmation came from that source." In their original form, therefore, the first two essays have the character of grand inferential constructions that happen somehow – almost incidentally, one might say – to coincide with or catch up a good deal of the truth. Based on experience of some kind, they are nonetheless not primarily empirical in nature but are systematic and relatively coherent reworkings of glimpses into, intuitions of, and insights about hidden truths which still remain partly hidden.

II

In order to gain some sense of how this work might have affected its early readers, let us reconstitute in a general way part of the argument of the text of 1905. (I will of course refer to later additions and revisions when it seems appropriate.) Freud begins the first essay on "The Sexual Aberrations" by making an axial distinction. He divides all sexual behavior into two categories. One has to do with the "sexual object," the person towards whom sexual activity is directed or sexual desire felt. The second has to do with the "sexual aim," the act towards which the sexual instinct inclines. Both of these categories contain numerous deviations, and Freud classifies these deviations by means of this first distinction. The first class of aberrations contains those sexual activities that are deviant in respect of the sexual object. The most important and largest population in this class consists of adults whose sexual object has been "inverted." These inverts, or homosexuals as they are ordinarily called, "vary greatly in their behavior in several respects." Freud divides such behavior according to exclusiveness at one end of a scale and contingency at the other. He also notes variations that have to do with the subjective views of inverts towards their own behavior and with the date of onset and persistency of such behavior. Although the range of variation is great, the variations seem nonetheless connected, and he is forced to conclude that they form "a connected series." If there is a totality here it is organized heterogeneously.

When he turns to contemporary explanations of this aberration, he finds that the explanations explain very little. As for the currently popular medical ascription that inversion is "an innate indication of nervous degeneracy," Freud rejects both parts of the diagnosis as inadequate in classificatory precision and explanatory value. Inversion occurs among too many otherwise normal and indeed gifted and highly developed people to be regarded as a sign of some kind of organic degeneration. As for the argument about whether homosexuality is "innate" or "acquired," Freud refuses to choose exclusively between the two opposed alternatives. He then turns to certain theories of bisexuality. He cannot accept those explanations of homosexuality that ascribe it to either somatic or psychical hermaphroditism, nor does he think that it can be traced to certain localized centers of the brain. Nevertheless, partly because of the evolutionary evidence in normal human anatomy that points towards "an originally bisexual disposition," Freud accepts the notion that this disposition "is somehow concerned in inversion, though we do not know in what that disposition exists, beyond anatomical structure." Along with this, which explains nothing, he accepts the hypothesis that in confronting inversion "we have to deal with disturbances that affect the sexual instinct in the course of its development," which is a little better.

He turns next to homosexuals' attitudes towards their sexual objects and demonstrates that there is no uniformity of attitude to be found. And the same variety exists in respect of sexual aim – a whole array of activities characterizes homosexual behavior, not any exclusive kind of activity. What Freud is doing here is refusing to accept homosexuality as a simple or single entity; indeed he does the opposite. He stresses its complexity and hints that it may consist of more than one entity. And he continued to place stress in this direction. In 1915, he added as part of a long footnote the following reflection:

Psycho-analytic research is most decidedly opposed to any attempts at separating off homosexuals from the rest of mankind as a group of a special character. By studying sexual excitations other than those that are manifestly displayed, it has found that all human beings are capable of making a homosexual object-choice and have in fact made one in their unconscious. . . . Thus from the point of view of psycho-analysis the exclusive sexual interest felt by men for women is also a problem that needs elucidation and is not a self-evident fact based upon an attraction that is ultimately of a chemical nature.

In refusing to separate out homosexuals from other "normal"

human beings, Freud was emphasizing the continuity and related-ness that exists between both groups – or between pathology and non-pathology, if you will. And in adding that heterosexual normality is itself problematical, unelucidated, and not self-evident, he was drawing attention to the uncertain and complex character of what we ordinarily take to be the natural human norm.

Freud concludes this section by remarking that the present state of knowledge does not provide a position on which to base "a satisfactory explanation of the origin of inversion." Nevertheless, his "investi-gation" of the material before him has led him to discover that the connection between the sexual instinct and the sexual object is not as intimate as is commonly supposed.

> Experience of the cases that are considered abnormal has shown us that in them the sexual instinct and the sexual object are merely soldered together – a fact which we have been in danger of overlooking in consequence of the uniformity of the normal picture, where the object appears to form part and parcel of the instinct. We are thus warned to loosen the bond that exists in our thoughts between instinct and object. It seems probable that the sexual instinct is in the first instance independent of its object; nor is its origin likely to be due to its object's attraction.

In this passage of speculative flight Freud is making a number of theoretical proposals. He is suggesting that the sexual instinct is plastic and labile, that it can be displaced, that it is not entirely dependent upon its object – or the object world – and that it may indeed be at first independent and without an object. All of these suggestions will lead to momentous consequences later on.[5]

Deviations in respect to the sexual aim comprise those practices that are known as "perversions." They begin for Freud with activities in which the mouth is brought into contact with the genitals of another person. Such practices, Freud remarks, "have no doubt been common among mankind from primeval times." And those who condemn these acts as perversions "are giving way to an unmistakable feeling of *disgust*, which protects them from accepting sexual aims of the kind. The limits of such disgust are, however, often purely conventional." In other words, perversions are commonly known or recognized by the subjective feeling of disgust that their contem-plation elicits; moreover, this subjective sign is for Freud in part a historical and conventional circumstance. It is in some measure a socially induced force, and its action leads "to a restriction of the sexual aim." Nevertheless, Freud wryly adds, "the sexual instinct in its strength enjoys overriding this disgust." The same holds true for those activities which make sexual use of the anal orifice.

The sexual instinct extends its interest to other parts of the body as well, and in those activities described as fetishism we see one such extension. These activities can extend to inanimate objects as well, such as "a piece of clothing or underlinen." What is interesting about such practices – and about all the other perversions as well – is that they are in some degree "habitually present in normal love," especially in its preliminary aims. And Freud regards them as pathological only when they take the place of the normal sexual aims and object "in *all* circumstances," when they take on the "characteristics of exclusiveness and fixation." Such characteristics apply as well to the perversions that have to do with looking and being looked at, namely voyeurism and exhibitionism. These connected symptoms occur in both active and passive forms, which leads Freud on to "the most common and the most significant of all the perversions," sadism and masochism. He finds the roots of sadism in the "element of *aggressiveness*" that is usually part of the sexuality of most male human beings. In sadism, the "aggressive component of the sexual instinct . . . has become independent and exaggerated and, by displacement, has usurped the leading position." Masochism is a more complex and mysterious phenomenon, and in 1905 Freud had to content himself with the remark that "no satisfactory explanation of this perversion has been put forward and . . . it seems possible that a number of mental impulses are combined in it to produce a single resultant."

Yet sadism and masochism have a further interest because both are "habitually found to occur together in the same individual." This co-presence of opposites, Freud remarks, has "a high theoretical significance," and he proceeds to connect these opposites "with the opposing masculinity and femininity which are combined in bisexuality – a contrast which often has to be replaced in psychoanalysis by that between activity and passivity." At this point even a casual reader cannot escape the sense that a large theoretical design is beginning to take shape.

As he moves towards a conclusion of this section, Freud notes once again that the sexual life of healthy adults is rarely without perverse constituents in it, and he repeats his admonition that when it comes to the sphere of sexuality "we are brought up against peculiar and, indeed, insoluble difficulties as soon as we try to draw a sharp line to distinguish mere variations within the range of what is physiological from pathological symptoms." This "most unruly of all the instincts" can lead people whose behavior is in other respects normal to activities of the most astonishing and repulsive kind. In such activities, Freud observes, it is impossible to overlook the important role played by the mind in the transformations of the sexual instinct. "It is impossible to deny that in their case a piece of mental work has been performed which, in spite of its horrifying result, is the equivalent of an idealization of the instinct." It was the ancients, one recalls, that Freud describes as idealizing the instinct; and the inference must follow that in the perversions the past survives in the present, and that there is something archaic about these expressions of sexuality in which the highest and the lowest intersect and are joined. Indeed some perversions are intelligible only if we assume such a convergence. "If such perversions admit of analysis," Freud concludes, "that is, if they can be taken to pieces, then they must be of a composite nature. This gives us a hint that perhaps the sexual instinct itself may be no simple thing, but put together from components which have come apart again in the perversions." The obscure circularity of this chain of reasoning may be interpreted as follows. The sexual instinct is not a single or unitary entity. It is made up of different components that are brought together – amalgamated, aggregated, or synthesized – in normal adult sexual activity. In the perversions, however, we see that the components have come apart again; they have decomposed, and some of them have been recomposed to form these alternate kinds of behavior. The disaggregation and decomposition that Freud had chosen as the analytic and expository form in which to treat the sexual aberrations is now revealed to be an essential attribute in the formation and structure of those aberrations themselves. The fit between form and content or analytic intellectual style and material structure is very snug indeed.

At this point, Freud abruptly shifts gears and begins without warning or transition a new section entitled "The Sexual Instinct in Neurotics." At once the reader becomes aware that the territory has been shifted as well, as has the pitch of explanatory discourse. Persons who suffer from such complaints as hysteria or obsessional neuroses, Freud begins, are approximately closer to the normal than the aberrants with whom he has just finished his preliminary dealings. Nevertheless, psychoanalytic investigation has determined that the sexual instinct is fundamental in the maintenance of neurotic symptoms; it provides the most important "source of energy" of the neuroses, and as a consequence the sexual life of neurotics tends in varying degree to be expressed in their symptoms. Indeed, Freud continues, "the symptoms constitute the sexual activity of the patient." The symptoms are in fact substitutes – "transcriptions as it were" – for certain highly charged wishes and desires which have undergone the peculiar and unexplained mental process called repression and have as a result been lost to consciousness. They have not, however, lost their force, and since they cannot be discharged by conscious mental representation, they find expression in "somatic phenomena." By means of another mysterious process called "conversion," they appear as the somatic symptoms – the paralyses, tics, convulsions, blindnesses – of hysteria. Hysteria is thus an embodiment or exemplification of the mind–body problem, one expression of that apparently insoluble – and indissoluble – relation. Moreover, hysterics are excessively civilized persons. In them the restrictive forces of "shame, disgust and morality," which are overriden in the perversions, act with decisive power against sexual desire. Yet their excessive aversion to sexuality is regularly combined with a characterizing opposite, an "exaggerated sexual craving," although this craving is also fated to become at some point unconscious. Torn between sexual strivings and his aversion to sexuality, the hysteric chooses illness as a means of escaping his conflict. Unfortunately illness "does not solve his conflict, but seeks to evade it by transforming his libidinal impulses into symptoms."

At the same time, it would be misleading to assert that such symptoms originate either solely or exclusively at the cost of normal adult sexuality – though that, Freud notes, is what he is commonly taken to be saying. Neurotic symptoms also express perverse or abnormal sexual instincts and ideas and are formed in part out of them. Hence, Freud concludes, rising to his large formulation, *"neuroses are, so to say, the negative of perversions."* Inversion, all the perversions, and all the "component instincts" in their paired opposites – including sadism and masochism – appear "without exception" in the "unconscious mental life" of neurotics. We suddenly see what Freud is doing. In a bewilderingly brief few pages on the neuroses he has recapitulated the entire structure of the earlier part of the essay, which was, one recalls, about actually perverse sexual behavior. But the recapitulation is now on the level of the neurotic symptom, of unconscious mental life, of fantasies, ideas, and mental representations. It is, in other words, on the level of theory. Just as for Marx political economy was the theory of capitalism, so for Freud the neuroses contain the theory of sexual behavior in both its normal and aberrant modes of expression. They contain that theory, and with Freud's help they will contain it in an integrated form. Having decomposed the perversions into component parts, he has at once recomposed them in the neuroses. In the neuroses the language of sexuality begins to speak articulately, coherently, and theoretically.[6]

But Freud is not content with letting the neuroses speak just yet. Instead he begins to speak himself about "Component Instincts and

Erotogenic Zones," and of the linkage of the two in both perversions and psychoneuroses. He reminds us again of the role played by perverse impulses in both the neuroses and normal life, and of the unbroken series of gradients that connect "the neuroses in all their manifestations and normality." He reaches the conclusion that "there is indeed something innate lying behind the perversions but that it is something innate in *everyone*, though as a disposition it may vary in its intensity and may be increased by the influences of actual life." He is speaking about the democracy of instinctual, biological life; and what is at stake are the "innate constitutional roots of the sexual instinct." In one class of persons – those with perversions – these roots "may grow into the actual vehicles of sexual activity." In another – the neurotics – they have undergone insufficient repression and persist as symptoms. And in "the most favorable cases" they have undergone such restrictions and modifications that somehow "what is known as normal sexual life" is brought about or achieved. In addition, he remarks, these roots and this constitution will only be demonstrable in children.

> A formula begins to take shape which lays it down that the sexuality of neurotics has remained in, or been brought back to, an infantile state. Thus our interest turns to the sexual life of children, and we will now proceed to trace the play of influences which govern the evolution of infantile sexuality till its outcome in perversion, neurosis or normal sexual life.

The recomposition that was summarily demonstrated in the neuroses has now been displaced in historical time. In order to make the full demonstration of recomposition Freud is going back to the very beginning. The theory will exist in fully integrated coherence only after – having first disassembled the perversions – Freud has been able to take the fragments and components of infantile sexual life and show how they develop historically and emerge in adulthood into integrated coherence themselves – or into the deformed coherences of the neuroses and sexual aberrations. Once again the discursive form taken by the theoretical structure is inseparable from the experiential form taken by the material content of which that structure is the theory.

III

Freud begins the essay on infantile sexuality by noting that as far as he is aware "not a single author has clearly recognized the regular existence of a sexual instinct in childhood." He is indeed so struck by the boldness of this assertion that he has gone through the literature on the subject yet once more to test its validity. It remains valid.[7] What Freud means is that no one before him had unequivocally recognized the pleasure-seeking activities of infancy and childhood as both sexual and normal. There was in fact a wealth of literature on childhood sexuality published during the Victorian period, but that literature tended almost uniformly to regard the sexual experiences or activities of children as pathological, abnormal, and deplorable. In the growing literature that was concerned with the development of the child, sexuality was not included as part of that development, nor did it have a special development in childhood itself. Freud sets out to repair this neglect, this cultural amnesia that is the counterpart to the personal infantile amnesia in which we all cloak this decisive period of life.

We cannot follow Freud in any detail as he develops his exposition – and as it additionally develops in the much-revised text across a period of twenty years. In brief, Freud sees both the occurrence of sexuality in childhood and the building up of restrictions against it and inhibitions of it in a double sense. Both the sexuality and the constraining structures are in the first instance organically determined and arise endogenously or endosomatically in the course of normal growth. At the same time both sexual impulses and the constraining structures are open to influences from the outside, are affected by experience and education; and the final form which they will take will bear upon it the marks of such influences.

Freud begins with the phenomenon of thumb-sucking or sensual sucking. This early behavior itself refers back to a still earlier one, and is a search for a pleasure that is remembered. The child's "first and most vital activity, his sucking at his mother's breast" is also his first experience of pleasure. This first experience arises out of and is associated with a vital organic function; moreover, the membranes of the lips and mouth of the child function as an erogenous zone. The experience is exemplary and determinative. "No one," writes Freud, in one of his most famous remarks, "who has seen a baby sinking back satiated from the breast and falling asleep with flushed cheeks and a blissful smile can escape the reflection that this picture persists as a prototype of the expression of sexual satisfaction in later life." Later on, or when the mother is not present, the child's need to repeat this pleasure becomes "detached from the need for taking nourishment." The child then can take a part of its own body – his thumb – to suck on and recapture the pleasure. The pleasure is therefore autoerotic, which leads Freud to remark that at first the sexual instinct in childhood is without an object – a speculative construction of considerable theoretical depth and resonance.

The oral phase is followed by activities at the other end of the alimentary canal. The anal zone is the second area of erotegenic pleasure. The sexual excitements of this zone are both active and passive and involve both the stimulation of the mucous membrane and the control (and release) of the sphincter muscle. As with the oral phase, the persistence of significance into later life of the erotogenic importance of this zone has a determining influence on what character or personality will be like. The third erotogenic zone in children is the genitals. This zone is also connected with a vital function, urination. Although it is not the site or vehicle of the oldest sexual impulses, it is "destined to great things in the future." It is easily and regularly stimulated, and "it is scarcely possible to avoid the conclusion that the foundations for the future primacy over sexual activity exercised by this erotogenic zone are established by early infantile masturbation, which scarcely a single individual escapes." Freud also distinguishes two kinds of infantile masturbation – that which is associated with early infancy and that which revives during the later-named phallic and Oedipal phases.

It should be noted that although Freud represented infantile sexuality from the very beginning as a matter of overlapping periodicities and interlocking phases, in 1905 he was not yet able to particularize with full concreteness what those periodicities and phases are and when they specifically occur. One corollary of this uncertainty was that he put his theoretical system together in such a way that revisions of, deletions from, and additions to it could be conveniently and easily made. This combination of openness to new experience and material with genuine systematic coherence at a high level of abstract theoretical generality is one of the identifying qualities of Freud's thinking. As is the similar alliance in him of a simultaneous commitment to the idea of the determination, and overdetermination, of all events and developments in mental and sexual life along with the idea that such events and developments are also contingent upon accidents of both disposition and experience. An essential part of the distinction of this text is to be found in the poised equilibrium in it of the open-ended and the systematic, the concrete and the abstract, and the contingent and the determined – and in the delicacy with which that equilibrium is sustained.[8] It is what leads Freud to emphasize repeatedly, for example, that "persons who remain normal may have had the same experiences in their childhood" as those who become neurotic or perverse later on. In other words, there is no single causal or developmental scenario that leads to a particular adult outcome. Different scenarios may in fact lead to the same outcome in maturity. And the converse is also possible and demonstrable: a single scenario may lead in different persons to different adult outcomes. Hence, although it is true that "under the influence of seduction children can become polymorphously perverse, and can be led into all possible kinds of sexual irregularities," it is equally true that: (1) "seduction is not required in order to arouse a child's sexual life; that can also come about spontaneously from internal causes"; and (2) it is "impossible not to recognize that this same disposition to perversions of every kind is a general and fundamental human characteristic."

Freud proceeds with his recapitulation of the first essay and his recomposition of the adult aberrations out of the normal development of sexuality in childhood. He turns to those component instincts in childhood "which from the very first involve other people as sexual objects." These are scopophilia, exhibitionism, and cruelty. Freud followed the discussion of these developments by adding in 1915 two entirely new sections on the sexual researches of childhood and the phases of development of the sexual organization in which the "pregenital organizations" of childhood are brought into full explicitness. He closes the essay with a section in which he brings forward some additional sources in childhood of sexual stimulation, excitation and satisfaction.

With the arrival of puberty a further series of transformations take place. New objects appear along with a new sexual aim. And the component instincts must now be brought together, assembled, integrated and subordinated to "the primacy of the genital zone."[9] Freud rehearses in his customary, compact style the three sources of stimuli that impinge on the developing organism. These are stimuli that come from the external world, from the organic interior, and from mental life, "which is itself a storehouse for external impressions and a receiving post for internal excitations." He takes up for a second time the puzzling and many-sided problem of the nature of sexual tension or excitation and its relation to pleasure, describes how the erotogenic zones "fit themselves into the new arrangements" as forepleasures, and relates once again these forepleasures to the mechanism of the perversions. He passes on to the extremely complex question of the differentiation between men and women, a differentiation in which the notion of bisexuality makes an important return. In addition, this transformation involves for women a further change. In little girls, genital sexuality is experienced on a phallic model or prototype, with the clitoris as the organ of stimulation and pleasure. When a girl turns into a woman, this organ both enlarges and relinquishes a part of its function: "When at last the sexual act is permitted and the clitoris itself becomes excited, it still retains a function: the task, namely, of transmitting the excitation to the adjacent female sexual parts, just as – to use a simile – pine shavings can be kindled to set a log of harder wood on fire." In view of the tragicomedy that so much subsequent discussion of female sexuality has turned out to be, it is appropriate to bring forward this early and largely neglected remark, including the homely and half-inappropriate metaphor that Freud enlists to illustrate it. The clitoris does not altogether give up its excitability;[10] what it does is to transfer "susceptability to stimulation" to "the vaginal orifice." It ceases to be the exclusive or leading zone for female sexual activity. For 1905 that is not an altogether condemnable formulation.

Yet we cannot let the matter rest there. In the first essay there is an important theoretical subsection on the "over-valuation of the sexual object," which contains the following passage:

> The significance of the factor of sexual overvaluation can be best studied in men, for their erotic life alone has become accessible to research. That of women – partly owing to the stunting effect of civilized conditions and partly owing to their conventional secretiveness and insincerity – is still veiled in an impenetrable obscurity.

If we juxtapose these remarks with those taken from the third essay, we are left with a series of questions. Where did Freud get the information that he construes into the theoretical construction of the third essay, information which, in addition, he denies having access to in the first? From the street? from folklore? from experience? out of his ear? from the observations he said he was unable to make? from unconscious hints let drop by his patients? Are the two passages compatible or incompatible? It is quite impossible to say, and the matter remains veiled in impenetrable obscurity.[11]

Nevertheless, along with the establishment of genital primacy at puberty, there takes place as well the completion of the process that permits the organism to seek and find a sexual object. Here too psychical preparations have been made from a very early date. "At a time at which the first beginnings of sexual satisfaction are still linked with the taking of nourishment, the sexual instinct has a sexual object outside the infant's body in the shape of his mother's breast. It is only later that the instinct loses that object, just at the time, perhaps, when the child is able to form a total idea of the person to whom the organ that is giving him satisfaction belongs." It is then, Freud writes inconsistently, that the instinct becomes autoerotic, and not until latency has been passed through is it ready to resume and restore the original relation. The inconsistency has to do with his earlier statement that at first, at its origin, the sexual instinct in infants has no object. And since he is making conjectural inferences about such occluded matters as the origin and formation of object relations – matters about which reliable data are still today very hard to come by – one can understand his lack of certitude and oscillation. His conclusion, however, has a sturdy coherence to it. "There are thus good reasons," he wrote, "why a child sucking at its mother's breast has become the prototype of every relation of love. The finding of an object is in fact a refinding of it." The past is the prehistory of the present in the sense that it is the necessary precondition of present existence. And history repeats and recapitulates prehistory, though at a further stage of organization and development.

Hence the child's relations with those who care for it – especially its mother – are sexual in character. And the mother in turn regards the child "with feelings that are derived from her own sexual life," as she mothers and nurses and nurtures it. There is nothing to be horrified at in recognizing the sexual nature of this relation, Freud quickly adds. Moreover, "if the mother understood more of the high importance of the part played by instincts in mental life as a whole – in all its ethical and psychical achievements – she would spare herself any self-reproaches even after her enlightenment. She is only fulfilling her task in teaching the child to love." Although love takes many forms, the kind of love Freud has ideally in mind is associated with the idea of a vigorous and autonomous adult human being.

This autonomy is a goal that cannot be reached directly. For the object that is found in adult life cannot be the identical refound object of infancy and early childhood. The Oedipal experience must be gone through and resolved. The barrier against incest – "a cultural demand made by society" – must be iternalized, along with other prohibitions and restraints. When at puberty the incestuous fantasies are rearoused, they must again be overcome and repudiated. If this work is gone through successfully, "one of the most significant, but also one of the most painful, psychical achievements of the pubertal period is completed: detachment from parental authority, a process that alone makes possible the opposition, which is so important for the progress of civilization, between the new generation and the old." In view of the widespread tendency to regard Freud's thinking as essentially classical and conservative in affinity, it is helpful to be reminded of such a remark. Freud is also one of the last great legatees of the Romantic tradition in European thought. His theories are grounded in the idea of conflict, and this conflict exists in the realm of the normal as much as it does in the pathological. Even his conceptions of integration are touched by it. He sees integration as falling within the larger contexts of conflict and of incompatible needs, contradictory aims, and implacably opposed demands. Such integration as he finds is never complete, rarely adequate, and more often than not unstable. He never envisages the human or the social world as composing now or in the future to some harmonious order. There is the recognition and remembrance of bliss and satisfaction in his world, but there is no music of the spheres. In his world men and women go through a long development of striving for autonomy, but the achievement of such autonomy is arduous, unpredictable, and easily subverted.

At this point Freud closes his exposition. He adds to it a "Summary" in which the arguments of the three separate essays are rehearsed together and a few further theoretical observations put down. He closes with a reminder of the importance for all later development of the experiences of childhood, "a period which is regarded as being devoid of sexuality." After writing this text Freud was to live for more than thirty years. During that period he would continue to write and develop his ideas. But with the *Three Essays* now fitted in alongside of *The Interpretation of Dreams*, the new theoretical paradigm – and the new vision of human existence – that he was to introduce into the consciousness of the Western world was there in its essentials. He and his followers would go on filling in new details, adding observations, plugging up gaps, throwing out new explanatory epicycles. They would, in short, begin to operate – as they are operating today – on the analogy of normal science. But the fundamental theory was there in 1905. That it was a theory fully deserving of the name is in part suggested to us in the circumstance that nothing has come along in seventy years that remotely resembles it in explanatory power, coherence, and integrity. No intellectually serious challenges to it have taken or lasted. The superseders of it that have been regularly announced have just as regularly fallen away. And Freud's own followers continue working on the boundaries of knowledge, about four inches ahead of where Freud left off. Such a circumstance is no discredit to them; it is one more illustration of how rarely genius of revolutionary proportions occurs in both science and other theoretical disciplines. And it illustrates as well how when such a genius occurs the world changes.

Notes

1   Ernest Jones, *The Life and Work of Sigmund Freud*, 3 Vols (New York, 1953–7), Vol. 2, p. 286.

2   About the only kind of innocence that Freud allowed of was a small class of "innocent jokes."

3   At the end of the text Freud offers the following related observation: "in consequence of the inverse relation holding between civilization and the free development of sexuality, of which the consequences can be followed far into the structure of our existences, the course taken by the sexual life of a child is just as unimportant for later life where the cultural or social level is relatively low as it is important where that level is relatively high." Whatever one may wish to make of the last part of this statement, the opposition between civilization and "the free development of sexuality" is a notion that Freud obdurately held to throughout his life; behind this notion is a further idea that human cultural evolution is founded on a deep-seated set of contradictions.

4   In a footnote situated further on in the 1905 text, he did make the admission in respect to homosexuals.

5   One of them is to be found in a footnote that he added in 1910. "The most striking distinction between the erotic life of antiquity and our own no doubt lies in the fact that the ancients laid the stress upon the instinct itself, whereas we emphasize its object. The ancients glorified the instinct and were prepared on its account to honour even an inferior object; while we despise the instinctual activity itself, and find excuses for it only in the merits of the object."

6   Some years later Freud remarked that "the theory of the neuroses is psychoanalysis itself", "Introductory Lectures on Psychoanalysis" (1916-17), *The Standard Edition of the Complete Psychological Works of Sigmund Freud*, 24 Vols (London, 1966-74), Vol. XVI, p. 379.

7   Some slight modifications of this claim have to be made. See Stephen Kern, "Freud and the Discovery of Child Sexuality," *History of Childhood Quarterly*, 1 (Summer 1973), 117-41, in which a number of partial anticipations of certain of Freud's findings are mentioned.

8   On a later occasion, Freud addressed this difficult subject directly. "So long as we trace the development from its final outcome backwards, the chain of events appears continuous, and we feel we have gained an insight which is completely satisfactory or even exhaustive. But if we proceed the reverse way, if we start from the premises inferred from the analysis and try to follow these up to the final result, then we no longer get the impression of an inevitable sequence of events which could not have been otherwise determined. We notice at once that there might have been another result, and that we might have been just as well able to understand and explain the latter. The synthesis is thus not so satisfactory as the analysis; in other words, from a knowledge of the premises we could not have foretold the nature of the result. ... But we never know beforehand which of the determining factors will prove the weaker or the stronger. We only say at the end that those which succeeded must have been the stronger. Hence the chain of causation can always be recognized with certainty if we follow the line of analysis, whereas to predict it along the line of synthesis is impossible." "The Psychogenesis of a Case of Homosexuality in a Woman" (1920), *Standard Edition*, Vol. XVIII, pp. 167-8. Such a passage suggests Freud's awareness that psychoanalytic theory, like the modern theory of evolution, is essentially a historical theory; its powers are explanatory rather than predictive.

9   In addition, "the sexual instinct is now subordinated to the reproductive function; it becomes, so to say, altruistic." This is at the other extreme from the archaic or primitive or perverse arrangements in which the instinct itself is idealized.

10 Freud is in this text undecided about the degree to which the clitoris has to "abandon its excitability," and the passage is ambiguous on this score.

11 One can add as a piece of crowning confusion the following leap in the dark from the second essay. In his discussion of the polymorphous perverse sexuality of children, Freud pauses for an illustration: "In this respect children behave in the same kind of way as an average uncultivated woman in whom the same poly-

morphous perverse disposition persists. Under ordinary conditions she may remain normal sexually, but if she is led on by a clever seducer she will find every sort of perversion to her taste, and will retain them as part of her own sexual activities. Prostitutes exploit the same polymorphous, that is, infantile, disposition for the purposes of their profession; and, considering the immense number of women who are prostitutes or who must be supposed to have an aptitude for prostitution without becoming engaged in it, it becomes impossible not to recognize that this same disposition to perversions of every kind is a general and fundamental human characteristic." One doesn't know where to look for a handle to these remarks. It is even difficult to frame a context that might make discussion of them pertinent. Perhaps we can do no better than repeat the waggish observation that it is very difficult to know the meaning of a statement about Freud being right or wrong since he is always both.

3 Freud and Dora: Story, History, Case History

It is generally agreed that Freud's case histories are unique. Today more than half a century after they were written they are still widely read. Even more, they are still widely used for instruction and training in psychoanalytic institutes. One of the inferences that such a vigorous condition of survival prompts is that these writings have not yet been superseded. Like other masterpieces of literature or the arts, these works seem to possess certain transhistorical qualities – although it may by no means be easy to specify what those qualities are. The implacable "march of science" has not – or has not yet – consigned them to "mere" history. Their singular and mysterious complexity, density, and richness have thus far prevented such a transformation and demotion.

This state of affairs has received less attention than it merits. Freud's case histories – and his works in general – are unique as pieces or kinds of writing, and it may be useful to regard them from the standpoint that this statement implies. I shall undertake, then, to examine one of Freud's case histories from the point of view of literary criticism, to analyze it as a piece of writing, and to determine whether this method of proceeding may yield results that other means have not. The assumption with which I begin, as well as the end that I hope to demonstrate, is that Freud is a great writer and that one of his major case histories is a great work of literature – that is to say, it is both an outstanding creative and imaginative performance and an intellectual and cognitive achievement of the highest order. And yet, as we shall see, this triumphant greatness is in part connected with the circumstance that it is about a kind of failure, and that part of the failure remains in fact unacknowledged and unconscious.[1]

"Fragment of an Analysis of a Case of Hysteria," better known to future readers as the case of Dora, is Freud's first great case history – oddly enough, he was to write only four others. It may be helpful for the reader if at the outset I refresh his or her memory by briefly reviewing some of the external facts of the case. In the autumn of 1900 Dora, an 18-year-old young woman, began treatment with Freud. She did so reluctantly and against her will, and, Freud writes, "it was only her father's authority which induced her to come to me at all." (22)[2] Neither Dora nor her father was a stranger to Freud. He had made separate acquaintance with both of them in the past, during certain episodes of illness that characterized their lives if not the life of the family as a whole. (Freud knew other members of the family as well.) Dora's father was a man "of rather unusual activity and talents, a large manufacturer in very comfortable circumstances." (18) In 1888 he had fallen ill with tuberculosis, which had made it necessary for the family to move to a small town with a good climate in some southern part of Austria; for the next ten years or so that remained their chief place of residence. In 1892 he suffered a detached retina which led to a permanent impairment of his vision. Two years later he fell gravely ill – it was "a confusional attack, followed by symptoms of paralysis and slight mental disturbances." (19) He was persuaded by a friend to come to Vienna and consult with Freud, who was then a rising young neurologist and psychiatrist. Freud settled upon the diagnosis of "diffuse vascular affection," a meningeal disturbance associated with the tertiary stage of syphilis; and since the patient admitted to having had a "specific infection" of syphilis before he married, Freud prescribed "an energetic course of anti-luetic treatment, as a result of which all the remaining disturbances passed off." (19) By 1899 his constitution had sufficiently recovered from the tuberculosis to justify the family's leaving the health resort and moving to "the town in which his factory was situated"; and in 1900 they moved again and settled permanently in Vienna.

Despite this long and protracted history of illness – he also at one time had apparently been infected with gonorrhea, which he may have passed on to his wife – Dora's father was clearly a dominating figure: vigorous, active, energetic, enterprising, and intelligent. Nothing of the sort could be said of Dora's mother, who from the accounts received of her by Freud appeared to his imagination as

> an uncultivated woman and above all as a foolish one, who had concentrated all her interests upon domestic affairs, especially since her husband's illness and the estrangement to which it led. She presented the picture, in fact, of what might be called the "housewife's psychosis." She had no understanding of her children's more active interests, and was occupied all day long in cleaning the house with its furniture and in keeping them clean – to such an extent as to make it almost impossible to use or enjoy them. (20)

The immediate family circle was completed by a brother, a year and a half older than Dora, who hardly figures in the account rendered by Freud and who seems to have escaped from his childhood and family experiences without severe disablements. In adult life he became a leading figure in Socialist politics and apparently led an active, successful, and distinguished career up to his death many years later.

As for Dora herself, her afflictions, both mental and physical, had begun in early childhood and had persisted and flourished with variations and fluctuating intensities until she was presented to Freud for therapy. Among the symptoms from which she suffered were to be found dyspnea, migraine, and periodic attacks of nervous coughing often accompanied by complete loss of voice during part of the episode. Dora had in fact first been brought by her father to Freud two years earlier, when she was 16 and suffering from a cough and hoarseness; he had then "proposed giving her psychological treatment," but this suggestion was not adopted, since "the attack in question, like the others, passed off spontaneously." (22) In the course of his treatment of Dora, Freud also learned of further hysterical – or hysterically connected – productions on her part, such as a feverish attack that mimicked appendicitis, a periodic limp, and a vaginal catarrh or discharge. Moreover, during the two-year interval between Dora's first visit and the occasion on which her father brought her to Freud a second time, and "handed her over to me for psychotherapeutic treatment" (19), "Dora had grown unmistakeably neurotic" in what today we would recognize as more familiar manifestations of emotional distress. Dora was now "in the first bloom of youth – a girl of intelligent and engaging looks." (23) Her character had, however, undergone an alteration. She had become chronically depressed and was generally dissatisfied with both herself and her family. She had become unfriendly towards the father, whom she had hitherto loved, idealized, and identified with. She was "on very bad terms" with her mother, for whom she felt a good deal of scorn. "She tried to avoid social intercourse, and employed herself – so far as she was allowed to by the fatigue and lack of concentration of which she complained – with attending lectures for women and with carrying on more or less serious studies."[3] (23) Two further events precipitated the crisis which led to her being delivered to Freud. Her parents found a written note in which she declared her intention to commit suicide because "as she said, she could no longer endure her life." Following this there occurred one day "a slight passage of words" between Dora and her father, which ended with Dora suddenly losing consciousness – the attack, Freud believed, was "accompanied by convulsions and delirious states," although it was lost to amnesia and never came up in the analysis.

Having outlined this array of affections, Freud dryly remarks that such a case "does not upon the whole seem worth recording. It is merely a case of '*petite hystérie*' with the commonest of all somatic and mental symtoms. ... More interesting cases of hysteria have no doubt been published ... for nothing will be found in the following pages on the subject of stigmata of cutaneous sensibility, limitation of the visual field, or similar matters." (24) This disavowal of anything sensational to come is of course a bit of shrewd disingenuousness on Freud's part, for what follows at once is his assertion that he is going to elucidate the meaning, origin, and function of every one of these symptoms by means of the events and experiences of Dora's life. He is going, in other words, to discover the "psychological determinants" that will account for Dora's illnesses; among these determinants he lists three principal conditions: "a psychical trauma, a conflict of affects, and ... a disturbance in the sphere of sexuality." (24) And so Freud begins the treatment by asking Dora to talk about her experiences. What emerges is the substance of the case history, a substance which takes all of Freud's immense analytic, expository, and narrative talents to bring into order. I will again very roughly and briefly summarize some of this material.

Sometime after 1888, when the family had moved to B — (the health resort where the father's tuberculosis had sent them), an intimate and enduring friendship sprang up between them and a couple named K. Dora's father was deeply unhappy in his marriage and apparently made no bones about it. The K.'s too were unhappily married, as it later turned out. Frau K. took to nursing Dora's father during these years of his illness. She also befriended Dora, and they behaved towards one another in the most familiar way and talked together about the most intimate subjects. Herr K., her husband, also made himself a close friend of Dora's – going regularly for walks with her and giving her presents. Dora in her turn befriended the K.'s two small children, "and had been almost a mother to them." What begins to be slowly if unmistakably disclosed is that Dora's father and Frau K. had established a sexual liaison and that this relation had by the time of Dora's entering into treatment endured for many years. At the same time Dora's father and Frau K. had tacitly connived at turning Dora over to Herr K., just as years later her father "handed her over to me [Freud] for psychotherapeutic treatment." And Dora had herself, at least at first, behaved towards Frau K.'s children in much the same way that Frau K. had behaved towards her. Up to a certain point, then, the characters in this embroilment were virtually behaving as if they were walking in their sleep. In some sense everyone was conspiring to conceal what was going on; and in some yet further sense everyone was conspiring to deny that anything was going on at all. What we have here, on one of its sides, is a classical Victorian domestic drama, that is at the same time a sexual and emotional can of worms.

Matters were brought to a crisis by two events that occurred to Dora at two different periods of her adolescence. When she was 14 Herr K. contrived one day to be alone with her in his place of business; in a state of sexual excitement, he "suddenly clasped the girl to him and pressed a kiss on her lips." (28) Dora responded with a "violent feeling of disgust," and hurried away. This experience, like those referred to in the foregoing paragraph, was never discussed with or mentioned to anyone, and relations continued as before. The second scene took place two years later in the summer when Dora was 16 (it was just after she had seen Freud for the first time). She and Herr K. were taking a walk by a lake in the Alps. In Dora's words, as they come filtered to us through Freud, Herr K. "had the audacity to make her a proposal." Apparently he had begun to declare his love for this girl whom he had known so well for so long. "No sooner had she grasped Herr K.'s intention than, without letting him finish what he had to say, she had given him a slap in the face and hurried away." (46) The episode as a whole will lead Freud quite plausibly to ask: "If Dora loved Herr K., what was the reason for her refusing him in the scene by the lake? Or at any rate, why did her refusal take such a brutal form, as though she were embittered against him? And how could a girl who was in love feel insulted by a proposal which was made in a manner neither tactless nor offensive?" (38) It may occur to us to wonder whether in the extended context of this case that slap in the face was a "brutal form" of refusal; but as for the other questions posed by Freud, they are without question rhetorical in character.

On this second occasion Dora did not remain silent. Her father was preparing to depart from the Alpine lake, and she declared her determination to leave at once with him. Two weeks later she told the story of the scene by the lake to her mother, who relayed it – as Dora had clearly intended – to her father. In due course Herr K. was "called to account" on this score, but he

denied in the most emphatic terms having on his side made any advances which could have been open to such a construction. He had then proceeded to throw suspicion upon the girl, saying that he had heard from Frau K. that she used to read Mantegazza's *Physiology of Love* and books of that sort in their house on the lake. It was most likely, he had added, that she had been over-excited by such reading and had merely "fancied" the whole scene she had described.(26)

Dora's father "believed" the story concocted by Herr – and Frau – K., and it is from this moment, more than two years before she came to Freud for treatment, that the change in Dora's character can be dated. Her love for the K.'s turned into hatred, and she became obsessed with the idea of getting her father to break off relations with them. She saw through the rationalizations and denials of her father and Frau K., and had "no doubt that what bound her father to this young and beautiful woman was a common love-affair. Nothing that could help to confirm this view had escaped her perception, which in this connection was pitilessly sharp." (32) Indeed, "the sharp-sighted Dora" was an excellent detective when it came to uncovering her father's clandestine sexual activities, and her withering criticisms of her father's character – that he was "insincere ... had a strain of baseness in his character ... only thought of his own enjoyment ... had a gift for seeing things in the light which suited him best" (34) – were in general concurred in by Freud. As he also agreed that there was something in her embittered if exaggerated contention that "she had been handed over to Herr K. as the price of his tolerating the relations between her father and his wife."[4] (34) Nevertheless, the cause of her greatest embitterment seems to have been her father's "readiness to consider the scene by the lake as a product of her imagination. She was almost beside herself at the idea of its being supposed that she had merely fancied something on that occasion." (46) And although Freud was in his customary way skeptical about such impassioned protestations and repudiations – and surmised that something in the way of an opposite series of thoughts or self-reproaches lay behind them – he was forced to come to "the conclusion that Dora's story must correspond to the facts in every respect." (46) If we try to put ourselves in the place of this girl between her sixteenth and eighteenth years, we can at once recognize that her situation was a desperate one. The three adults to whom she was closest, whom she loved the most in the world, were apparently conspiring – separately, in tandem, or in concert – to deny her the reality of her experience. They were conspiring to deny Dora her reality and reality itself. This betrayal touched upon matters that might easily unhinge the mind of a young person; for the three adults were not betraying Dora's love and trust alone, they were betraying the structure of the actual world. And indeed, when Dora's father handed her over to Freud with the parting injunction "Please try and bring her to reason" (26), there were no two ways of taking what he meant. Naturally, he had no idea of the mind and character of the physician to whom he had dealt this leading remark.

Two other persons round out the cast of characters of this late-Victorian romance. And it seems only appropriate that they should come directly from the common stock of Victorian literature and culture, both of them being governesses. The first of these was Dora's own governess, "an unmarried woman, no longer young, who was well read and of advanced views." (36) This woman "used to read every book on sexual life and similar subjects, and talked to the girl about them," at the same time enjoining Dora to secrecy about such conversations. She had long since divined the goings-on between Dora's father and Frau K. and had in the past tried in vain to turn Dora against both Frau K. and her father. Although she had turned a blind eye to this side of things, Dora very quickly penetrated into the governess's real secret: she, too, was in love with Dora's father. And when Dora realized that this governess was actually indifferent to her – Dora's – welfare, she "dropped her." At the same time Dora had dimly to realize that there was an analogy between the governess's behavior in Dora's family and Dora's behavior in relation to the children of the K.'s and Herr K. The second governess made her appearance during Dora's last analytic hour; the appearance was brilliantly elicited by Freud, who remarked that Dora's decision to leave him, arrived at, she said, a fortnight beforehand, "'sounds just like a maid servant or governess – a fortnight's warning.'" (105) This second governess was a young girl employed by the K.'s at the time of Dora's fateful visit to them at the Alpine lake some two years before. She was a silent young person, who seemed totally to ignore the existence of Herr K. Yet a day or two before the scene at the lake she took Dora aside and told her that Herr K. had approached her sexually, had pleaded his unhappy cause with her, had in fact seduced her, but had quickly ceased to care for her. He had, in short, done to her what in a day or two he was going to try to do again with Dora. The girl said she now hated Herr K., yet she did not go away at once, but waited there hoping that Herr K.'s affections would turn again in her direction. Dora's response at the lake and afterward was in part a social one – anger at being treated by Herr K. as if she were a servant or governess; but it was also in part a response by identification, since she, too, did not tell the story at once but waited perhaps for something further from Herr K. And when, after the two-week interval, she did tell the story, Herr K. did not renew "his proposals but ... replied instead with denials and slanders" (108) in which he was aided and abetted by Dora's father, and Frau K. Dora's cup of bitterness was full to overflowing, as the following two years of deep unhappiness and deepening illness undeniably suggest.

II

Dora began treatment with Freud sometime in October, 1900, for on the fourteenth of that month Freud writes Fliess that "I have a new patient, a girl of eighteen; the case has opened smoothly to my collection of picklocks." According to this statement the analysis was proceeding well, but it was also not proceeding well. The material produced was very rich, but Dora was there more or less against her will. Moreover, she was more than usually amnesic about events in her remote past and about her inner and mental life – a past and a life towards which Freud was continually pressing her – and met many or even most of his interpretations with statements such as "I don't know," and with a variety of denials, resistances, and grudging silences. The analysis found its focus and climax in two dreams. The first of these was the production by Dora of a dream that in the past she had dreamed recurrently.[5] Among the many messages concealed by it, Freud made out one that he conveyed to his patient: "'you have decided to give up the treatment,'" he told her, adding, "'to which, after all, it is only your father who makes you come.'" (70). It was a self-fulfilling interpretation. A few weeks after the first dream, the second dream occurred. Freud spent two hours elucidating it, and at the beginning of the third, which took place on December 31, 1900, Dora informed him that she was there for the last time. Freud pressed on during this hour and presented Dora with a series of stunning and outrageously intelligent interpretations. The analysis ended as follows: "Dora had listened to me without any of her usual contradictions. She seemed to be moved; she said good-bye to me very warmly, with the heartiest wishes for the New Year, and – came no more." (109) Dora's father subsequently called on Freud two or three times to reassure him that Dora was returning, but Freud knew better than to take him at his word. Fifteen months later, in April 1902, Dora returned for a single visit; what she had to tell Freud on that occasion was of some interest, but he knew that she was done with him, as indeed she was.

Dora was actuated by many impulses in breaking off the treatment; prominent among these partial motives was revenge – upon men in general and at that moment Freud in particular, who was standing for those other men in her life who had betrayed and injured her. He writes rather ruefully of Dora's "breaking off so unexpectedly, just when my hopes of a successful termination of the treatment were at their highest, and her thus bringing those hopes to nothing – this was an unmistakeable act of vengeance on her part." And although Dora's "purpose of self-injury" was also served by this action, Freud goes on clearly to imply that he felt hurt and wounded by her behavior. Yet it could not have been so unexpected as all that, since as early as the first dream, Freud both understood and had communicated this understanding to Dora that she had already decided to give up the treatment.[6] What is suggested by this logical hiatus is that although Dora had done with Freud, Freud had not done with Dora. And this supposition is supported by what immediately followed. As soon as

Dora left him, Freud began writing up her case history – a proceeding that, as far as I have been able to ascertain, was not in point of immediacy a usual response for him. He interrupted the composition of the *Psychopathology of Everyday Life* on which he was then engaged and wrote what is substantially the case of Dora during the first three weeks of January 1901. On January 25 he wrote to Fliess that he had finished the work the day before and added, with that terrifying self-confidence of judgement that he frequently revealed, "Anyhow, it is the most subtle thing I have yet written and will produce an even more horrifying effect than usual." (4) The title he had at first given the new work – "Dreams and Hysteria" – suggests the magnitude of ambition that was at play in him. This specific case history, "in which the explanations are grouped round two dreams ... is in fact a continuation of the dream book. It further contains solutions of hysterical symptoms and considerations on the sexual-organic basis of the whole condition." As the provisional title and these further remarks reveal, it was to be nothing less than a concentrated synthesis of Freud's first two major works, *Studies on Hysteria* (1895) and *The Interpretation of Dreams* (1900), to which there had been added the new dimension of the "sexual-organic basis," that is, the psycho-sexual developmental stages that he was going to represent in fuller detail in the *Three Essays on the Theory of Sexuality* (1905). It was thus a summation, a new synthesis, a crossing point and a great leap forward all at once. Dora had taken her revenge on Freud, who in turn chose not to behave in kind. At the same time, however, Freud's settling of his account with Dora took on the proportions of a heroic inner and intellectual enterprise.

Yet that account was still by no means settled, as the obscure subsequent history of this work dramatically demonstrates. In the letter of January 25, 1901, Freud had written to Fliess that the paper had already been accepted by Ziehen, joint editor of the *Monatsschrift für Psychiatrie und Neurologie*, by which he must mean that the acceptance did not include a reading of the piece, which had only been "finished" the day before. On February 15, in another letter to Fliess, he remarks that he is now finishing up *The Psychopathology of Everyday Life*, and that when he has done so, he will correct it and the case history – by which he apparently means that he will go through one last revision of the mss. and then "send them off, etc." That "etc." is covering considerable acreage. About two months later, in March 1901, according to Ernest Jones, Freud showed "his notes of the case" – whatever *that* may mean – to his close friend Oscar Rie. The reception Rie gave to them was such, reports Freud, that "I thereupon determined to make no further effort to break down my state of isolation."[7] That determination was less than unshakable, and on May 8, 1901, Freud wrote to Fliess that he had not yet "made up his mind" to send off the work. One month later he made up his mind and sent it off, announcing to Fliess that "it will meet the gaze of an astonished public in the autumn." (4) But nothing of the sort was to occur, and what happened next was, according to Jones, "entirely mysterious" and remains so. Freud either sent it off to Ziehen, the editor who had already accepted it and then having sent it, asked for it back. Or he sent it off to another magazine altogether, the *Journal für Psychologie und Neurologie*, whose editor, one Brodmann, refused to publish it, basing his outright rejection, it has been surmised, on the grounds of the improprieties and indiscretions that would be perpetrated by such a publication (Jones, *Life and Work of Sigmund Freud*, Vol. II, pp. 255 f.). The upshot of all those circlings and countercirclings was that Freud returned the manuscript to a drawer for four more years. And when he did at last send it into print, it was in the journal that had accepted it in the first place.

But we are not out of the darkness and perplexities yet, for when Freud finally decided in 1905 to publish the case, he revised the work once again. As James Strachey remarks, "there is no means of deciding the extent" of these revisions, meaning no certain, external, or physical means. Strachey nonetheless maintains that "all the internal evidence suggests ... that he changed it very little." According to my reading, Strachey is incorrect, and there is considerable internal evidence that intimates much change. But this is no place to argue such matters, and anyway, who can say precisely what Strachey means by "little" or what I mean by "much"? There is one further touch of puzzlements to top it all off. Freud got the date of his case wrong. When he wrote or rewrote it, either in January 1901, or in 1905, he assigned the case to the autumn of 1899 instead of 1900. And he continued to date it incorrectly, repeating the error in 1914 in the "History of the Psychoanalytic Movement" and again in 1923 when he added a number of new footnotes to the essay on the occasion of its publication in the eighth volume of his *Gesammelte Schriften*. Among the many things suggested by this recurrent error is that in some sense he had still not done with Dora, as indeed I think we shall see he had not. The modern reader may be inclined to remark that all this hemming and hawing about dates and obscurities of composition, questions of revision, problems of textual status, and authorial uncertainties of attitude would be more suitable to the discussion of a literary text – a poem, play, or novel – than to a work of "science." If this is so, one has to reply to this hypothetical reader that he is barking up the wrong discourse, and that his conception of the nature of scientific discourse – particularly the modes of discourse that are exercised in those disciplines which are not preponderantly or uniformly mathematical or quantitative – has to undergo a radical revision.

The final form into which Freud casts all this material is as original as it is deceptively straightforward. It is divided into five parts. It opens with a short but extremely dense and condensed series of "Prefatory Remarks." There follows the longest section of the work, called "The Clinical Picture" (*Der Krankheitszustand*). In this part Freud describes the history of Dora's family and of how he got to know them, presents an account of Dora's symptoms and how they seemed to have been acquired, and informs the reader of the process by which she was brought to him for treatment. He also represents some of the progress they had made in the first weeks of the treatment. Throughout he intersperses his account of Dora's illness and treatment with excursions and digressions of varying lengths on an assortment of theoretical topics that the material of the case brought into relevant prominence. The third part of the essay, "The First Dream," consists of the reproduction in part of the analysis of Dora's recurrent dream. Part of it is cast in dramatic dialogue, part in indirect discourse, part in a shifting diversity of narrative and expository modes, each of which is summoned up by Freud with effortless mastery. The entire material of the case up to now is reviewed and re-enacted once more: new material ranging from Dora's early childhood through her early adolescence and down to the moment of the analysis is unearthed and discussed, again from a series of analytic perspectives and explanatory levels that shift about so rapidly that one is inclined to call them rotatory. The fourth part, "The Second Dream," is about the final three sessions of the treatment, and Freud invents yet another series of original compositional devices to present the fluid mingling of dramatic, expository, narrative, and analytic materials that were concentrated in the three hours. The final part of the essay, "Postscript," written indeed after the case was officially "closed" but at an utterly indeterminate set of dates, is true to its title. It is not a conclusion in the traditional sense of neatly rounding off through a final summary and group of generalizations the material dealt with in the body of the work – although it does do some of that. It is rather a group of added remarks, whose effect is to introduce still further considerations, and the work is brought to its proper end by opening up new and indeterminate avenues of exploration; it closes by giving us a glimpse of unexplored mental vistas in whose light presumably the entire case that has gone before would be transfigured yet again.

The general form, then, of what Freud has written bears certain suggestive resemblances to a modern experimental novel. Its narrative and expository course, for example, is neither linear nor rectilinear; instead, its organization is plastic, involuted, and heterogeneous, and follows spontaneously an inner logic that seems frequently to be at odds with itself; it often loops back around itself and is multi-dimensional in its representation of both its material and itself. Its continuous innovations in formal structure seem unavoidably to be dictated by its substance, by the dangerous, audacious, disreputable, and problematical character of the experiences being represented and dealt with, and by the equally scandalous intentions of the author and the outrageous character of the role he has had the presumption to assume. In content, however, what Freud has written is in parts rather like a play by Ibsen, or more precisely, like a series of Ibsen's plays. And as one reads through the case of Dora, scenes and characters from such works as *Pillars of Society*, *A Doll's House*, *Ghosts*, *An Enemy of the People*, *The Wild Duck*, and *Rosmersholm* rise up and flit through the mind. There is, however, this difference. In this Ibsen-like drama, Freud is not only Ibsen, the creator and playwright; he is also and directly one of the characters in the action, and in the end suffers in a way that is comparable to the suffering of the others.

What I have been reiterating at excessive length is that the case of Dora is first and last an extraordinary piece of writing, and it is to this circumstance in several of its most striking aspects that we should direct our attention. For it is a case history, a kind of genre of writing – a particular way of conceiving and constructing human experience in written language – which in Freud's hands became something that it never was before.[8]

III

The ambiguities and difficulties begin with the very title of the work, "Fragment of an Analysis of a Case of Hysteria." In what sense or senses is this piece of writing that the author describes as "a detailed report of the history of a case" a fragment? (7) Freud himself supplies us with a superabundant wealth of detail on this count. It is a fragment in the sense that its "results" are "incomplete." The treatment was "broken off at the patient's own wish," at a time when certain problems "had not been attacked and others had only been imperfectly elucidated." It follows that the analysis itself is "only a fragment," as are "the following pages" of writing which present it. (12) To which the modern reader, flushed with the superior powers of his educated irony, is tempted to reply: how is it that this fragment is also a whole, an achieved totality, an integral piece of writing called a case history? And how is it, furthermore, that this "fragment" is

fuller, richer, and more complete than the most "complete" case
histories of anyone else? But there is no more point in asking such
questions of Freud – particularly at this preliminary stage of
proceedings – than there would be in posing similar "theoretical"
questions to Joyce or Proust. And indeed Freud has barely begun.

The work is also fragmentary, he continues, warming to his
subject, because of the very method he has chosen to pursue; on this
plan, that of non-directional free association, "everything that has to
do with the clearing-up of a particular symptom emerges piecemeal,
woven into various contexts, and distributed over widely separate
periods of time." Freud's technique itself is therefore fragmentary;
his way of penetrating to the micro-structure – the "finer structure,"
as he calls it – of a neurosis is to allow the material to emerge
piecemeal. At the same time these fragments only *appear* to be
incoherent and disparate; in actuality they eventually will be
understood as members of a whole. Still, in the present instance the
results were more than usually unfinished and partial, and to explain
what in the face of such difficulties he has done, he resorts to one of
his favorite metaphorical figures:

> I had no choice but to follow the example of those discoverers
> whose good fortune it is to bring to the light of day after their long
> burial the priceless though mutilated relics of antiquity. I have
> restored what is missing, taking the best models known to me from
> other analyses; but, like a conscientious archaeologist, I have not
> omitted to mention in each case where the authentic facts end and
> my constructions begin. (12)[9]

Here the matter has complicated itself one degree further. The
mutilated relics or fragments of the past also remain fragments; what
Freud has done is to restore, construct, and reconstruct what is
missing – an activity and a group of conceptions that introduce an
entirely new range of contingencies. And there is more of this in the
offing as well.

Furthermore, Freud goes on, there is still another "kind of
incompleteness" to be found in this work, and this time it has been
"intentionally introduced." He has deliberately chosen not to
reproduce "the process of interpretation to which the patient's
associations and communications had to be subjected, but only the
results of that process." That is to say, what we have before us is not a
transcription in print of a tape recording of eleven weeks of analysis
but something that is abridged, edited, synthesized, and constructed
from the very outset. And as if this were not enough, Freud
introduces yet another context in which the work has to be regarded

as fragmentary and incomplete. It is obvious, he argues, "that a single case history, even if it were complete and open to no doubt, cannot provide an answer to all questions arising out of the problem of hysteria." One case of hysteria, in short, cannot exhaust the structure of all the others. And so in this sense too the work is a particle or component of a larger entity or whole. It nevertheless remains at the same time a whole in itself and has to stand by itself in its own idiosyncratic way – which is to be simultaneously fragmentary and complete. Thus, like a modernist writer – which in part he is – Freud begins by elaborately announcing the problematical status of his undertaking and the dubious character of his achievement.

Even more, like some familiar "unreliable narrator" in modernist fiction, Freud pauses at regular intervals to remind the reader of this case history that "my insight into the complex of events composing it [has] remained fragmentary," that his understanding of it remains in some essential sense permanently occluded. This darkness and constraint are the result of a number of converging circumstances, some of which have already been touched on and include the shortness of the analysis and its having been broken off by Dora at a crucial point. But it also includes the circumstance that the analysis – any analysis – must proceed by fragmentary methods, by analyzing thoughts and events bit by discontinuous bit. Indeed, at the end of one virtuoso passage in which Freud demonstrates through a series of referential leaps and juxtapositions the occurrence in Dora's past of childhood masturbation, he acknowledges that this is the essence of his procedure. "Part of this material," he writes, "I was able to obtain directly from the analysis, but the rest required supplementing. And, indeed, the method by which the occurrence of masturbation in Dora's case has been verified has shown us that material belonging to a single subject can only be collected piece by piece at various times and in different connections." (80) The method is hence a fragmentary construction and reconstruction which in the end amount to a whole that simultaneously retains its disjointed character – in sum it resembles "reality" itself, a word that, as writers today like to remind us, should always be surrounded by quotation marks.

At the same time, however, Freud protests too much in the opposite direction, as when he remarks that "it is only because the analysis was prematurely broken off that we have been obliged in Dora's case to resort to framing conjectures and filling in deficiencies." (85) At an earlier moment he had asserted that "if the work had been continued, we should no doubt have obtained the fullest possible enlightenment upon every particular of the case." (19) We shall return later to these and other similar remarks, but in the present connection what they serve to underscore is Freud's effort to persuade us, and himself, of how much more he could have done – an effort which, by this point in the writing, the reader is no longer able to take literally.[10] And this tendency to regard such assertions with a certain degree of skepticism is further reinforced when at the end of the essay – after over 100 pages of dazzling originality, of creative genius performing with a compactness, complexity, daring, and splendor that seem close to incomparable in their order – he returns to this theme, which was, we should recall, set going by *the very first word* of his title. He begins the "Postscript" with a statement whose modesty is by now comically outrageous. "It is true," he writes, "that I have introduced this paper as a fragment of an analysis; but the reader will have discovered that it is incomplete to a far greater degree than its title might have led him to expect." (112) This disclaimer is followed by still another rehearsal of what has been left out. In particular, he writes, he has "in this paper entirely left out of account the technique," and, he adds, "I found it quite impracticable ...to deal simultaneously with the technique of analysis and with the internal structure of a case of hysteria." In any event, he concludes, "I could scarcely have accomplished such a task, and if I had, the result would have been almost unreadable." (112) And if the reader is not grateful for these small mercies, Freud goes on a few pages later to speak of this essay as a "case of whose history and treatment I have published a fragment in these pages." In short, this fragment is itself only a fragment of a fragment. If this is so – and there is every reason to believe that Freud is seriously bandying about with words – then we are compelled to conclude that in view of the extreme complexity of this fragment of a fragment, the conception of the whole that Freud has in mind is virtually unimaginable and inconceivable.

We are then obliged to ask – and Freud himself more than anyone else has taught us most about this obligation – *what else* are all these protestations of fragmentariness and incompleteness about? Apart from their slight but continuous unsettling effect upon the reader, and their alerting him to the circumstances that there is an author and a series of contingencies behind the solid mass of printed matter that he is poring over, plowing through, and browsing in, as if it were a piece of nature and not a created artifact – apart from this, what else do these protestations refer to? They refer in some measure, as Freud himself indicates in the postscript, to a central inadequacy and determining incompleteness that he discovered only after it was too late – the "great defect" (118) of the case was to be located in the undeveloped, misdeveloped, and equivocal character of the "trans-ference," of the relation between patient and physician in which so much was focused. Something went wrong in the relation between

Freud and Dora or – if there are any analysts still reading – in the relation between Dora and Freud. But the protestations refer, I believe, to something else as well, something of which Freud was not entirely conscious. For the work is also fragmentary or incomplete in the sense of Freud's self-knowledge, both at the time of the actual case and at the time of his writing it. And he communicates in this piece of writing a less than complete understanding of himself, though like any great writer, he provides us with the material for understanding some things that have escaped his own understanding, for filling in some gaps, for restoring certain fragments into wholes.

How else can we finally explain the fact that Freud chose to write up this particular history in such extensive detail? The reasons that he offers in both the "Prefatory Remarks" and the "Postscript" aren't entirely convincing – which doesn't of course deny them a real if fractional validity. Why should he have chosen so problematic a case, when presumably others of a more complete yet equally brief kind were available? I think this can be understood in part through Freud's own unsettled and ambiguous role in the case; that he had not yet, so to speak, "gotten rid" of it; that he had to write it out, in some measure, as an effort of self-understanding – an effort, I think we shall see, that remained heroically unfinished, a failure that nonetheless brought lasting credit with it.

IV

If we turn now to the "Prefatory Remarks," it may be illuminating to regard them as a kind of novelistic framing action, as in these few opening pages Freud rehearses his motives, reasons, and intentions and begins at the same time to work his insidious devices upon the reader. First, exactly like a novelist, he remarks that what he is about to let us in on is positively scandalous, for "the complete elucidation of a case of hysteria is bound to involve the revelation of intimacies and the betrayal of ... secrets." (8) Second, again like a writer of fiction, he has deliberately chosen persons, places, and circumstances that will remain obscure; the scene is laid not in metropolitan Vienna but "in a remote provincial town." He has from the beginning kept the circumstance that Dora was his patient such a close secret that only one other physician – "in whose discretion I have complete confidence" – knows about it. He has "postponed publication" of this essay for "four whole years," also in the cause of discretion, and in the same cause has "allowed no name to stand which could put a non-medical reader on the scent." (8) Finally, he has buried the case even deeper by publishing it "in a purely scientific and technical periodical" in order to secure yet another "guarantee against unauthorized readers." He has, in short, made his own mystery within a mystery, and one of the effects of such obscure preliminary goings-on is to create a kind of Nabokovian frame – what we have here is a history framed by an explanation which is itself slightly out of focus.[11]

Third, he roundly declares, this case history is science and not literature: "I am aware that – in this city, at least – there are many physicians who (revolting though it may seem) choose to read a case history of this kind not as a contribution to the psychopathology of neuroses, but as a *roman à clef* designed for their private delectation." (9) This may indeed be true; but it is equally true that nothing is more literary – and more modern – than the disavowal of all literary intentions. And when Freud does this again later on towards the end of "The Clinical Picture," the situation becomes even less credible. The passage merits quotation at length.

I must now turn to consider a further complication to which I should certainly give no space if I were a man of letters engaged upon the creation of a mental state like this for a short story, instead of being a medical man engaged upon its dissection. The element to which I must now allude can only serve to obscure and efface the outlines of the fine poetic conflict which we have been able to ascribe to Dora. This element would rightly fall a sacrifice to the censorship of a writer, for he, after all, simplifies and abstracts when he appears in the character of a psychologist. But in the world of reality, which I am trying to depict here, a complication of motives, an accumulation and conjunction of mental activities – in a word, overdetermination – is the rule (59 f.)

In this context it is next to impossible to tell whether Freud is up to another of his crafty maneuverings with the reader or whether he is actually simply unconscious of how much of a modern and modernist writer he is. For when he takes to describing the difference between himself and some hypothetical man of letters and writer of short stories he is in fact embarked upon an elaborate obfuscation. That hypothetical writer is nothing but a straw man; and when Freud in apparent contrast represents himself and his own activities, he is truly representing how a genuine creative writer writes. And this passage, we must also recall, came from the same pen that only a little more than a year earlier had written passages about Oedipus and Hamlet that changed for good the ways in which the civilized world would henceforth think about literature and writers.[12] What might be thought of as this sly unliterariness of Freud's turns up in other contexts as well.

If we return to the point in the "Prefatory Remarks" from which we have momentarily digressed, we find that Freud then goes on to describe other difficulties, constraints, and problematical circumstances attaching to the situation in which he finds himself. Among them is the problem of "how to record for publication" (10) even such a short case – the long ones are as yet altogether impossible. We shall presently return to this central passage. Moreover, since the material that critically illuminated this case was grouped about two dreams, their analysis formed a secure point of departure for the writing. (Freud is of course at home with dreams, being the unchallenged master in the reading of them.) Yet this tactical solution pushes the *entire problematic* back only another step further, since Freud at once goes on to his additional presupposition, that only those who are already familiar with "the interpretation of dreams" – that is, *The Interpretation of Dreams* (1900), whose readership in 1901 must have amounted to a little platoon indeed – are likely to be satisfied at all with the present account. Any other reader "will find only bewilderment in these pages." (11) As much as it is like anything else, this is like Borges – as well as Nabokov. In these opening pages Freud actively and purposefully refuses to give the reader a settled point of attachment, and instead works at undercutting and undermining his stability by such slight manipulations as this: i.e., in order to read the case of Dora which the reader presumably has right in front of him, he must also first have read the huge, abstruse, and almost entirely unread dream book of the year before. This offputting and disconcerting quality, it should go without saying, is characteristically modern; the writer succumbs to no impulse to make it easy for the reader; on the contrary, he is by preference rather forbidding and does not extend a cordial welcome. But Freud has not yet finished piling Pelion upon Ossa, and he goes on to add for good measure that the reader really ought to have read *Studies on Hysteria* as well, if only to be confounded by the differences between this case and those discussed at much briefer length there. With this and with a number of further remarks about the unsatisfactory satisfactory character of what he has done and what is to come, Freud closes this frame of "Prefatory Remarks," leaving what audience he still has left in a bemused, uncertain, and dislocated state of mind. The reader has been, as it were, "softened up" by his first encounter with this unique expository and narrative authority; he is thoroughly off balance and is as a consequence ready to be "educated," by Freud. By the same token, however, if he has followed these opening few pages carefully, he is certainly no longer as prepared as he was to assert the primacy and priority of his own critical sense of things. He is precisely where Freud – and any writer – wants him to be.

At the opening of Part I, "The Clinical Picture," Freud tells us that he begins his "treatment, indeed, by asking the patient to give me the whole story of his life and illness," and immediately adds that "the information I receive is never enough to let me see my way about the case." (16) This inadequacy and unsatisfactoriness in the stories his patients tell is in distinct contrast to what Freud has read in the accounts rendered by his psychiatric contemporaries, and he continues by remarking that "I cannot help wondering how it is that the authorities can produce such smooth and exact histories in cases of hysteria. As a matter of fact the patients are incapable of giving such reports about themselves." There is an immense amount beginning to go on here. In the first place, there is the key assumption that everyone – that every life, every existence – has a story, to which there is appended a corollary that most of us probably tell that story poorly. There follows at once Freud's statement of flat disbelief in the "smooth and exact" histories published by his colleagues who study hysteria. The implications that are latent in this negation are at least twofold: (1) these authorities are incompetent and may in some sense be "making up" the histories they publish; (2) real case histories are neither "smooth" nor "exact," and the reader cannot expect to find such qualities here in the "real" thing. Furthermore, the relations at this point in Freud's prose between the words "story," "history," and "report" are unspecified, undifferentiated, and unanalyzed and in the nature of the case contain and conceal a wealth of material.

Freud proceeds to specify what it is that is wrong with the stories his patients tell him. The difficulties are in the first instance formal shortcomings of *narrative*: the connections, "even the ostensible ones – are for the most part incoherent," obscured and unclear; "and the sequence of different events is uncertain." In short, these narratives are disorganized, and the patients are unable to tell a coherent story of their lives. What is more, he states, "the patients' inability to give an ordered history of their life in so far as it coincides with the history of their illness is not merely characteristic of the neurosis. It also possesses great theoretical significance." (16) Part of this significance comes into view when we regard this conjecture from its obverse side, which Freud does at once in a footnote.

> Another physician once sent his sister to me for psychotherapeutic treatment, telling me that she had for years been treated without success for hysteria (pains and defective gait). The short account which he gave me seemed quite consistent with the diagnosis. In my first hour with the patient I got her to tell me her history herself. When the story came out perfectly clearly and connectedly

in spite of the remarkable events it dealt with, I told myself that the case could not be one of hysteria, and immediately instituted a careful physical examination. This led to the diagnosis of a not very advanced stage of tabes, which was later on treated with Hg injections ... with markedly beneficial results. (16 f.)

What we are led at this juncture to conclude is that Freud is implying that a coherent story is in some manner connected with mental health (at the very least, with the absence of hysteria), and this in turn implies assumptions of the broadest and deepest kind about both the nature of coherence and the form and structure of human life. On this reading, human life is, ideally, a connected and coherent story, with all the details in explanatory place, and with everything (or as close to everything as is practically possible) accounted for, in its proper causal or other sequence. And inversely, illness amounts at least in part to suffering from an incoherent story or an inadequate narrative account of oneself.

Freud then describes in technical detail the various types and orders of narrative insufficiency that he commonly finds; they range from disingenuousness both conscious and unconscious to amnesias and paramnesias of several kinds and various other means of severing connections and altering chronologies. In addition, he maintains, this discomposed memory applies with particular force and virulence to "the history of the illness" for which the patient has come for treatment. In the course of a successful treatment, this incoherence, incompleteness, and fragmentariness are progressively transmuted, as facts, events, and memories are brought forward into the forefront of the patient's mind.

> The paramnesias prove untenable, and the gaps in his memory are filled in. It is only towards the end of the treatment that we have before us an intelligible, consistent, and unbroken case history. Whereas the practical aim of the treatment is to remove all possible symptoms and to replace them by conscious thoughts, we may regard it as a second and theoretical aim to repair all the damages to the patient's memory. (18)

And he adds as a conclusion that these two aims "are coincident" – they are reached simultaneously and by the same path.[13] Some of the consequences that can be derived from these tremendous remarks are as follows. The history of any patient's illness is itself only a sub-story (or a sub-plot), although it is at the same time a vital part of a larger structure. Furthermore, in the course of psychoanalytic treatment, nothing less than "reality" itself is made, constructed, or reconstructed. A complete story – "intelligible, consistent, and unbroken" – is the theoretical, created end story. It is a story, or a fiction, not only because it has a narrative structure but also because the narrative account has been rendered in language, in conscious speech, and no longer exists in the deformed language of symptoms, the untranslated speech of the body. At the end – at the successful end – one has come into possession of one's own story. It is a final act of self-appropriation, the appropriation by oneself of one's own history. This is in part so because one's own story is in so large a measure a phenomenon of language, as psychoanalysis is in turn a demonstration of the degree to which language can go in the reading of all our experience. What we end with, then, is a fictional construction which is at the same time satisfactory to us in the form of the truth, and as the form of the truth.

No larger tribute has ever been paid to a culture in which the various narrative and fictional forms had exerted for centuries both moral and philosophical authority and which had produced as one of its chief climaxes the great bourgeois novels of the nineteenth century. Indeed, we must see Freud's writings – and method – as themselves part of this culmination, and at the same moment, along with the great modernist novels of the first half of the twentieth century, as the beginning of the end of that tradition and its authority. Certainly the passages we have just dealt with contain heroic notions and offer an extension of heroic capabilities if not to all men then to most, at least as a possibility. Yet we cannot leave this matter so relatively unexamined, and must ask ourselves how it is that this "story" is not merely a "history" but a "case history" as well. We must ask ourselves how these associated terms are more intimately related in the nexus that is about to be wound and unwound before us. To begin to understand such questions, we have to turn back to a central passage in the "Prefatory Remarks." Freud undertakes therein "to describe the way in which I have overcome the *technical* difficulties of drawing up the report of this case history." (9) Apparently "the report" and the "case history" referred to in this statement are two discriminable if not altogether discrete entities. If they are, then we can further presume that, ideally at any rate, Dora (or any patient) is as much in possession of the "case history" as Freud himself. And this notion is in some part supported by what comes next. Freud mentions certain other difficulties, such as the fact that he "cannot make notes during the actual session ... for fear of shaking the patient's confidence and of disturbing his own view of the material under observation." (9) In the case of Dora, however, this obstacle was partly overcome because so much of the material was grouped about two dreams, and "the wording of these dreams was recorded immediately after the session" so that "they thus afforded a secure point of attachment for the chain of interpretations and recollections which proceeded from there." Freud then writes as follows:

> The case history itself was only committed to writing from memory after the treatment was at an end, but while my recollection of the case was still fresh and was heightened by my interest in its publication. Thus the record is not absolutely – phonographically – exact, but it can claim to possess a high degree of trustworthiness. Nothing of any importance has been altered in it except in some places the order in which the explanations are given; and this has been done for the sake of presenting the case in a more connected form. (10)

Such a passage raises more questions than it resolves. The first sentence is a kind of conundrum in which case history, writing, and memory dance about in a series of logical entwinements, of possible alternate combinations, equivalences, and semi-equivalences. These are followed by further equivocations about "the record," "phonographic" exactitude, and so forth – the ambiguities of which jump out at one as the terms begin to be seriously examined. For example, is "the report" the same thing as "the record"; and if "the record" were "phonographically" exact, would it be a "report"? Like the prodigious narrative historian that he is, Freud is enmeshed in an irreducible paradox of history: that the term itself refers to both the activity of the historian – the writing of history – and to the objects of his undertaking, what history is "about." I do not think, therefore, that we can conclude that Freud has created this thick context of historical contingency and ambiguity out of what he once referred to as Viennese *schlamperei*.

The historical difficulties are further compounded by several other sequential networks that are mentioned at the outset and that figure discernibly throughout the writing. First, there is the virtual Proustian complexity of Freud's interweaving of the various strands of time in the actual account; or, to change the figure, his geological fusing of various time strata – strata which are themselves at once fluid and shifting. We observe this most strikingly in the palimpsest-like quality of the writing itself; which refers back to *Studies on Hysteria* of 1895; which records a treatment that took place at the end of 1900 (although it mistakes the date by a year); which then was written up in first form during the early weeks of 1901; which was then exhumed in 1905 and was revised and rewritten to an indeterminable extent before publication in that year; and to which additional critical comments in the form of footnotes were finally appended in 1923. All of these are of course held together in vital connection and interanimation by nothing else than Freud's consciousness. But we must take notice as well of the co-presence of still further different time sequences in Freud's presentation – this co-presence being itself a historical or novelistic circumstance of some magnitude. There is first the connection established by the periodically varied rehearsal throughout the account of Freud's own theory and theoretical notions as they had developed up to that point; this practice provides a kind of running applied history of psychoanalytic theory as its development is refracted through the embroiled medium of this particular case. Then there are the different time strata of Dora's own history, which Freud handles with confident and loving exactitude. Indeed, he is never more of a historical virtuoso than when he reveals himself to us as moving with compelling ease back and forth between the complex group of sequential histories and narrative accounts with divergent sets of diction and at different levels of explanation that constitute the extraordinary fabric of this work. He does this most conspicuously in his analytic dealings with Dora's dreams, for every dream, he reminds us, sets up a connection between two "factors," an "event during childhood" and an "event of the present day – and it endeavors to reshape the present on the model of the remote past." (71) The existence or re-creation of the past in the present is in fact "history" in more than one of its manifold senses. And such a passage is also one of Freud's many analogies to the following equally celebrated utterance.

> Men make their own history, but they do not make it just as they please; they do not make it under circumstances chosen by themselves, but under circumstances directly encountered, given and transmitted from the past. The tradition of all the dead generations weighs like a nightmare on the brain of the living. And just when they seem engaged in revolutionising themselves and things, in creating something that has never yet existed, precisely in such periods of revolutionary crisis they anxiously conjure up the spirits of the past to their service and borrow from them names, battle cries, and costumes in order to present the new scene of world history in this time-honored disguise and this borrowed language.[14]

And just as Marx regards the history-makers of the past as sleepwalkers, "who required recollections of past world history in order to drug themselves concerning their own content," so Freud similarly regards the conditions of dream-formation, of neurosis itself, and even of the cure of neurosis, namely, the analytic experience of transference. They are all of them species of living past history in the present. If the last of these works out satisfactorily, then a case history is at the end transfigured. It becomes an inseparable part of an integral life history. Freud is of course the master historian of those transfigurations.[15]

V

We cannot in prudence follow Freud's written analysis of the case in anything like adequate detail. What we can do is try to trace out the persistence and development of certain themes. And we can try as well to keep track of the role – or some of the roles – played by Freud in the remainder of this case out of whose failure this triumph of mind and of literature emerged. At the very beginning, after he had listened to the father's account of "Dora's impossible behavior," Freud abstained from comment, for, he remarks, "I had resolved from the first to suspend my judgement of the true state of affairs till I had heard the other side as well." (26) Such a suspension inevitably recalls an earlier revolutionary project. In describing the originating plan of *Lyrical Ballads*, Coleridge writes that it "was agreed that my endeavours should be directed to persons and characters super- natural, or at least romantic; yet so as to transfer from our inward nature a human interest and a semblance of truth sufficient to procure for these shadows of imagination that willing suspension of disbelief for the moment, which constitutes poetic faith."[16] We know very well that Freud had a more than ordinary capacity in this direction, and that one of the most dramatic moments in the prehistory of psychoanalysis had to do precisely with his taking on faith facts that turned out to be fantasies. Yet Freud is not only the reader suspending judgement and disbelief until he has heard the other side of the story; and he is not only the poet or writer who must induce a similar process in himself if he is to elicit it in his audience. He is also concomitantly a principal, an actor, a living character in the drama that he is unfolding in print before us. Moreover, that suspension of disbelief is in no sense incompatible with a large body of assumptions, many of them definite, a number of them positively alarming. I think that before we pursue any further Freud's spectacular gyrations as a writer, we had better confront the chief of these presuppositions.

They have to do largely with sexuality and in particular with female sexuality. They are brought to a focus in the central scene of Dora's life (and case), a scene that Freud "orchestrates" with inimitable richness and to which he recurs thematically at a number of junctures with the tact and sense of form that one associates with a classical composer of music (or with Proust, Mann, or Joyce). Dora told this episode to Freud towards the beginning of their relation, after "the first difficulties of the treatment had been overcome." It is the scene between her and Herr K. which took place when she was 14 years old – that is, four years before the present tense of the case – and that acted, Freud said, as a "sexual trauma." The reader will recall that on this occasion Herr K. contrived to get Dora alone "at his place of business" in the town of B —, and then without warning or preparation "suddenly clasped the girl to him and pressed a kiss upon her lips." Freud then asserts that "this was *surely* just the situation to call up a *distinct* feeling of sexual excitement in a *girl* of *fourteen* who had *never before* been approached. But Dora had at that moment a violent feeling of disgust, tore herself free from the man, and hurried past him to the staircase and from there to the street door." [all italics are mine] (28). She avoided seeing the K.'s for a few days after this, but then relations returned to "normal" – if such a term survives with any permissible sense in the present context. She continued to meet Herr K., and neither of them ever mentioned "the little scene." Moreover, Freud adds, "according to her account Dora kept it a secret till her confession during the treatment," and he pretty clearly implies that he believes this.

This episode preceded by two years the scene at the lake that acted as the precipitating agent for the severe stage of Dora's illness; and it was this later episode and the entire structure that she and others had elaborated about it that she had first presented to Freud, who continues thus:

> In this scene – second in order of mention, but first in order of time – the behavior of this child of fourteen was already entirely and completely hysterical. I should without question consider a person hysterical in whom an occasion for sexual excitement elicited feelings that were preponderantly or exclusively unpleasurable; and I should do so whether or no the person were capable of producing somatic symptoms.(28)

As if this were not enough, he proceeds to produce another rabbit out of his hat. In Dora's feeling of disgust an obscure psychical mechanism called the "reversal of affect" was brought into play; but so was another process, and here Freud introduces – casually and almost as a throwaway – one more of his grand theoretical-clinical formulations, namely, the idea of the "*displacement* of sensation," or, as it has more commonly come to be referred to, the "displacement upwards." "Instead of the genital sensation which would certainly have been felt by a healthy girl in such circumstances, Dora was overcome by the unpleasurable feeling which is proper to the tract of mucous membrane at the entrance to the alimentary canal – that is by disgust." Although the disgust did not persist as a permanent symptom but remained behind residually and potentially in a general distaste for food and poor appetite, a second displacement upward was the resultant of this scene "in the shape of a sensory hallucination which occurred from time to time and even made its appearance while she was telling me her story. She declared that she could still feel upon the upper part of her body the pressure of Herr K.'s embrace." Dipping into the hat once again, and taking into account certain other of Dora's "inexplicable" – and hitherto unmentioned – "peculiarities" (such as her phobic reluctance to walk past any man she saw engaged in animated conversation with a woman), Freud "formed in my own mind the following reconstruction of the scene. I believe that during the man's passionate embrace she felt not merely his kiss upon her lips but also his erect member against her body. The perception was revolting to her; it was dismissed from her memory, repressed, and replaced by the innocent sensation of pressure upon her thorax, which in turn derived an excessive intensity from its repressed source." (30) This repressed source was located in the erotogenic oral zone, which in Dora's case had undergone a developmental deformation from the period of infancy. And thus, Freud concludes, "the pressure of the erect member probably led to an analogous change in the corresponding female organ, the clitoris; and the excitation of this second erotogenic zone was referred by a process of displacement to the simultaneous pressure against the thorax and became fixed there." (30)

This passage of unquestionable genius contains at the same time something questionable and askew. In it Freud is at once dogmatically certain and very uncertain. He is dogmatically certain of what the normative sexual response in young and other females is, and asserts himself to that effect. At the same time he is, in my judgement, utterly uncertain about where Dora is, or was, developmentally. At one moment in the passage he calls her a "girl," at another a "child" – but in point of fact he treats her throughout as if this 14-, 16-, and 18-year-old adolescent had the capacities for sexual response of a grown woman – indeed, at a later point he conjectures again that Dora either responded, or should have responded, to the embrace with specific genital heat and moisture. Too many determinations converge at this locus for us to do much more than single out a few of the more obvious influencing circumstances. In the first instance, there was Freud's own state of knowledge about such matters at the time, which was better than anyone else's but still relatively crude and undifferentiated. Second, we may be in the presence of what can only be accounted for by assuming that a genuine historical-cultural change has taken place between then and now. It may be that Freud was expressing a legitimate partial assumption of his time and culture when he ascribes to a 14-year-old adolescent – whom he calls a "child" – the normative responses that are ascribed today to a fully developed and mature woman.[17] This supposition is borne out if we consider the matter from the other end, from the standpoint of what has happened to the conception of adolescence in our own time. It begins now in pre-puberty and extends to – who knows when? Certainly its extensibility in our time has reached well beyond the age of 30. Third, Freud is writing in this passage as an advocate of nature, sexuality, openness, and candor – and within such a context Dora cannot hope to look good. The very framing of the context in such a manner is itself slightly accusatory. In this connection we may note that Freud goes out of his way to tell us that he knew Herr K. personally and that "he was still quite young and of prepossessing appearance."[18] If we let Nabokov back into the picture for a moment, we may observe that Dora is no Lolita, and go on to suggest that *Lolita* is an anti-*Dora*.

Yet we must also note that in this episode – the condensed and focusing scene of the entire case history – Freud is as much a novelist as he is an analyst. For the central moment of this central scene is a "reconstruction" that he "formed in my own mind." This pivotal construction becomes henceforth the principal "reality" of the case, and we must also observe that this reality remains Freud's more than Dora's, since he was never quite able to convince her of the plausibility of the construction; or, to regard it from the other pole of the dyad, she was never quite able to accept this version of reality, of what "really" happened. Freud was not at first unduly distressed by this resistance on her side, for part of his understanding of what he had undertaken to do in psychoanalysis was to instruct his patients – and his readers – in the nature of reality. This reality was the reality that modern readers of literature have also had to be educated in. It was conceived of as a *world of meanings*. As Freud put it in one of those stop-you-dead-in-your-tracks footnotes that he was so expert in using strategically, we must at almost every moment "be prepared to be met not by one but by several causes – by *overdetermination*." (31) Thus the world of meanings is a world of multiple and compacted causations; it is a world in which everything has a meaning, which means that everything has more than one meaning. Every symptom is a concrete universal in several senses. It not only embodies a network of significances but also "serves to represent several unconscious mental processes simultaneously." (58) By the same token, since it is a world almost entirely brought into existence, maintained and mediated through a series of linguistic transactions between patient and physician, it partakes in full measure of the virtually limitless complexity of language, in particular its capacities for producing statements characterized by multiplicity, duplicity, and ambiguity of significance. Freud lays particular stress on the ambiguity, is continually on the lookout for it, and brings his own formidable skills in this direction to bear most strikingly on the analyses of Dora's dreams. The first thing he picks up in the first of her dreams is in fact an ambiguous statement, with which he at once confronts her. While he is doing so, he is also letting down a theoretical footnote for the benefit of his readers.

> I laid stress on these words because they took me aback. They seemed to have an ambiguous ring to them. . . . Now, in a line of associations ambiguous words (or as we may call them, 'switch-words') act like points at a junction. If the points are switched across from the position in which they appear to lie in the dream, then we find ourselves on another set of rails; and along this second track run the thoughts which we are in search of but which still lie concealed behind the dream.(65)[19]

As if this were not sufficient, the actual case itself was full of such literary and novelistic devices or conventions as thematic analogies, double plots, reversals, inversions, variations, betrayals, etc. – full of what the "sharp-sighted" Dora as well as the sharp-sighted Freud thought of as "hidden connections" – though it is important to add that Dora and her physician mean different things by the same phrase. And as the case proceeds Freud continues to confront Dora with such connections and tries to enlist her assistance in their construction. For example, one of the least pleasant characteristics in Dora's nature was her habitual reproachfulness – it was directed mostly towards her father but radiated out in all directions. Freud regarded this behavior in his own characteristic manner. "A string of reproaches against other people," he comments, "leads one to suspect the existence of a string of self-reproaches with the same content." (35) Freud accordingly followed the procedure of turning back "each simple reproach on the speaker herself." When Dora reproached her father with malingering in order to keep himself in the company of Frau K., Freud felt "obliged to point out to the patient that her present ill-health was just as much actuated by motives and was just as tendentious as had been Frau K.'s illness, which she had understood so well." (42) At such moments Dora begins to mirror the other characters in the case, as they in differing degrees all mirror one another as well.

Yet the unity that all these internal references and correspondences points to is not that of a harmony or of an uninflected linear series. And at one moment Freud feels obliged to remark that

> my experience in the clearing-up of hysterical symptoms has shown that it is not necessary for the various meanings of a symptom to be compatible with one another, that is, to fit together into a connected whole. It is enough that the unity should be constituted by the subject-matter which has given rise to all the various phantasies. In the present case, moreover, compatibility even of the first kind is not out of the question. ... We have already learned that it quite regularly happens that a single symptom corresponds to several meanings *simultaneously*. We may now add that it can express several meanings *in succession*. In the course of years a symptom can change its meaning or its chief meaning, or the leading role can pass from one meaning to another. (53)

To which it may be added that what is true of the symptom can also be true of the larger entity of which it is a part. The meaning in question may be a contradictory one; it may be constituted out of a contradictory unity of opposites, or out of a shifting and unstable set of them. Whatever may be the case, the "reality" that is being both constructed and referred to is heterogeneous, multi-dimensional and open-ended – novelistic in the fullest sense of the word.

Part of that sense, we have come to understand, is that the writer is or ought to be conscious of the part that he – in whatever guise, voice, or persona he chooses – invariably and unavoidably plays in the world he represents. Oddly enough, although there is none of his writings in which Freud is more vigorously active than he is here, it is precisely this activity that he subjects to the least self-conscious scrutiny, that he almost appears to fend off. For example, I will now take my head in my hands and suggest that his extraordinary analysis of Dora's first dream is inadequate on just this count. He is only dimly and marginally aware of his central place in it (he is clearly incorporated into the figure of Dora's father), comments on it only as an addition to Dora's own addendum to the dream, and does nothing to exploit it. (73 f.) Why he should choose this course is a question to which we shall shortly return. Instead of analyzing his own part in what he has done and what he is writing, Freud continues to behave like an unreliable narrator, treating the material about which he is writing as if it were literature but excluding himself from both that treatment and that material. At one moment he refers to himself as someone "who has learnt to appreciate the delicacy of the fabric of structures such as dreams" (87), intimating what I surmise he incontestably believed, that dreams are natural works of art. And when in the analysis of the second dream, we find ourselves back at the scene at the lake again; when Dora recalls that the only plea to her of Herr K. that she could remember is "You know I get nothing out of my wife"; when these were precisely the same words used by Dora's father in describing to Freud his relation to Dora's mother; and when Freud speculates that Dora may even "have heard her father make the same complaint . . . just as I myself did from his own lips" (98, 106) – when a conjunction such as this occurs, then we know we are in a novel, probably by Proust. Time has recurred, the repressed has returned, plot, double plot, and counterplot have all intersected, and "reality" turns out to be something that for all practical purposes is indistinguishable from a systematic fictional creation.

Finally, when at the very end Freud turns to deal – rudimentarily as it happens – with the decisive issue of the case, the transferences, everything is transformed into literature, into reading and writing. Transferences, he writes, "are new editions of facsimiles" or tendencies, fantasies, and relations in which "the person of the physician" replaces some earlier person. When the substitution is a simple one, the transferences may be said to be "merely new impressions or reprints": Freud is explicit about the metaphor he is using. Others "more ingeniously constructed . . . will no longer be new impressions, but revised editions." (116) And he goes on, quite carried away by these figures, to institute a comparison between dealing with the transference and other analytic procedures. "It is easy to learn how to interpret dreams," he remarks, "to extract from the patient's associations his unconscious thoughts and memories, and to practise similar explanatory arts: for these the patient himself will always provide the text." The startling group of suppositions contained in this sentence should not distract us from noting the submerged ambiguity in it. The patient does not merely provide the text; he also *is* the text, the writing to be read, the language to be interpreted. With the transference, however, we move to a different degree of difficulty and onto a different level of explanation. It is only after the transference has been resolved, Freud concludes, "that a patient arrives at a sense of conviction of the validity of the connections which have been constructed during the analysis." (117) I will refrain from entering the veritable series of Chinese boxes opened up by that last statement, and will content myself by proposing that in this passage as a whole Freud is using literature and writing not only creatively and heuristically – as he so often does – but defensively as well.

The writer or novelist is not the only partial role taken up unconsciously or semi-consciously by Freud in the course of this work. He also figures prominently in the text in his capacity as a nineteenth-century man of science and as a representative Victorian critic – employing the seriousness, energy, and commitment of the Victorian ethos to deliver itself from its own excesses. We have already seen him affirming the positive nature of female sexuality, "the genital sensation which would certainly have been felt by a healthy girl in such circumstances" (37), but which Dora did not feel. He goes a good deal further than this. At a fairly early moment in the analysis he faces Dora with the fact that she has "an aim in view which she hoped to gain by her illness. That aim could be none other than to detach her father from Frau K." Her prayers and arguments had not worked; her suicide letter and fainting fits had done no better. Dora knew quite well how much her father loved her, and, Freud continues to address her,

> I felt quite convinced that she would recover at once if only her father were to tell her that he had sacrificed Frau K. for the sake of her health. But, I added, I hoped he would not let himself be persuaded to do this, for then she would have learned what a powerful weapon she had in her hands, and she would certainly not fail on every future occasion to make use once more of her liability to ill-health. Yet if her father refused to give way to her, I was quite sure she would not let herself be deprived of her illness so easily. (42)

This is pretty strong stuff, considering both the age and her age. I think, moreover, that we are justified in reading an over-determination out of this utterance of Freud's and in suggesting that he had motives additional to strictly therapeutic ones in saying what he did.

In a related sense Freud goes out of his way to affirm his entitlement to speak freely and openly about sex – he is, one keeps forgetting, the great liberator and therapist of speech. The passage is worth quoting at some length.

> It is possible for a man to talk to girls and women upon sexual matters of every kind without doing them harm and without bringing suspicion upon himself, so long as, in the first place, he adopts a particular way of doing it, and, in the second place, can make them feel convinced that it is unavoidable. . . . The best way of speaking about such things is to be dry and direct; and that is at the same time the method furthest removed from the prurience with

which the same subjects are handled in "society," and to which girls and women alike are so thoroughly accustomed. I call bodily organs and processes by their technical names. ...*J'appelle un chat un chat*. I have certainly heard of some people – doctors and laymen – who are scandalized by a therapeutic method in which conversations of this sort occur, and who appear to envy either me or my patients the titillation which, according to their notions, such a method must afford. But I am too well acquainted with the respectability of these gentry to excite myself over them. ... The right attitude is: "*pour faire une omelette il faut casser des oeufs.*" (48 f.)

I believe that Freud would have been the first to be amused by the observation that in this splendid extended declaration about plain speech (at this point he takes his place in a tradition coming directly down from Luther), he feels it necessary to disappear not once but twice into French. I think he would have said that such slips – and the revelation of their meanings – are the smallest price one has to pay for the courage to go on. And he goes on with a vengeance, immediately following this passage with another in which he aggressively refuses to moralize in any condemnatory sense about sexuality. As for the attitude that regards the perverse nature of his patient's fantasies as horrible –

I should like to say emphatically that a medical man has no business to indulge in such passionate condemnation. . . . We are faced by a fact; and it is to be hoped that we shall grow accustomed to it, when we have learned to put our own tastes on one side. We must learn to speak without indignation of what we call the sexual perversions. ... The uncertainty in regard to the boundaries of what is to be called normal sexual life, when we take different races and different epochs into account, should in itself be enough to cool the zealot's ardor. We surely ought not to forget that the perversion which is the most repellent to us, the sensual love of a man for a man, was not only tolerated by a people so far our superiors in cultivation as were the Greeks, but was actually entrusted by them with important social functions. (49 f.)

We can put this assertion into one of its appropriate contexts by recalling that the trial and imprisonment of Oscar Wilde had taken place only five years earlier. And the man who is speaking out here has to be regarded as the greatest of Victorian physicians, who in this passage is fearlessly revealing one of the inner and unacknowledged meanings of the famous "tyranny of Greece over Germany."[20] And as we shall see, he has by no means reached the limits beyond which he will not go.

How far he is willing to go begins to be visible as we observe him sliding almost imperceptibly from being the nineteenth-century man of science to being the remorseless "teller of truth," the character in a play by Ibsen who is not to be deterred from his "mission." In a historical sense the two roles are not adventitiously related, any more than it is adventitious that the "truth" that is told often has unforeseen and destructive consequences and that it can rebound upon the teller. Sometimes we can see this process at work in the smallest details. For instance, one day when Freud's "powers of interpretation were at a low ebb," he let Dora go on talking until she brought forth a recollection that made it clear why she was in such a bad mood. Freud remarks of this recollection that it was "a fact which I did not fail to use against her." (59) There can be no mistaking the adversary tone, however slight, of this statement. It may be replied that Freud is writing with his customary dry irony; yet this reply must be met by observing that irony is invariably an instrument with a cutting edge. But we see him most vividly at this implacable work in the two great dream interpretations, which are largely "phono-graphic" reproductions of dramatic discourse and dialogue. Very early on in the analysis of the first dream, Freud takes up the dream element of the "jewel-case" and makes the unavoidable symbolic interpretation of it. He then proceeds to say the following to this Victorian maiden who has been in treatment with him for all of maybe six weeks:

> "So you are ready to give Herr K. what his wife withholds from him. That is the thought which has had to be repressed with so much energy, and which has made it necessary for every one of its elements to be turned into its opposite. The dream confirms once more what I had already told you before you dreamt it – that you are summoning up your old love for your father in order to protect yourself against your love for Herr K. But what do all these efforts show? Not only that you are afraid of Herr K., but that you are still more afraid of yourself, and of the temptation you feel to yield to him. In short, these efforts prove once more how deeply you love him."(70)

He immediately adds that "Naturally Dora would not follow me in this part of the interpretation," but this does not deter him for a moment from pressing on with further interpretations of the same order; and this entire transaction is in its character and quality prototypical for the case as a whole. The Freud we have here is not the

sage of the Berggasse, not the master who delivered the incomparable
Introductory Lectures of 1916–17, not the tragic Solomon of
Civilization and Its Discontents. This is an earlier Freud, the Freud of
the Fliess letters, to certain passages of which I would now like to
turn.

In May 1895 Freud writes to Fliess to tell him why he has not been
writing to him. Although he has been overburdened with work,
patients, and so on, he is aware that such excuses are in part pretexts.

> But the chief reason was this: a man like me cannot live without a
> hobby-horse, a consuming passion – in Schiller's words a tyrant. I
> have found my tyrant, *and in his service I know no limits*. My tyrant
> is psychology; it has always been my distant, beckoning goal and
> now, since I have hit on the neuroses, it has come so much the
> nearer. [italics mine]

Three weeks later he writes to Fliess to inform him that he has started
smoking again after an abstinence of fourteen months "because I
must treat that mind of mine decently, or the fellow will not work for
me. I am demanding a great deal of him. Most of the time the burden
is superhuman." In March of the next year he tells Fliess that "I keep
coming back to psychology; it is a compulsion from which I cannot
escape." A month later he communicates the following:

> When I was young, the only thing that I longed for was
> philosophical knowledge, and now that I am going over from
> medicine to psychology I am in the process of attaining it. I have
> become a therapist against my will; I am convinced that, granted
> certain conditions in the person and the case, I can definitely cure
> hysteria and obsessional neurosis.[21]

And in May 1897 he writes: "No matter what I start with, I always
find myself back again with the neuroses and the psychical apparatus.
It is not because of indifference to personal or other matters that I
never write about anything else. Inside me there is a seething
ferment, and I am only waiting for the next surge forward." This is
the Freud of the case of Dora as well. It is Freud the relentless
investigator pushing on no matter what. The Freud that we meet with
here is a demonic Freud, a Freud who is the servant of his *daimon*.
That *daimon* in whose service Freud knows no limits is the spirit of
science, the truth, or "reality" – it doesn't mattter which; for him they
are all the same. Yet it must be emphasized that the "reality" Freud
insists upon is very different from the "reality" that Dora is claiming
and clinging to. And it has to be admitted that not only does Freud

overlook for the most part this critical difference; he also adopts no measures for dealing with it. The demon of interpretation has taken hold of him, and it is this power that presides over the case of Dora.

In fact, as the case history advances, it becomes increasingly clear to the careful reader that Freud and not Dora has become the central character in the action. Freud the narrator does in the writing what Freud the first psychoanalyst appears to have done in actuality. We begin to sense that it is his story that is being written and not hers that is being retold. Instead of letting Dora appropriate her own story, Freud became the appropriator of it. The case history belongs progressively less to her than it does to him. It may be that this was an inevitable development, that it is one of the typical outcomes of an analysis that fails, that Dora was under any circumstances unable to become the appropriator of her own history, the teller of her own story. Blame does not necessarily or automatically attach to Freud. Nevertheless, by the time he gets to the second dream he is able to write: "I shall present the material produced during the analysis of this dream in the somewhat haphazard order in which it recurs to my mind." (95) He makes such a presentation for several reasons, most of which are legitimate. But one reason almost certainly is that by this juncture it is his *own* mind that chiefly matters to him, and it is *his* associations to her dream that are of principal importance.

At the same time, as the account progresses, Freud has never been more inspired, more creative, more inventive; as the reader sees Dora gradually slipping further and further away from Freud, the power and complexity of the writing reach dizzying proportions. At times they pass over into something else. We have already noted that at certain moments Freud permits himself to say such things as: if only Dora had not left "we should no doubt have obtained the fullest possible enlightenment upon every particular of the case" (13); or that there is in his mind "no doubt that my analytic method" can achieve "complete elucidation" of a neurosis (32); or that "it is only because the analysis was prematurely broken off that we have been obliged ... to resort to framing conjectures and filling in deficiencies." (85) Due allowance has always to be made for the absolutizing tendency of genius, especially when as in the case of Dora the genius is writing with the license of a poet and the ambiguity of a seer. But Freud goes quite beyond this. There are passages in the case of Dora which, if we were to find them, say, in a novel, would prompt us to conclude that either the narrator or the character who made such an utterance was suffering from *hubris*; in the context of psychoanalysis one supposes that the appropriate term would be *chutzpah*. For example, after elucidating the symbolism of the jewel-case and Dora's reticule, Freud goes on to write:

There is a great deal of symbolism of this kind in life, but as a rule we pass it by without heeding it. When I set myself the task of bringing to light what human beings keep hidden within them, not by the compelling power of hypnosis, but by observing what they say and what they show, I thought the task was a harder one than it really is. He that has eyes to see and ears to hear may convince himself that no mortal can keep a secret. If his lips are silent, he chatters with his finger-tips; betrayal oozes out of him at every pore. And thus the task of making conscious the most hidden recesses of the mind is one which it is quite possible to accomplish (77 f.)

This, we are forced to recall, is from the Freud who more than anyone else in the history of Western civilization has taught us to be critically aware of fantasies of omniscience, and who on other occasions could be critical of such tendencies in himself. But not here where the demon of interpretation is riding him, riding him after Dora, whom it had ridden out. And it rides him still further, for he follows the passage I have just quoted with another that in point of mania quite surpasses it. Dora had complained for days on end of gastric pains. Freud quite plausibly connected these sensations with a series of other events and circumstances in her life that pointed to a repressed history of childhood masturbation. He then continues:

It is well known that gastric pains occur especially often in those who masturbate. According to a personal communication made to me by Wilhelm Fliess, it is precisely gastralgias of this character which can be interrupted by an application of cocaine to the "gastric spot" discovered by him in the nose, and which can be cured by the cauterization of the same spot.

At this juncture we have passed beyond interpretation and are in the positive presence of demented and delusional science. This passage was almost certainly written in 1901 as part of the first draft of the text; but it must remain a matter of puzzlement that neither in 1905, when he published the revised version, nor at any time thereafter did Freud think it necessary to amend or strike out those mythological observations.[22]

Anyone who goes on like this – and as Freud has gone on with Dora – is, as they say, asking for it. *Chutzpah's* reward is poetic justice. When Dora reports her second dream, Freud spends two hours of inspired insight in elucidating some of its meanings. "At the end of the second session," he writes, "I expressed my satisfaction at the results." (105) The satisfaction in question is in large measure self-satisfaction, for Dora responded to Freud's expression of it with the following words uttered in "a depreciatory tone: 'Why, has anything so remarkable come out?'" That satisfaction was to be of short duration, for Dora opened the third session by telling Freud that this was the last time she would be there – it was December 31, 1900. Freud's remarks that "Her breaking off so unexpectedly, just when my hopes of a successful termination of the treatment were at their highest, and her thus bringing those hopes to nothing – this was an unmistakable act of vengeance on her part" (109) are only partly warranted. There was, or should have been, nothing unexpected about Dora's decision to terminate; indeed, Freud himself on the occasion of the first dream had already detected such a decision on Dora's part and had communicated this finding to her. Moreover, his "highest" hopes for a successful outcome of the treatment seem almost entirely without foundation. The case, as he himself presents it, provides virtually no evidence on which to base such hopes – Dora stonewalled him from the beginning right up to the very end. In such a context the hopes of success almost unavoidably become a matter of self-reference and point to the immense *intellectual* triumph that Freud was aware he was achieving with the material adduced by his patient. On the matter of "vengeance," however, Freud cannot be faulted; Dora was, among many other things, certainly getting her own back on Freud by refusing to allow him to bring her story to an end in the way he saw fit. And he in turn is quite candid about the injury he felt she had caused him. "No one who, like me," he writes, "conjures up the most evil of those half-tamed demons that inhabit the human breast, and seeks to wrestle with them, can expect to come through the struggle unscathed." (109)

This admission of vulnerability, which Freud artfully manages to blend with the suggestion that he is a kind of modern combination of Jacob and Faust, is in keeping with the weirdness and wildness of the case as a whole and with this last hour. That hour recurs to the scene at the lake, two years before, and its aftermath. And Freud ends his final hour with the following final interpretation. He reminds Dora that she was in love with Herr K.; that she wanted him to divorce his wife; that even though she was quite young at the time she wanted "'to wait for him, and you took it that he was only waiting till you were grown up enough to be his wife. I imagine that this was a perfectly serious plan for the future in your eyes.'" But Freud does not say this in order to contradict it or categorize it as a fantasy of the adolescent girl's unconscious imagination. On the contrary, he had very different ideas in view, for he goes on to tell her:

You have not even got the right to assert that it was out of the

question for Herr K. to have had any such intention; you have told
me enough about him that points directly towards his having such
an intention. Nor does his behaviour at L — contradict this view.
After all, you did not let him finish his speech and do not know
what he meant to say to you.

He has not done with her yet, for he then goes on to bring in the other
relevant parties and offers her the following conclusion:

> Incidentally, the scheme would by no means have been so
> impracticable. Your father's relation with Frau K. ... made it
> certain that her consent to a divorce could be obtained; and you can
> get anything you like out of your father. Indeed, if your temptation
> at L — had had a different upshot, this would have been *the only
> possible solution for all the parties concerned*. (108) [italics mine]

No one – at least no one in recent years – has accused Freud of being a
swinger, but this is without question a swinging solution that is being
offered. It is of course possible that he feels free to make such a
proposal only because he knows that nothing in the way of action can
come of it; but with him you never can tell – as I hope I have already
demonstrated. One has only to imagine what in point of ego-strength,
balance, and self-acceptance would have been required of Dora *alone*
in this arrangement of wife-and-daughter-swapping to recognize at
once its extreme irresponsibility, to say the least.[23] At the same time
we must bear in mind that such a suggestion is not incongruent with
the recently revealed circumstance that Freud analyzed his own
daughter. Genius makes up its own rules as it goes along – and breaks
them as well. This "only possible solution" was one of the endings
that Freud wanted to write to Dora's story; he had others in mind
besides, but none of them was to come about. Dora refused or was
unable to let him do this; she refused to be a character in the story that
Freud was composing for her, and wanted to finish it herself. As we
now know, the ending she wrote was a very bad one indeed.[24]

VI

Let us move rapidly to a conclusion long overdue. In this
extraordinary work Freud and Dora often appear as unconscious,
parodic refractions of each other. Both of them insist with implacable
will upon the primacy of "reality," although the realities each has in
mind differ radically. Both of them use reality, "the truth," as a
weapon. Freud does so by forcing interpretations upon Dora before
she is ready for them or can accept them. And this aggressive truth

bounds back upon the teller, for Dora leaves him. Dora in turn uses her version of reality – it is "outer" reality that she insists upon – aggressively as well. She has used it from the outset against her father, and five months after she left Freud she had the opportunity to use it against the K.'s. In May 1901 one of the K.'s children died. Dora took the occasion to pay them a visit of condolence –

> and they received her as though nothing had happened in the last three years. She made it up with them, she took her revenge on them, and she brought her own business to a satisfactory conclusion. To the wife she said: 'I know you have an affair with my father'; and the other did not deny it. From the husband she drew an admission of the scene by the lake which he had disputed, and brought the news of her vindication home to her father. Since then she had not resumed her relations with the family. (121)

She told this to Freud fifteen months after she had departed when she returned one last time to visit him – to ask him, without sincerity, for further help, and "to finish her story." (120). She finished her story, and as for the rest, Freud remarks, "I do not know what kind of help she wanted from me, but I promised to forgive her for having deprived me of the satisfaction of affording her a far more radical cure for her troubles." (122)

But the matter is not hopelessly obscure, as Freud himself has already confessed. What went wrong with the case, "Its great defect, which led to its being broken off prematurely," was something that had to do with the transference; and Freud writes that "I did not succeed in mastering the transference in good time." (118) He was in fact just beginning to learn about this therapeutic phenomenon, and the present passage is the first really important one about it to have been written. It is also in the nature of things heavily occluded. Instead of trying to analyze at what would be tedious length its murky reaches, let me state summarily my sense of things. On Dora's side the transference went wrong in several senses. In the first place, there was the failure on her part to establish an adequate positive transference to Freud. She was not free enough to respond to him erotically – in fantasy – or intellectually – by accepting his interpretations: both or either of these being prerequisites for the mysterious "talking cure" to begin to work. And in the second, halfway through the case a negative transference began to emerge, quite clearly in the first dream. Freud writes that he "was deaf to this first note of warning," and as a result this negative "transference took me unawares, and, because of the unknown quantity in me which reminded Dora of Herr K., she took her revenge on me as she wanted to take her revenge on him, and deserted me as she believed herself to have been deceived and deserted by him." This is, I believe, the first mention in print of the conception that is known as "acting out" – out of which, one may incidentally observe, considerable fortunes have been made.

We are, however, in a position to say something more than this. For there is a reciprocating process in the analyst known as the counter-transference, and in the case of Dora this went wrong too. Although Freud describes Dora at the beginning of the account as being "in the first bloom of youth – a girl of intelligent and engaging looks," almost nothing attractive about her comes forth in the course of the writing. (31) As it unwinds, and it becomes increasingly evident that Dora is not responding adequately to Freud, it also becomes clear that Freud is not responding favorably to this response, and that he doesn't in fact like Dora very much.[25] He doesn't like her negative sexuality, her inability to surrender to her own erotic impulses. He doesn't like "her really remarkable achievements in the direction of intolerable behavior." (91) He doesn't like her endless reproachfulness. Above all, he doesn't like her inability to surrender herself to him. For what Freud was as yet unprepared to face was not merely the transference, but the counter-transference as well – in the case of Dora it was largely a negative counter-transference – an unanalyzed part of himself.[26] I should like to suggest that this cluster of unanalyzed impulses and ambivalences was in part responsible for Freud's writing of this great text immediately after Dora left him. It was his way – and one way – of dealing with, mastering, expressing, and neutralizing such material. Yet the neutralization was not complete; or we can put the matter in another way and state that Freud's creative honesty was such that it compelled him to write the case of Dora as he did, and that his writing has allowed us to make out in this remarkable Fragment a still fuller picture. As I have said before, this Fragment of Freud's is more complete and coherent than the fullest case studies of anyone else. Freud's case histories are a new form of literature – they are creative narratives that include their own analysis and interpretation. Nevertheless, like the living works of literature that they are, the material they contain is always richer than the original analysis and interpretation that accompany it; and this means that future generations will recur to these works and will find in them a language they are seeking and a story they need to be told.

Notes

1   The empirical rule that literary criticism generally follows is to trust the tale and not the teller; indeed, it was the empirical rule pursued by Freud himself.

2   All quotations have been drawn from *The Standard Edition of the Complete Psychological Works of Sigmund Freud*. Vol. VII, pp. 3–122. Numbers in parentheses represent pages from which quotations have been taken. The Strachey translation has been checked against the text in *Gesammelte Werke*, Vol. V, pp. 163–286. In a few places the translation has been corrected.

3   It is worth noting that Freud tells us nothing more about these activities.

4   Later on, Freud adds to this judgement by affirming that "Dora's father was never entirely straightforward. He had given his support to the treatment so long as he could hope that I should 'talk' Dora out of her belief that there was something more than a friendship between him and Frau K. His interest faded when he observed that it was not my intention to bring about that result." (109)

5   Since this dream will be referred to frequently in what is to come, it may be helpful to the reader if I reproduce its wording: "A house was on fire. My father was standing beside my bed and woke me up. I dressed quickly. Mother wanted to stop and save her jewel-case; but Father said: 'I refuse to let myself and my two children be burnt for the sake of your jewel-case.' We hurried downstairs, and as soon as I was outside I woke up." (64)

6   It is also permissible to question why Freud's hopes for a successful termination were at that moment at their highest – whether they were in fact so, and what in point of fact his entire statement means. We shall return to this passage later.

7   Ernest Jones, *The Life and Work of Sigmund Freud*, 3 Vols (New York, 1953–7), Vol. 1, p. 362. Oscar Rie was a pediatrician who had earlier worked as Freud's assistant at Kassowitz's Institute for Children's Diseases; he became a member of Freud's intimate circle, was a partner at the Saturday night tarok games, and was at the time the Freud family physician.

8   Freud's chief precursors in this, as in so much else, are the great poets and novelists. There are a number of works of literature that anticipate in both form and substance the kind of thing that Freud was to do. I shall mention only one. Wordsworth's small masterpiece "Ruth" can in my judgement be most thoroughly understood as a kind of proto-case history, as a case history, so to speak, before the fact.

9   From almost the outset of his career, images drawn from archaeology worked strongly in Freud's conception of his own creative activity. In *Studies on Hysteria* Freud remarks that the procedure he followed with Fräulein Elisabeth von R. was one "of clearing away the pathogenic psychical material layer by layer, and we liked to compare it with the technique of excavating a buried city." In a closely related context, he observes that he and Breuer "had often compared the symptomatology of hysteria with a pictographic script which has become intelligible after the discovery of a few bilingual inscriptions." And his way of representing the "highly involved trains of thought" that were determinants in certain of the hysterical attacks of Frau Cäcilie was to compare them to "a series of pictures with explanatory texts." (*Standard Edition*, Vol. II, pp. 139, 129, 177).

10   In later years, and after much further experience, Freud was no longer able to make such statements. In *Inhibitions, Symptoms and Anxiety* (1926) he writes: "Even the most exhaustive analysis has gaps in its data and is insufficiently documented." (*Standard Edition*, Vol. XXI, p. 107).

11   One is in a position now to understand rather better the quasi-meretricious fits of detestation that overtake Nabokov whenever Freud's name is mentioned. That "elderly gentleman from Vienna" whom Nabokov has accused of "inflicting his dreams upon me" was in fact a past master at all the tricks, ruses, and sleights-of-hand that Nabokov has devoted his entire career to. The difference is this: that in Freud such devices are merely a minor item in the immense store of his literary resources.

Nabokov's revenge has been such cuties as "Dr Sig Heiler," "Sigismund Lejoyeux," and one "Dr Froit of Signy-Mondieu-Mondieu." At an entirely different level an analogous relation existed between Charlie Chaplin and W. C. Fields. The latter often tried to get his own back on the comic genius by calling him "that god-damned juggler" along with similar phrases of endearment.

12 Some years earlier Freud had been more candid and more innocent about the relation of his writing to literature. In *Studies on Hysteria* he introduces his discussion of the case of Fräulein Elisabeth von R. with the following disarming admission:

> I have not always been a psychotherapist. Like other neuropathologists, I was trained to employ local diagnosis and electro-prognosis, and it still strikes me myself as strange that the case histories I write should read like short stories and that, as one might say, they lack the serious stamp of science. I must console myself with the reflection that the nature of the subject is evidently responsible for this, rather than any preference of my own. The fact is that local diagnosis and electrical reactions lead nowhere in the study of hysteria, whereas a detailed description of mental processes such as we are accustomed to find in the works of imaginative writers enables me, with the use of a few psychological formulas, to obtain at least some kind of insight into the course of that affection. Case histories of this kind are intended to be judged like psychiatric ones; they have, however, one advantage over the latter, namely, an intimate connection between the story of the patient's sufferings and the symptoms of his illness – a connection for which we still search in vain in the biographies of other psychoses. (*Standard Edition*, Vol. II, pp. 160 f.)

13 There is a parodic analogue to this passage of some contemporary significance. It is taken from the relatively esoteric but influential field of general systems theory, one of whose important practitioners suffered from severe disturbances of memory. Indeed, he could hardly remember anything. He nonetheless insisted that there was nothing wrong with his memory; in fact, he went on to argue, he had a perfect memory – it was only his retrieval system that wasn't working. In the light of such a comment, it is at least open to others to wonder whether other things as well weren't working.

14 K. Marx, *The Eighteenth Brumaire of Louis Bonaparte*, pt I.

15 Erik H. Erikson has waggishly observed that a case history is an account of how someone fell apart, while a life history is an account of how someone held together.

16 *Biographia Literaria*, ch. 14.

17 Freud may at this point be thinking within an even more historically anachronistic paradigm than the one that normally applied in the late-Victorian period or in the Vienna of the time. In both pre- and early-industrial Europe sexual maturity was commonly equated – especially for women – with reproductive maturity, and both were regarded as conterminous with marriageability. Ironically it was Freud more than any other single figure who was to demonstrate the inadequacy and outmodedness of this paradigm. See John H. Gagnon and William Simon, *Sexual Conduct: the Social Sources of Human Sexuality* (Chicago, 1973), p. 296.

18 There is a fourth influencing circumstance that deserves to be mentioned. Freud appears to have worked in this case with a model in mind, but it turned out that the model either didn't fit or was the wrong one. In the case of "Katharina" in *Studies on Hysteria*, Freud had performed a kind of instant analysis with a fair degree of success. Katharina was the 18-year-old daughter of the landlady of an Alpine refuge hut that Freud had climbed to one summer's day. This "rather sulky-looking girl" had served Freud his meal and then approached him for medical advice, having seen his signature in the Visitors' Book. She was suffering from various hysterical symptoms – many of which resembled those that afflicted Dora – and the story that came out had to do with attempted sexual seductions by her father, followed by her actually catching her father in the act with a young cousin – a discovery that led to the separation and divorce of the parents. The symptoms and the experiences seemed very closely connected, and as Freud

elicited piecemeal these stories from her she seemed to become "like someone transformed" before his eyes. He was very pleased and said that he "owed her a debt of gratitude for having made it so much easier for me to talk to her than to the prudish ladies of my city practice, who regard whatever is natural as shameful." (*Standard Edition*, Vol. I, pp. 125–34). The circumstances of her case and of Dora's are analogous in a number of ways, but Dora was no rustic Alpine *Jungfrau* who spoke candidly and in dialect (which Freud reproduces); she was in truth one of the prudish ladies of his city practice who was frigid then and remained so all her life.

19 Such a passage serves to locate Freud's place in a set of traditions in addition to those of literature. It is unmistakable that such a statement also belongs to a tradition that includes Hegel and Marx at one end and Max Weber and Thomas Mann somewhere near the other. It was Weber who once remarked that "the interests of society are the great rails on which humanity moves, but the ideas throw the switches." *Gesammelte Aufsätze zur Religionssoziologie* (Tübingen, 1922) Vol. I, p. 252. And Mann for his part regularly gave off such observations as: "Relationship is everything. And if you want to give it a more precise name, it is ambiguity." *Doctor Faustus*, ch. VII.

20 "When the social historian of the future looks back to the first half of the twentieth century with the detachment that comes with the passage of time, it will by then be apparent that amongst the revolutionary changes to be credited to that period, two at least were of vital importance to the development of humanism: the liberation of psychology from the fetters of conscious rationalism, and the subsequent emancipation of sociology from the more primitive superstitions and moralistic conceptions of crime. It will also be apparent that this twin movement towards a new liberalism owed its impetus to the researches of a late-Victorian scientist, Sigmund Freud, who first uncovered the unconscious roots of that uniquely human reaction which goes by the name of 'guilt'." Edward Glover, *The Roots of Crime* (New York, 1960), p. ix.

21 One might have thought that such a passage would have at least slowed the endless flow of nonsense about Freud's abstention from philosophical aspirations. To be sure, Freud is himself greatly responsible for the phenomenon. I am referring in part to the famous passage in *Inhibitions, Symptoms and Anxiety* (1926):

> I must confess that I am not at all partial to the fabrication of *Weltanschauungen*. Such activities may be left to the philosophers, who avowedly find it impossible to make their journey through life without a Baedeker of that kind to give them information on every subject. Let us humbly accept the contempt with which they look down on us from the vantage-ground of their superior needs. But since *we* cannot forgo our narcissistic pride either, we will draw comfort from the reflection that such "Handbooks to Life" soon grow out of date and that it is precisely our short-sighted, narrow, and finicky work which obliges them to appear in new editions, and that even the most up-to-date of them are nothing but attempts to find a substitute for the ancient, useful and all-sufficient Church Catechism. We know well enough how little light science has so far been able to throw on the problems that surround us. But however much ado the philosophers may make, they cannot alter the situation. Only patient, persevering research, in which everything is subordinated to the one requirement of certainty, can gradually bring about a change. The benighted traveller may sing aloud in the dark to deny his own fears; but, for all that, he will not see an inch beyond his nose.

This is splendid and spirited writing; but I cannot resist suggesting that Freud is using philosophy here as a kind of stalking horse and that the earlier passage is in some senses closer to his enduring meaning. What Freud meant there by "philosophical knowledge" was knowledge or comprehension of the veritable nature of reality itself, and I do not believe he ever abandoned his belief in such knowledge.

In any case, too much has been made – on both sides – of the "antagonism" between psychoanalysis and philosophy.

22 It is pertinent to the present discussion to add that on at least one occasion in 1895 Freud directly addressed Fliess as "Demon" or "You Demon." (*Daimonie warum schreibst Du nicht? Wie geht es Dir? Kummerst Du ich gar nicht mehr, was ich treibe?*) Furthermore, the treatment described by Freud in the foregoing paragraph was administered by Fliess to Freud himself on several occasions during the 1890s. Throughout that decade Freud suffered at irregular intervals from migraine headaches and colds. He applied cocaine locally (one supposes that he took a healthy sniff), permitted Fliess to perform a number of nasal cauterizations, and at one point seems to have undergone minor surgery of the turbinate bone in the nasal passage at Fliess's hands.

The pertinence of the displacement of Freud's relation to Fliess into the case of Dora becomes clearer if we recall that in this friendship – certainly the most important relation of its kind in his life – Freud was undergoing something very like a transference experience, without wholly understanding what was happening to him. In this connection, the case of Dora may also be regarded as part of the process by which Freud began to move towards a resolution of his relation with Fliess – and perhaps vice versa as well.

That relation is still not adequately understood, as the documents that record it have not been fully published. As matters stand at present, one has to put that relation together from three sources: (1) *The Origins of Psychoanalysis*, ed. Ernst Kris (New York, 1950); this volume contains some of Freud's letters to Fliess, many of them in fragmentary or excerpted form, plus drafts and notes of various projects; (2) Ernest Jones, *The Life and Work of Sigmund Freud* (New York, 1953-7); (3) Max Schur, *Freud: Living and Dying* (New York, 1972). The last work provides the fullest account yet available, but does not stand by itself and must be supplemented by material drawn from the other two sources.

23 Fifteen years later, when Freud came to write about Ibsen, the character and situation that he chose to analyze revealed the closest pertinence to the case of Dora. In "Some Character-Types Met with in Psycho-Analytic Work" he devotes a number of pages to a discussion of Rebecca West in *Rosmersholm*. Rebecca, the new, liberated woman, is one of those character-types who are wrecked by success." The success she is wrecked by is the fulfillment – partly real, partly symbolic – in mature life of her Oedipal fantasies, the precise fulfillment that Freud, fifteen years earlier, had been capable of regarding as the "only solution" for Dora, as well as everyone else involved in the case (see *Standard Edition*, Vol. XIV, pp. 324-31).

24 For what happened to Dora in later life, see Felix Deutsch, "A Footnote to Freud's 'Fragment of an Analysis of a Case of Hysteria,'" *Psychoanalytic Quarterly*, XXVI (1957), pp. 159-67. The story is extremely gruesome. For some further useful remarks, see Erik H. Erikson, "Psychological Reality and Historical Actuality," *Insight and Responsibility* (New York, 1964), pp. 166-74.

25 Dora seems indeed to have been an unlikeable person. Her death, which was caused by cancer of the colon, diagnosed too late for an operation, "seemed a blessing to those who were close to her." And Dr Deutsch's informant went on to describe her as "'one of the most repulsive hysterics' he had ever met."

26 That the counter-transference was not entirely negative is suggested in the very name that Freud chose to give to his patient in writing this case history. Freud's favorite novel by Dickens was *David Copperfield*. Like David, Freud was born with or in a caul – an augury of a singular destiny. On at least one occasion, Freud described his father as a Micawber-like figure. The first book he sent as a gift to Martha Bernays shortly after they had met was a copy of *David Copperfield*.

Dora, of course, was David Copperfield's first love and first wife. She is at once a duplication of David's dead mother and an incompetent and helpless creature, who asks David to call her his "child-wife." She is also doomed not to survive, and Dickens kills her off so David can proceed to realize himself in a fuller way. One could go on indefinitely with such analogies, but the point should be sufficiently clear: in the very name he chose, Freud was in a manner true to his method, theory, and mind, expressing the overdeterminations and ambivalences that are so richly characteristic of this work as a whole.

For the relevant biographical material, see Jones, *Life and Work of Sigmund Freud*, Vol. 1, pp. 2, 4, 104, 174.

4 Freud and the Rat Man

I

Freud's "Notes Upon a Case of Obsessional Neurosis" (1909, *Standard Edition*, Vol. III, pp. 153–318), his celebrated account of the Rat Man, is one of the richest, most complex and opaque pieces of his major writings. In contrast to the equally famous case of Dora, it has been from the outset widely and regularly commented upon in the literature of the discipline itself – although the quality and sometimes even the simplest literal accuracy of such discussions have varied with striking unevenness. The work continues because of its unique qualities to be used today as a text for training psychoanalysts. In what follows I shall try once again to ascertain how far certain habits of reading, procedures of enquiry, and modes of analysis developed by literary criticism can, when applied to so complex and problematical an account, bring to light goings on, ways of conceiving the world and constructing meaning through an analysis dramatically represented or rendered in a written text that other methods of investigation have hitherto overlooked. I shall also, once again, try to say or imply something of the significance of such circumstances for certain kinds of humanistic enquiry: psychoanalysis and literary criticism being on this view – and among other things – related rather than disparate or divergent disciplines of the cultural sciences. Both of them form part of the organized examination of the human world as it creates its own meanings and, in a variety of ways and at a number of pitches of discourse, reflect simultaneously upon these same processes.

I shall retreat from these abstrusenesses and begin, as literary criticism has tended traditionally to do, with the humble external circumstances of the case. These suggest without much possibility of mistake that Freud was from the outset aware of the peculiar value of this particular case. The Rat Man first appeared in Freud's consulting room on October 1, 1907. By the 30th of that month Freud was prepared to present an account of where the case had gotten to before the weekly meeting of the Vienna Psychoanalytic Society. This account and the discussion that followed it took up both that meeting and the one that came directly after it on November 6. Freud made three further and shorter reports to the Society on the progress of the case, on November 20 of the same year and then again on January 22 and April 8, 1908. Later that month, the First International Psychoanalytical Conference took place at Salzburg. Freud was naturally the leading speaker at the opening session. He took advantage of the occasion to report on the case – which was still in progress – and in his autobiography, Ernest Jones records what was for him and the others present a memorable morning's experience.

> Delivered without any notes, it [Freud's discourse] began at eight-o-clock and at eleven he offered to bring it to a close. We had all been so enthralled, however, at his fascinating exposition that we begged him to go on, and he did so for another hour. I had never been so oblivious of the passage of time. ... [Freud's] ease of expression, his masterly ordering of complex material, his perspicacious lucidity, and his intense earnestness made a lecture by him ... both an intellectual and an artistic feast.[1]

According to Freud's account (186), the analysis was completed sometime in September 1908, that termination coinciding with "the complete restoration of the patient's personality, and ... the removal of his inhibitions." (155) This outcome was in marked contrast to Freud's experience with Dora, as was much of the subsequent history of the publication of Freud's account of the matter – which in the case of Dora was mysteriously delayed for almost five years.

In May and June 1908 Freud wrote to Jung that the case of the Rat Man was one of the current projects preoccupying his attention. He did not, however, get around to writing out the case history until the summer of 1909; and he did so, as it were, as part of the final preparation for his first and only trip to America, his reception of an honorary degree, and the public recognition on a transatlantic scale of his personal and intellectual achievements. On June 3, 1909, he writes to Jung that "I suddenly feel like writing about the Salzburg rat man," and says that he can have the piece ready for the second number of the new yearbook of psychoanalytic studies of which Jung had been appointed editor. He began writing during that month, devoted much of his energy to it, and on the last day of June reported to Jung on his progress:

> I am finding it very difficult; it is almost beyond my powers of perception; the paper will probably be intelligible to no one outside our immediate circle. How bungled our reproductions are, how wretchedly we dissect the great art works of psychic nature! Unfortunately this paper in turn is becoming too bulky. It just pours out of me, and even so it's inadequate, incomplete and therefore untrue. ... I am determined to finish it before leaving and to do nothing more before setting sail for America.

On July 7, 1909, still complaining and dissatisfied, he sent a copy of the draft manuscript to Jung.

In October, shortly after their return from the triumphant overseas adventure, Jung wrote Freud in praise of the case. Freud was naturally very pleased with this response of his chosen successor, but still felt that the piece had "obvious shortcomings," some of which he even tried to explain away.

> It seemed to me that since the emergence of the *Jahrbuch* I could change my mode of presentation. Ψ now has an audience and I am justified in writing for this audience. It is no longer necessary to restate our most elementary assumptions and refute the most primitive objections in every single paper. It is just as absurd for people to expect to understand our papers without the prerequisite training as to pick up a treatise on integral calculus without having gone beyond elementary arithmetic.

There is a certain amount of truth in this passage mixed in with a good deal of special pleading. For although it may help to explain in part why the case of the Rat Man has none of the grand narrative sweep, lucidity, and analytic thoroughness and fullness of the case of Dora, it says nothing at all about the equal presence of similar qualities of coherence, expository fullness, narrative virtuosity, and sustained sinuosity of episodic, incremental development in Freud's other major cases. It does nothing to account for these qualities in either the case of Little Hans, written shortly before the Rat Man and published in the previous and first number of the *Jahrbuch*, or in the cases of Schreber and the Wolf Man both of them written afterwards. Yet all of these writings share, along with the case of Dora, a coherent narrative, novelistic power, a particularized clarity within the detailed and multiplex historical complexity of one narrative made up of several intertwined and simultaneous evolving sub-narratives. Such qualities characterize these cases outstandingly, yet claims to a similar set of literary and narrative virtues cannot be made on behalf of the case of the Rat Man.

In the same letter of October 17, 1909, Freud immediately goes on to remark to Jung that "Last week the newspapers carried the Rat Man's announcement of his engagement to the 'lady'; he is facing life with courage and ability. The one point that still gives him trouble (father-complex and transference) has shown up clearly in my conversation with this intelligent and grateful man." One of the things that these remarks seem to suggest – apart from Freud's sustained friendly feelings for his patient – is that although the analysis of the Rat Man had terminated about a year earlier, he and

Freud may have remained in some kind of personal communication. From what we learn from the original case and the subsequently published addendum to it, this speculation appears to be at least plausible. We learn one other thing as well. In a footnote added in 1923 to the very end of the case Freud writes that "Like so many other young men of value and promise, he perished in the Great War." Like his contemporary, Hans Castorp, the Rat Man was life's delicate child who did not survive to enjoy the pleasures and rigors of existence after the trials he had manfully undergone, if not on the *Zauberberg* then at least in the *Berggasse*.

One's suspicion about the quality of special pleading in the remarks made to Jung is markedly supported by the opening pages of the essay. For Freud begins it with a set of positions, of polar or binary pairings, not to say outright contradictions. On the one hand, he tells the reader, this case, by reason of its length, injurious effects, and the patient's own view of it, is to be thought of as moderately severe; at the same time the patient's experience in Freud's therapy has led to a completely successful outcome, or, as Freud puts it in a passage I have already referred to, "the complete restoration of the patient's personality, and ... the removal of his inhibitions." On the other hand, Freud goes on, his presentation of the relevant material will be as remote from completeness or adequacy as can be conceived. The matter he is to put forward will be of "two kinds." First, he will "give some fragmentary extracts" from the history of the case; and second, "starting out from this case, and ... taking other cases into account which I have previously analysed, I shall make some disconnected statements of an aphoristic character upon the genesis and finer psychological mechanism of obsessional processes, and ... thus hope to develop my first observations on the subject, published in 1896" (155). Hence at the very outset we are confronted with contrarieties: a completely successful course of a revolutionary mental therapy which has led to the restoration of wholeness to a patient's personality is going to be presented in a fragmentary, disjointed, disconnected and aphoristic [sic!] variety of discursive forms. The intractably opposed character of these two tendencies may serve to alert the informed reader that one of the grand themes of the neurosis about to undergo analysis and reconstruction is itself intractable ambivalence.

These two ambivalences are, however, unconscious at this moment of writing in both the patient and Freud, and the latter proceeds to explain why his program of communicating in this form should be so incorrigible and unsatisfactory – all his palaver to Jung about his new professionalized audience is put aside as the pretentiousness, rationalization, and self-exculpation that it largely is. Freud acknowledges two kinds of obstacles to which his writings on these

matters must accommodate themselves. The first are external. He
cannot offer a full account of his patient's life because disclosure of
the details of that life would immediately lead to destruction of the
patient's privacy. "The importunate interest of a capital city," of all
Vienna, Freud writes, is now "focussed with particular attention
upon my medical activities," and thus he is forbidden from "giving a
faithful picture of the case." The period of Freud's career that he
thought of as "splendid isolation" has clearly drawn to a close.
Moreover, the distortions conventionally resorted to by physicians in
presenting their cases have come for Freud to seem increasingly
"useless and objectionable." If the disguises are too slight they fail in
their purpose of protecting the patient from unwelcome curiosity.
And if the camouflagings go beyond this, the sacrifice they exact is
that "they destroy the intelligibility of the material, which depends
for its coherence precisely upon the small details of real life." And
from this there follows the inconvenient and paradoxical consequence that "it is far easier to divulge the patient's most intimate
secrets than the most innocent and trivial facts about him." And since
"real life" is made up of both kinds of details, the censorship of one
kind leads to drastic curtailment, incomplete coherence, intelligibility that is less than wholly perspicuous – to an account in other
words that seems to resemble in no way the four-hour uninterrupted
intellectual aria that made so unforgettable an impression on Ernest
Jones and his other colleagues at Salzburg.

But apart from these external obstacles there are internal
difficulties that are more telling and cogent still in respect of the
"disconnected results" that are all Freud has to report. "I must
confess," he writes,

> that I have not yet succeeded in completely penetrating the
> complicated texture of a *severe* case of obsessional neurosis, and
> that, if I were to reproduce the analysis, it would be impossible for
> me to make the structure, such as by the help of analysis we know
> or suspect it to be, visible to others through the mass of therapeutic
> work superimposed on it.

Freud is making here a methodological observation of considerable
interest, but its density needs to be dispersed and illuminated.
Perhaps we can usefully do so by juxtaposing against it for the
purposes of analogy this passage from Marx's Afterword to the
second German edition of Volume I of *Das Kapital*.

> Of course the method of presentation must differ in form from that
> of inquiry. The latter has to appropriate the material in detail, to

analyse its different forms of development, to trace out their inner connexion. Only after this work is done, can the actual movement be adequately described. If this is done successfully, if the life of the subject-matter is ideally reflected as in a mirror, then it may appear as if we had before us a mere a priori construction.

Marx is trying both to explain and justify his way of going about things in *Kapital*, which begins, the reader may recall, with a long, abstract discussion – definition, expansion, and construction – of the commodity as a kind of ideal philosophical conception; and only after that has been achieved does he go on to progressively more particular and historical problems and analyses. Marx is saying that this proce-dure is in some senses the reverse of how he actually went about doing his work – which was to begin with the piece-by-piece appropriation of the historical material in detail and to work out the inner connections and hence the theories from that mass of concrete kinds of evidence and disparate orders of data. Freud, in a sense, pursued a course that tended to reverse Marx, though as we have seen he was confronting analogous difficulties. Freud begins the case of the Rat Man with seven sections that he calls "Extracts from the Case History." These are, as we shall see, not all of them extracts in the same or in a single sense. And he ends the piece with a second section consisting of three separate groups of generalizing remarks, to which in 1924 he added the heading "Theoretical."

Indeed the reader can easily surmise, as the reader of the case history itself will have already almost surely concluded, that Freud is less successful in these compositional and structural strategies than Marx was in Volume I of *Kapital*. (I suppose this needs to be said, since this represents one of the rare occasions on which such a comparison holds.) And Freud himself is quick to point out the shortcomings of both his method and what he has achieved. Not only is he unable within the limits circumscribed for himself and by that material to set out the endless "resistances of the patients" and the manifold "forms in which they are expressed." He is even unable to assert that he really understands an obsessional neurosis – certainly, he observes, he understands hysteria better. And this is somewhat surprising, for we should have expected the contrary.

> The language of an obsessional neurosis – the means by which it expresses its secret thoughts – is, as it were, only a dialect of the language of hysteria; but it is a dialect in which we ought to be able to find our way about more easily, since it is more nearly related to the forms of expression adopted by our conscious thought than is the language of hysteria. Above all, it does not involve the leap from a mental process to a somatic innervation – hysterical

conversion – which can never be fully comprehensible to us. (156–7)

As he so often does, Freud resorts to a metaphor drawn from language itself when he wants to discuss questions that have to do with understanding neuroses. But he does so here in an odd way – he asserts that an obsessional neurosis is "only a dialect of the language of hysteria." What is implied in this statement is *not* that obsessional neuroses and hysterias are each of them different dialects of some common, fundamental language – the language, say, of the unconscious as it expresses itself in what Freud then called the psychoneuroses of defense. No; what he is saying is that obsessional neuroses are to hysteria as the language spoken in Bavaria, Swabia, or Vienna was to some idealized and normative, Prussianized High German of the Wilhelmine Empire. This is an extremely dubious assertion. (It is also sloppy, and what Freud probably means is that he had learned to speak, decipher, translate, and decode the language/ dialect of hysteria before he managed to do the same for obsessions.) Moreover, a further cause of puzzlement, for Freud, is to be found in the circumstance that we understand less about obsessions than we do about hysteria, when we should, it seems, expect to understand more. This expectation is justified by the observation that the language of obsessional neuroses is "more nearly related to the forms of expression adopted by our conscious thought than is the language of hysteria." In other words, obsessional neuroses are virtually pure or purely mental disorders: they are disorders of thought or of language as it remains confined within the domain broadly defined as thought – which can include in addition to ideas, impulses, affects, speech, and even certain ritual behaviors expressive of these latter phenomena. Above all, the utterly obscure transition from mind to body in the form of the hysterical symptoms of conversion is missing from the typical obsessional neurosis – and Freud at this moment despairs of ever understanding the processes that are involved in that mysterious leap. In addition, he has also changed his mind about how well he understands in a comparative sense these entities – as he was subsequently to do again and with regularity throughout his career. In 1895, for example, he had written to Fliess that "the course of events in obsessional neurosis is what is clearest to me, because I have come to know it best."[2] By 1909, his knowledge had, apparently, developed further in the reverse direction.

He goes on to supply a number of reasons to account for his conviction that he is "less familiar" with the inner structures of obsessional neuroses than he is with hysteria, and concludes that "in these circumstances there is no alternative but to report the facts in the imperfect and incomplete fashion they are known." What he has to pass on, he continues, are "crumbs of knowledge ... laboriously enough collected ... [and] not in themselves very satisfying." Perhaps other investigators will take these remarks up as starting-points for further investigation. Freud had made similar protestations of inadequacy and incompleteness at the beginning – as well as throughout – the case of Dora; but the context of those self-exculpating remarks were in sharp contrast to the context confronting us here. The analysis of Dora was unsuccessful, short, fragmentary and broken off by the patient's deserting Freud before he could satisfy his own sense of understanding the problems she presented. In the present instance we will have to seek elsewhere for the causes of Freud's intuition of radical insufficiency and defectiveness.

Finally, there is one further prefatory matter that remains to be touched upon. Some part of Freud's "original record of the earlier parts of this treatment" has survived. (154) How and why it did has not been explained; Freud's usual practice was to destroy the written material on which his publications were based after the works appeared in print. After Freud's death in London, these manuscript notes were found among his papers. Part of these notes was published for the first time in translation in Volume 10 of the *Standard Edition* in 1955. In that section of the published essay that Freud entitled "Extracts from the Case History," he writes in a footnote that "What follows is based upon notes made on the evening of the day of treatment, and adheres as closely as possible to my recollection of the patient's words." But this statement holds true only for the first seven or eight sessions of the analysis (according to how one counts the hour in which the patient first appeared in Freud's office). Thereafter Freud sometimes made daily notes, sometimes let days pass without putting anything down, and then caught up with a subsequent summary of "arrears," and sometimes omitted to do even that. The record that survives breaks off, Strachey tells us, "for no explained reason after the entry dated January 20th (1908)." (253) The analysis was then in its fourth month, and the only possible significance, of a perhaps external kind, that I can provisionally attach to this date – if it does in fact represent the end of Freud's note-taking in this case and not merely the end of such notes as survive – is that two days later, on January 22, Freud was to make the third of his reports on the case to the Vienna Psychoanalytic Society, and that in this brief communication he reveals a good deal about the inner dynamics of the obsession at stake and obsessions in general.

But we do not have a translated version of those original notes either. For the sake of intelligibility and convenience of reading, the Stracheys have enlarged or filled in Freud's "telegraphic style" of taking notes, have translated abbreviations into whole words, supplied omitted pronouns and other words and in general expanded the ellipses in which most of these notes were apparently first written down. They have also changed some names, and have, with the exception of the preliminary interview, left out the entire first third of the original record, which covers the first seven full sessions of the analysis, and on which sections A–D (159–86) of the case history are based. We do not, then, have anything in print that closely resembles what they state is the "Original Record of the Case." We have a very valuable, edited version of Freud's notes, but sooner or later someone will have to have access to the original.

Nevertheless, the value that has been added by the publication of this edition of Freud's notes on the case cannot easily be underestimated. These notes, along with the first half of the case history, permit us to see more closely than anywhere else Freud's representation of himself at work. They permit us as well to see what he includes as relevant material and, sometimes even more pertinently and surprisingly, what he chooses to leave out or not to discuss. And they permit us to learn about some minor historical matters: for example, if one consults a perpetual calendar along with the notes, one soon discovers that it was then Freud's custom to hold psychoanalytic sessions on Saturdays, and that regular psychoanalytic patients had the expectation of meeting with Freud for six sessions (each lasting fifty-five minutes) per week.[3] The notes inform us additionally about Freud's attitudes towards his patients, and the nature and style of intervention in the therapy that he then regarded as either appropriate or useful. They permit us as well to observe what, after due hesitation, I find myself resigned to call the creative process in Freud. I mean by this cliché to refer first to the observable movement back and forth between notes and case history being written for publication. But I mean also to refer to the reverse of this observable datum: to the fact that some things appear in the essay and not in the notes and vice versa; that the principle of selectivity pursued by Freud in this connection is not always consistent and is sometimes opaque if not incomprehensible; and that there is often no way to get from material in the notes to formulations in the essay. In other words, something mysterious is going on; the case history does not, as it were, simply emerge from the notes; nor do the history and the notes taken together make up an intelligible and coherent whole. Nor in certain senses does the history taken by itself; and Freud is being more than conventionally modest in his authorial role when he complains about the intellectual and formal shortcomings of this piece of work.

He is in my view quite precise in these critical reservations. The case remains full of obscurities. The story of the Rat Man never really becomes clear or gets clearly told. The narrative form is broken, struck aside and abandoned, now here for the purpose of analytic, thematic study of the neurosis, now there in order to pursue the exploration of the character of the Rat Man and what that character represents, now somewhere else for an exposition of the dynamic psychic processes of both pathology and defense that make up so much of the Rat Man's existence – an existence which by the time he has gotten around to consulting Freud has been almost entirely invaded and taken over by his mental affliction. Indeed, the entire narrative-expository form, rich and complex as it is, is less traditionally satisfying and adequate as a story than the case of Dora or than any of Freud's other major case histories. One of our problems is to demonstrate how and why this should be so, why in some measure it has to be, and why despite these radical if conventional imperfections a piece of writing of enduring importance as writing is at the same time being prompted into existence. But before we do this we will have to take several steps backwards.

II

The first of those steps has to do with the identification of an error in the first paragraph of the case history. Freud refers there to his "first observations on the subject" of the "genesis and finer psychological mechanisms of obsessional processes," and lists the essay of 1896, "Further Remarks on the Neuro-Psychoses of Defence," and Section II of that essay, as the locus of those observations. This is incorrect, as the very title of the essay might lead us to suspect, and Freud's initial theoretical remarks directed to the present context were made in 1894, in the essay "The Neuro-Psychoses of Defence," in Section II of that earlier essay (*Standard Edition*, Vol. III, pp. 51–8). There he first distinguishes obsessional neuroses from hysteria by asserting that the characteristic defense of an obsession is that it secures itself against the intrusion into the field of consciousness of an incompatible (usually a sexual) idea by "separating" that idea "from its affect." That affect, which has become momentarily free, then by a process that goes unexplained, *"attaches itself to other ideas which are not in themselves incompatible; and, thanks to this 'false connection,' those ideas turn into obsessional ideas."* A mechanism has been succinctly described, but not very much has been explained.

The mechanism in question is to be known as a "displacement of affect"; and the obsession that results "represents a substitute or surrogate for the incompatible sexual idea and has taken its place in

consciousness." The incompatible idea remains outside of consciousness, and the transaction that has taken place represents a kind of
metonymic shift in unconscious psychic space (whatever that may be).
Moreover, once the physician recognizes that the affect of an obsession
appears to be *"dislodged"* or "transposed," his efforts will be to
"retranslate" this obsession back *"into sexual terms"* [all the emphases
are in the original].

Freud does not at this point in his career think very highly of this
kind of maneuver as offering its subject much in the way of defense, for
the distressing affect "from which the ego has suffered remains as it was
before, unaltered and undiminished." Like phobias, to which they are
related, but unlike hysterias, obsessions confine all their transformations "to the psychical sphere," and it is in the psychical sphere
that they remain. Freud then proceeds to provide some illustrations of
obsessions suffered by his patients which demonstrate a variety of
manifestations, ranging from psychosis to phobias, not all of them
uniform in their illuminating power but uniform in their covert sexual
content. Nor is Freud always careful at this early juncture to distinguish
between sexual affects and ideas and the guilts and self-reproaches
suffered as a result of their occurrence and as part of the defenses
mounted against them. What he does do in his therapy at this time, he
tells us, is in large measure a work of "translation back of the
obsessional idea into sexual terms." He does this principally "by
leading back the attention of patients with phobias and obsessions to the
repressed sexual ideas in spite of all their protestations, and, wherever
possible, by stopping up the sources from which those ideas sprang."
Psychoanalysis, we should recall, had not yet been born; and Freud is
directive, suggestive, and traditionally authoritarian in the medical
sense with his patients. Protestations are overridden, and the sources of
pathological thought are mysteriously stopped up – presumably, and
ipso facto, by some sort of fiat. Nevertheless, despite this general
atmosphere of grim forbiddingness, we should also note that change is
largely brought about by a shifting in the direction and focus of
attention on the part of the patient. It is mind-bending, to be sure, but
that is for the most part *all* it is.

Freud returned to this subject at least twice more in 1895.
"Obsessions and Phobias: The Psychical Mechanism and their
Aetiology" (*Standard Edition*, Vol. III, pp. 71–82) was originally
written and published in French (a German translation was published
during the same year). The first distinction of substance that Freud
makes in this short paper is that in phobias, the prevailing affect, or
emotional state, is always anxiety, "while in true obsessions other
emotional states, such as doubt, remorse or anger, may occur just as
well as anxiety." In addition – he continues in amplification and

clarification of his earlier paper – in obsessions the affect or emotional state tends to persist, while the idea or ideas associated with it regularly vary. These ideas are always both associated with and substitutes for an original disturbing idea; as replacements for the antecedent unacceptable or "incompatible" idea they are always "ill-adapted" or inappropriate, and "it is this *mésalliance* between the emotional state and the associated idea that accounts for the absurdity so characteristic of obsessions." Freud has here introduced a new descriptive category: among the neuroses, the obsessions occupy pre-eminently the realm of the absurd, and this circumstance, as we shall see, creates for them an additional context of significant affiliations.

He then presents a number of clinical vignettes as exemplifications of his hypothesis; they are sufficiently absurd, as is at least one of his interpretations of them. The motive behind all these substitutions remains defense of the ego against an incompatible (almost invariably sexual) idea, but as the instances accumulate we see that the notion of the substitution of a particular idea for an anterior one slides into the formulation of the displacement of idea from affect, which in turn can be rephrased in terms of a splitting within the ego. In addition, these displacements or defenses can now occur in relation to space, time, content or context – thus enlarging still further the range of permutations of which the syndrome is inclusive. Freud concludes by sharply distinguishing again obsessions from phobias, a demarcation that he will also in due course severely qualify.

Freud returned to these problems again before the year 1895 was out in his "Christmas Fairy Tale" about "The Neuroses of Defence" that he sent to Fliess. He is in this piece writing very much at his ease, and in the spirit of free speculation pays relatively little attention to consistency or precision. Still, one can observe that many of Freud's abiding powers as a thinker are to be found in his qualities of originality and speculative boldness, in the audacity of connections he imputes, rather than in the scholarly precision or academic tidiness and formality of his presentations – and it is this former set of qualities that are in foremost evidence throughout his communications to Fliess.

All the neuroses of defense, Freud begins, have a number of things in common; chief among these is that they are all "pathological aberrations of normal psychical affective states." The obsessional neuroses are pathological aberrations of unconscious "*self-reproach*."[4] In the course of his general speculations about neuroses, Freud presents in this text the first known dynamic model for the formation of the neuroses as a whole. This model begins with a sexual experience that is traumatic and hence creates inner conflict; this conflict is defensively dealt with at first by repression, which is temporarily successful, but also leaves as its displaced residue a single, primary (and usually isolated) symptom. In time this successful defense proves vulnerable, the repression breaks down, and the repressed returns in the form of a more widely distributed neurotic illness which expresses both the repressed impulses or ideas and the repressing agencies in new symptoms which are simultaneously new defenses as well. The clearest representative of this "course of events," Freud observes, is to be found among the obsessional neuroses, for this is the form of neurosis that in 1895, he states, he has come to know best.

When in an obsessional neurosis we attain the stage of the return of the repressed, the unaltered "*self-reproach*" recurs, emerging first as a "pure sense of guilt without any content," but then quickly becoming linked with (or mediated by) a double distortion – of both time and content. Time is distorted by displacing the troubling obsession onto some action that is either contemporary or thought to lie in the future; content is distorted by substitution – a surrogate idea "is chosen from the category of what is analogous." The rhetoric of obsessional composition, therefore, reveals itself as being produced by and being itself "a product of compromise, correct as regards affect and category but false owing to chronological displacement and substitution by analogy." The introduction of the category of compromise into the strategy of symptom-construction connects this process to the as yet unelaborated theory of dreams and their formation. Moreover, this rhetoric of compromise has its cultural analogue in G. K. Chesterton's idea of the "Victorian compromise," a notion proposed within a few years of Freud's but undoubtedly without any awareness of it. The two conceptions, however, are notable for the circumstance that they are at once both successes and failures; they are strategic holding actions against forces from beneath or below, concerted efforts of resistance that in due time wear out or fail or cease to sustain themselves in their function.

As the obsession takes its place within the domain of the "conscious ego," that agency first regards the presence of this intrusive entity "as something alien to it"; indeed it withholds belief from the reality of the idea by enlisting "the antithetic idea of conscientiousness formed long before." Its first line of defense, accordingly, is what was to become widely known as reaction-formations; and from this perspective the neurosis was consciously perceived as an alien presence not native to a previously integral inner person. But it can also happen that the "ego is overwhelmed by the obsession," that it is invaded, overrun, and entirely occupied in all its energies by it. And it is precisely the curious alternation between these contradictory states of mind, between an ego whose perceived center holds firm in defending itself against an alien set of neurotic impulses and formations and an ego whose center has been displaced and profoundly altered by that entity (which can no longer be considered alien to it in the same earlier sense) that characterizes a considerable part of what happens in Freud's dealings with the Rat Man.

Freud then goes on to enumerate part of the variety of defensive symptoms to be found in obsessional neuroses and the sets of transformations through which they can typically be followed – from brooding to hoarding to obsessional ceremonials to drinking and back and forth among these and other familiar markings of affliction. In those cases in which "the affect of self-reproach has become admissible through transformation," Freud writes, one gets the impression "of a displacement having occurred along a chain of inferences: I reproach myself on account of an event – I am afraid other people know about it – therefore I feel ashamed in front of other people." As one link in the chain is repressed, the obsession jumps, so to speak, to another, each of the succeeding inferences themselves being both delusional and part of the defensive structure and struggle. The struggle terminates, Freud concludes, "in general doubting mania or in the development of the life of an eccentric with an indefinite number of secondary defensive symptoms – that is, if such a termination is reached at all." The defensive transformations terminate, in other words, in the production or the emergence of a character type rather than in the construction of a narrative. The fictional world being fabricated is one that is filled by character and its internal life rather than by narrative and the sequence of accumulating, meaningful events. The final state arrived at is highly mediated, protean, and the result of an almost unimaginable quantity of thinking; all of which can be translated virtually *ad infinitum* but which outpace exhaustive written description. The phenomenology of obsessive neuroses as a result seems to be located at the far end of a spectrum that has hysteria at its point of beginning.

During the next year Freud published the essay that he refers to at the opening of the case history of the Rat Man, where he mistakenly referred to it as his "first observations on the subject." In "Further Remarks on the Neuro-Psychoses of Defence," Section II concerns "The Nature and Mechanism of Obsessional Neurosis." (*Standard Edition*, Vol. III, pp. 168–74) Freud is now writing under the direct influence of his seduction theory of the etiology of neurosis; in this context obsessional neurosis differs from hysteria because the childhood experiences in question were those of "sexual activity" (rather than the passivity characterizing the suppositious seductions that lay in the unconscious childhood hinterlands of hysteria), of "acts of aggression carried out with pleasure and of pleasurable participation in sexual acts." The idea of actual seduction will of course later be mostly abandoned and largely modified; the acts of aggression will be translated into experiences located chiefly in the anal-sadistic phase of childhood development; and the sharp active-passive antithesis is at once collapsed by Freud himself when he writes that he finds a "*substratum of hysterical symptoms*" in all his cases of obsessional neuroses. The point of this act of intellectual obfuscation is confessed to at once by Freud: the truth is, he states, that "I can as yet give no definitive account of the aetiology of obsessional neurosis." It was to be a difficulty that would not go away in a hurry.

He nevertheless at once goes on to put forth his first full definition of the nosological entity in question. "*Obsessional ideas* are invariably transformed *self-reproaches* which have re-emerged from *repression* and which always relate to some *sexual* act that was performed with pleasure in *childhood*." Although Freud later criticized this definition as trying to condense or unify too many disparate elements and that it was therefore open to objection on formal grounds, the individual components that make up the formulation remain by and large unobjectionable.

Freud then proceeds to offer a hypothetical account of the etiology of such a neurosis. In the earliest period of childhood there will occur the "experiences of seduction that will later on make repression possible"; at a later date there will come "the acts of sexual aggression against the other sex, which will later appear in the form of acts involving self-reproach." I do not introduce these quotations as one further bit of entertainment in the gala called the folly of the history of science. Instead, despite their wrongness, I should like to direct attention to how little modification is needed to set them going in the correct direction, how close Freud was to the right discoveries. All that is needed, in fact, to set these erroneous formulations moving in the appropriate direction is to begin to *internalize* them – which is what Freud was soon to do. Shortly after his discovery that most of the seduction stories were fantasies, there followed his recognition, piecemeal as always, of the endogenous, spontaneous nature of infantile sexuality in all its polymorphous efflorescence. The early mental impressions of seduction will be referred to and transformed into experiences appropriate to the oral and passive-anal phases of development; and the acts of sexual aggression will be largely relegated to transformative tendencies in the anal–sadistic and phallic stages of the overlapping late pre-Oedipal and Oedipal periods.

Following these experiences in this dynamic model, there is the effort to "get rid," so to speak, of them by means of two defenses:

first repression, and second their replacement, in the absence that repression creates, by reaction-formations as "*primary symptom*[s] *of defence*" in the forms of "conscientiousness, shame, and self-distrust." These defenses will correspond to the later-to-be-developed period of latency, which is itself set about by the resolution of the Oedipal conflicts through the concomitant precipitation out of the institution of the super-ego. There follows the post-Oedipal and pre-pubescent period of apparent health or successful defense, this being succeeded in turn by the character-istically adolescent or post-adolescent failure of the defense, return of the repressed, and the elaboration of the neurosis of defense proper, along the lines of the transformations suggested in the introductory definition.

In this essay, however, Freud suggests a new classification and proposes to fill it with two discriminable forms of obsessive neurosis. The difference between them depends on what "forces an entrance into consciousness" in the return of the repressed: whether it is simply and solely the recollection of the event from the past, "the *mnemic content* of the act involving the self-reproach," or whether in addition to that recollection, "the self-reproachful *affect* connected with the act" returns as well. In the first of these there will occur the "typical obsessional ideas" (i.e., the "mnemic content" has already been transformed), accompanied by a vague and indefinite affect of unpleasure, rather than the appropriate, original self-condemnation. The obsessional idea itself is transformed in two ways in relation to the constituting act of childhood: "First, something contemporary is put in the place of something past; and secondly, something sexual is replaced by something analogous to it that is not sexual." That is to say, a double displacement has been constructed; a displacement in time is accompanied by a second displacement in content. As a result of this dual deformation of the original mental entity into something that is a logical self-contradiction, the compromise that will be arrived at, the consciously represented obsessional idea itself, will appear "absurd."

The second form of the neurosis will occur when what forces its way back to "representation in conscious psychic life" is the "repressed self-reproach" that accompanied the original act. When this takes place, Freud writes (less than clearly) "by means of some mental addition," the unconscious self-reproach can be "transformed into any other unpleasurable affect." But at this point there is no further reason for the affect to remain unconscious – since it has now been sufficiently disguised. And so the affect in turn goes through a series of thematic variations, which Freud immediately ripples off for us: self-reproach can easily turn into *shame* (he supplies an accompanying content for each of these metamorphoses), or into *hypochondriachal anxiety*, or into *social anxiety, religious anxiety, delusions of being noticed, fear of temptation*, "and so on." The variations themselves are aria-like – there seems no reason for them to end at any determinate place. But Freud has not yet caught his second wind, to give a good mix to the metaphor, for these "compromise symptoms" which he has just rehearsed with such bravura, figure forth only the first return of the repressed, which is itself a sign merely of the "collapse" of the first or original defensive constructions.

At this point in the developmental elaboration of the neurosis, the newly besieged ego "constructs a set of further symptoms." These Freud calls quite logically symptoms of "*secondary defence.*" All of these function as "*protective measures*" and have been called forward in one way or another before this as opponents in the struggle against obsessional ideas and affects. If these re-enlisted aids succeed at this juncture in once more fending off the symptoms that manifest the return of the repressed, "then the obsession is transferred to the protective measures themselves and creates a third form of 'obsessional neurosis' – *obsessional actions.*" Hence the secondary defenses become themselves integrated parts of the obessional neuroses, and Freud has now set up a grade of obsessions within the ego – obsessional ideas, affects, and actions, in that order of evolution. In addition, Freud asserts, obsessional actions "are never primary; they never contain anything but a defense – never an aggression." That is to say, they are a reversal of the hypothetically postulated origin of the neurosis; in addition, however, they give us a salient insight into Freud's conception of what, in human life, is primary and what is secondary. Which is also as much as to say that *obsessional actions* are ontologically more psychological in status than they are actional. Which leads Freud on to add some further links of a purely psychological kind to the endless chain of secondary defenses that he is in the midst of putting together. One form of secondary defense against the returning obsessional ideas may be to direct those ideas by forcible means onto other thoughts that are as remote from and contrary to them as possible. "This is why *obsessional brooding*, if it succeeds, regularly deals with abstract and *suprasensual* things," the repressed ideas being invariably of a sensual nature. Or else the patient may resort to his own powers of conscious logic and memory in trying to master his obsessional notions. This tactical swerve "leads to *obsessional thinking*, to a *compulsion to test things* and to *doubting mania.*" Such is the end of that particular strand of the chain of defenses genuine disorders of thinking form, the defenses themselves becoming sunk in the pathology they are trying to hold off. Along a similar line of elaboration, secondary defenses against obsessional affects lead to a still wider range of obsessional acts, which may be grouped or classified according to their purpose: "*penitential* measures (burdensome ceremonials, the observation of numbers), *precautionary* measures (all sorts of phobias, superstition, pedantry, increase of the primary symptoms of conscientiousness); measures to do with *fear of betrayal* (collecting scraps of paper, seclusiveness), or to ensure *numbing* [of the mind] (dipsomania)." And there is no reason to doubt that any of these can be transferred or transformed from one to another with bewildering speed, complexity, and tortuosity of logic. Once again amid this apparently endless play of permutations and combinations what appears as being constructed are representations of various characters and how such characters are built up, or what shape their internal structure might take. The only limit that Freud will place upon the combinations comes about through increasing severity of affliction; when the ego is over-whelmed by the symptoms, the relentless flux of variations is brought to an end: "the ceremonial actions" become "fixated," or "a general state of doubting mania" becomes permanent, or "a life of eccentricity conditioned by phobias" may be all that is at last possible. Such a gallery of characters has long been familiar to the student of literature.

Freud did not return at any length to this subject for another ten years, and when he did so it was in a very different context. That context is the essay "Obsessive Actions and Religious Practices" (1907) (*Standard Edition*, Vol. IX, pp. 117-27), Freud's first explicit enquiry into the psychology of religion. Ten years of additional experience have acted to chasten in some measure his assertiveness of claim; a decade before he had confidently offered an elegant definition of obsessional neuroses. Now, however, he finds himself incapable of putting forward a definition that is satisfactory in terms of both inclusiveness and rigor of distinction. "In place of a definition," he writes, "we must for the time being be content with obtaining a detailed knowledge of these states, since we have not yet been able to arrive at a criterion of obsessional neuroses; it probably lies very deep, although we seem to sense its presence everywhere in the manifestations of the illness." On the one side, this statement contains a considerable amount of intellectual undoing; on the other, it isn't entirely clear what it means, or how Freud is using the term "criterion." It isn't actually clear whether he means by this word primarily the characterizing marks or traits by which the neurosis may be distinguished, or whether he is referring to some abstract standard or definition by which a judgement or decision abstract the existence or presence of that entity may be enabled, or whether he means a bit of both.

This essay has become so much a part of cultural public property that there is no need to recapitulate its argument at any length. For our present purposes, however, one or two points merit notation and discussion. From a behavioral point of view, Freud writes, obsessions largely consist of "compulsions and prohibitions" (some things that have to be done, and some things that have *not* to be done). The connections between these private neurotic ceremonials and the sacred acts of religious ritual are clear and manifold – as far as structure, subjective meaning, and the special, circumscribed contextuality of each are concerned. The differences between them are equally striking and are by no means confined to the distinction of private/public realms. Most striking among these differences is the circumstance that "while the minutiae of religious ceremonial are full of significance and have a symbolic meaning, those of neurotics seem foolish and senseless. In this respect an obsessional neurosis represents a travesty, half comic and half tragic, of a private religion." Freud has written this last sentence with two purposes in mind. In his use of the term travesty he is introducing the insight that there is almost always perforce something literary and theatrical about obsessional neuroses. The point of a travesty has much to do with incongruity of style – characteristically a serious or dignified subject is dealt with in a frivolous, trivial, and most undignified set of ways. Travesty naturally suggests notions of parody and burlesque as well, and these bring in such modes of representational distortion as caricature and other dramatic means of communicating the uncomely and the ridiculous. And these qualities of representationality hold true as well of obsessions (as we have already seen and will see much further) that are confined to the realm of purely mental activity or thinking. (The half comic part of the obsession refers to the matter of style; the half tragic clearly refers to the subject and his suffering, both of which are out of control.)

But Freud's other purpose in composing this sentence is to lead us intellectually down the garden path (it is one of his favorite expository devices), for he at once goes on to say that "it is precisely this sharpest difference between neurotic and religious ceremonial which disappears when, with the help of the psychoanalytic technique of investigation, one penetrates to the true meaning of obsessive actions." Indeed, he concludes, after several pages of clinical illustrations "in obsessive actions everything has its meaning and can be interpreted." There is no doubt in my mind that Freud intends these remarks to have a generalized and generalizing force, and what they imply is that psychoanalysis is throughout an interpretative discipline, and that the problems, and the problematics, of interpretation are in psychoanalysis at every point inseparable from their counterparts in the realm of meaning. In other words, psychoanalysis is, among other things, a hermeneutical discipline, or cultural science, in which the puzzlements of interpretation and meaning converge in the multiple imponderables of representation. And as we have already begun to suggest, when it comes to the obsessional neuroses, and to the case of the Rat Man in particular, the problems of representation require extensive mediation or working through in both philosophical and literary spheres of discourse.

Hence all obsessional behaviors are both absurd and the reverse of absurd; they are at once foolish or crazy and at the same time have determinate, translatable and understandable significance and are filled with the force of intention. And ceremonial, obsessive actions arise partly as defenses against forbidden or unwelcome impulses and temptations and partly as protections in advance against the expected adverse consequences that such impulses and temptations will cause to come down upon one. And when the protective measures come to appear inadequate defenses against temptations, then prohibitions will be constructed to further distance one from situations that may give rise to such temptations. In this sense the restrictive prohibition which has replaced as a defense a previously contrived obsessive action functions in a way analogous to a phobia that has been constructed "to avert a hysterical attack." Moreover, in obsessional neuroses, as elsewhere, all manifestations of the affection are to be understood as representing "a compromise between the warring contents of the pleasure they are designed to prevent"; and this intentionality is expanded upon when Freud further remarks that "they serve the repressed instinct no less than the agencies which are repressing it." As the illness advances, this double dialectic of regression continues to pursue its course, "until actions which were originally mostly concerned with maintaining the defense come to approximate more and more to the proscribed actions through which the instinct was able to find expression in childhood." Yet the end reached is not the re-enactment of that proscribed childhood behavior, but generalized paralysis, mania of doubting, and an unsorted supermarket of maddeningly repeated ideas, expressions, gestures, tics, rituals, formulas of thought, speech and action, none of which make any immediate sense but pain to the agent and – metaphorically – absentee owner of these behaviors. At the same time, the principal mental process behind this myriad of manifestations is the "mechanism of psychical displacement." This device is itself a function of the plasticity of mental phenomena, in which the small can take the place of the large, the imaginary of the actual, the inanimate of the animate and yet the affect belonging to the original idea not disappearing along with it but often accompanying the transfer to the new mental or behavioral object. In this sense, obsessive neuroses are tropological afflictions and enlist at various moments in thought, language, and behavior such figures as metaphor, symbolism, synecdoche, metonymy, and all the various processes of displacement that go into both dream construction and the formation of other neurotic symptoms. They are afflictions, of course, because their aim is to escape, hide from, disguise, muffle, and elude meaning as much as it is to reveal it; and their failure to succeed in this aim is what permits Freud to begin to work at undoing them. In their fluidity, fecundity, and elaboration of bizarre choices of means by which to represent themselves they are surpassed only by dreams and psychoses – yet it is precisely their ordinariness, familiarity, and adjacency to the orderly businesses of daily life that Freud finds a matter of unfailing interest.

Freud returned to this matter once more before he wrote his case study. He returned to it, in point of fact, while the Rat Man was in analysis, and the essay "Character and Anal Eroticism" (1908) (*Standard Edition*, Vol. IX, pp. 169–75) was first published in March 1908. (For reasons known only to himself, as far as I have been able to ascertain, Strachey asserts that the analysis of the Rat Man "had been concluded shortly before," but there is no way to fit in eleven-plus months between October 1, 1907 and March 1908). Like the essay that had preceded it by a year, "Character and Anal Eroticism" is something of a trial venture into an area adjoining psychoanalysis proper and that would in time come to be known as applied analysis – in this instance Freud is discussing the nature of "character" in general as well as some "mechanisms" that go into its formation. At the same time, this essay is apparently about as far from the considerations of spirituality that inform the enquiry conducted in "Obsessive Actions and Religious Practices" as one might on first inspection imagine. But that, of course, is as usual part of Freud's strategy.

Freud begins by remarking that psychoanalytic observation of patients has repeatedly led him to postulate a connection between the presence of a "certain set of character-traits" and behavior that attached in the patient's recollected childhood to "one of his bodily functions and the organ concerned in it." We have here left the realm of purely or even chiefly psychic transactions and are back squarely in the domain where psychic and physical or somatic occurrences of a fundamental kind mysteriously interact.

These traits of character occur in "regular combination" and are commonly described by the words "*orderly, parsimonious* and *obstinate.*" In his customarily casual way, Freud draws no particular attention to the terms themselves, what has governed his choice of them, or their relations with one another; but I believe that we are compelled to do so, since there is nothing mandatory about any of the proceedings in question. To begin with, it may strike us to ask something about the quality of relation that may be ascribed to the three terms. Each of them, in the first instance, covers a "small group or series of inter-related character-traits." "Orderly" or orderliness is clearly a virtue and includes "the notion of bodily cleanliness, as well as of conscientiousness in carrying out small duties and trustworthiness." It can also be extended (in the German *ordentlich*) to touch on such English terms, Strachey notes, as "'correct,' 'tidy' ... as well as 'regular,' 'decent' and 'proper' in the more colloquial senses of those words." Its opposite would be "untidy" and "neglectful." Parsimony is a much more complicated word. Although it can be used in a positive sense to mean thrift, it almost never is, and is regularly brought forth to imply frugality in excess, niggardliness, stinginess, sparingness in expenditure of money, and avarice in general. Its chief familiar positive occurrence as suggesting economy in the use of specific means to an end is to be found in philosophy, in the phrase "the law of parsimony," otherwise known as Ockham's razor. Obstinacy, too, can be used in a positive way as when we say that someone is obstinate in defense of the truth; and the same holds true for "defiance," to which obstinacy is closely bound; but it becomes more difficult to regard such character traits as virtues when they occur together with "rage" and "revengefulness," as they very frequently do. Parsimony and obstinacy, Freud writes, are more closely linked with one another than they are with orderliness; they also supply the "more constant element" in the full complex of traits. Yet somehow all three, he believes, belong together.

They belong together, Freud has found, by virtue of common experiences of childhood. The bearers of such qualities of character in later life, he affirms, commonly took a long time in childhood to overcome their infantile faecal incontinence. "As infants they seem to have belonged to the class who refuse to empty their bowels when put on the pot because they derive a subsidiary pleasure from defecating; for they tell us that even in somewhat later years they enjoyed holding back their stool. and they remember ... doing all sorts of unseemly things with the faeces that had been passed." These idiosyncrasies pass with childhood and the loss of the direct erotogenic significance of the anal zone. Yet, Freud goes on to speculate, "it is to be suspected that the regularity with which this triad of properties is present in their [adult] character may be brought into relation with the disappearance of their anal eroticism."[5]

Freud is instantly aware that he has just written an essentially unintelligible sentence – leaving to one side the question of whether the state of affairs that he is describing is itself intelligible. His effort at further explanation drives him back to his fundamental theory of sexuality, with its origins in infantile experiences of sensual pleasure. The sexual instinct of humankind he had argued is anything but unitary: it is "highly complex and is put together from contributions made by numerous constituents and component instincts." Different parts and organs of the body make their due contribution and undergo a plurality of vicissitudes as in the course of individual development these various excitations are deflected from their sexual aims and directed towards others, and as during the historical period of latency reaction-formations such as "shame, disgust and morality" are built up in the mind to hedge them about further. Therefore, Freud concludes, it is at least plausible to suppose that the three character traits in question "which are so prominent in people who were formerly anal erotics, are to be regarded as the first and most constant results of the sublimation of anal eroticism." It may be plausible, but Freud himself admits that an "intrinsic necessity for this connection is not clear ... even to myself." All he can do is make certain suggestions and connections. For example, the virtues of "cleanliness, orderliness and trustworthiness give exactly the impression of a reaction-formation against an interest in what is unclean and disturbing and should not be part of the body." That is to say, these civilized virtues arise out of primitive defenses (by reversal or negation) against a once active but then interdicted interest and pleasure. Obstinacy presents a bit more of a problem for Freud, but he nonetheless puts forward three observations: (1) we should recall "that even babies show self-will about parting with their stool"; (2) it was a general practice then, and remains one today, for adults to spank children on their buttocks "in order to break their obstinacy and make them submissive"; and (3) an "invitation to a caress of the anal zone is still used today, as it was in ancient times, to express defiance or defiant scorn, and this in reality signifies an act of tenderness that has been overtaken by repression." That last stipulation is again by no means perspicuous, since much more than repression is patently involved in the evolution of the variety of expressions and gestures that have to do with arse-kissing. In addition, Freud leaves out the entire adaptive, civilized side of this complex of behaviors and says nothing about the relation of such traits to moral and intellectual independence, to personal autonomy, or to revolutionary strivings in a wide range of contexts.

The connections between money and defecation, however, are extensive, extremely well known, and hardly need to be mentioned. The associations between money and dirt or filth are part of the archaic heritage of thought that our civilization preserves within itself as part of its complex, uneven development: "wherever archaic modes of thought have predominated or persist – in the ancient civilizations, in myths, fairy tales and superstitions, in unconscious thinking, in dreams and in neuroses – money is brought into the most intimate relation to dirt." And Freud then goes on to provide illustrations from common speech and belief about the multitude of connections made in many civilizations between the devil, money, excrement, hell, and the general, repressed unconscious instinctual life of the race. Thus, he concludes, "in following the usage of the [sic] language, neurosis, here as elsewhere, is taking words in their original, significant sense, and where it appears to be using a word figuratively it is usually simply restoring its old meaning." And the contrast "between the most precious substance known to man and the most worthless" is precisely what has led to their specific identification as well. This double-sided relation is facilitated by the circumstance that the two parts of the equation are not chronologically in phase: the original erotic interest in defecation comes earlier and is destined in most to be extinguished; it is only in later years that "the interest in money makes its appearance as a new interest which had been absent in childhood." As a consequence the earlier impulsion, "which is in process of losing its aim," can in some measure be carried over to the newly emerging aim.

Freud is not sure how much he has succeeded in conveying in these speculations, and as yet he remains in ignorance about the processes of formation of other attributes of character. He tries nonetheless to conclude on a strong note of conviction and generality.

> We can at any rate lay down a formula for the way in which character in its final shape is formed out of the constituent instincts: the permanent character-traits are either unchanged prolongations of the original instincts, or sublimations of those instincts, or reaction-formations against them.

In this formulation Freud regards instincts themselves as being representatives (or presentations) *in the mind* of somatic processes. Their three-fold destiny is made possible because of their plasticity, a quality they share with other mental representatives of entities that emanate from the extra-mental world.

We have now summarily examined the chief of Freud's writings that are ancillary to the case of the Rat Man, and it is to a consideration of the case itself that we now may turn.

III

On Tuesday, October 1, 1907, a young man of about 30, who is referred to in the Strachey version of Freud's original notes as Dr Lorenz, appeared in Freud's office. He "introduced himself" to Freud by stating that he had suffered "from obsessions ever since childhood, but with particular intensity for the last four years." He presented himself, in other words, as being at the mercy of thoughts or ideas which caused him much pain and anguish and had prevented him from living what he considered to be a normal life. The thoughts that chiefly constituted the disorder that was oppressing him were of three general kinds. First, he was afflicted by *fears* "that something might happen to two people of whom he was very fond" – his father and a lady whom he admired. Second, he was consciously beset by *"compulsive impulses"* – for example, he said, an "impulse to cut his throat with a razor." And third, he also produced *"prohibitions* sometimes in connection with quite unimportant things." He had wasted years, he went on, fighting to no avail against these mental visitations, and as a result had fallen far behind in the course of life he had envisioned for himself.

He had tried various kinds of treatment before coming to see Freud, but none of these had been of any benefit to him, with the exception of one stay at a sanatorium. Moreover, he attributed the relief he experienced on this occasion to the fact that it was one of the very few times in his life that he had had the opportunity to experience frequent sexual intercourse. He then went on to speak at length about his sexual life in general, which he described as "stunted." Prostitutes disgusted him; masturbation played a minimal role in his existence. He had never had coitus before the age of 26. By the time he had said this much, Freud had already garnered the impression that this youngish man was "a clear-headed and shrewd person," and was bestirred to ask him what it was "that made him lay such stress upon telling me about his sexual life." The reply, surely not entirely a surprise, was that Lorenz knew that Freud's theories concerned sexuality, and that although he had never actually read any of Freud's writings, some short time before he had been "turning over the pages of one of my books" – it was *The Psychopathology of*

Everyday Life – and had there come across "the explanation of some curious verbal expressions which had so reminded him of some of his own 'efforts of thought' in connection with his ideas," that he had decided to "put himself in my hands." So ends the account of this preliminary session, and what we learn from it is that the patient had begun to build up a positive transference to Freud well before he arrived on the actual scene, and that Freud responded in a positive sense both to him and possibly to the signs of the already activated transference as well. We learn too what we will have ample opportunity to see throughout the case, that the patient was an uncommonly verbal and articulate man, that he led an extremely active mental life for which he found little difficulty in providing spoken expression.

But there are some things we do not learn as well, which pop out at us as soon as we compare Freud's published account of this preliminary session with the version of the same hour printed by the editors as part of the "Original Record of the Case" – this hour is the only one of the first eight sessions that they reproduce. (They thereby omit about one-third of the original record from their translation and edition, a circumstance that is slightly lamentable.) We learn from their edited version of Freud's original notes that Dr Lorenz was a lawyer and that in point of fact he had been so bound down by his tribulations that he "had only just now passed his final law examination." In this connection, we learn as well that his obsessions at this moment "only affected his professional work when it was concerned with criminal law." And connected either correlatively, associatively, or metonymically with this last circumstance was his perception that he "suffered from an impulse to do some injury to the lady that he admired. This impulse was usually silent in her presence, but came to the fore when she was not there. Being away from her, however, – she lives in Vienna – had always done him good." One can understand or interpret these omissions on the part of Freud on a number of grounds. The business about the law and the examination are expedient suppressions in the cause of confidentiality – all the more so, as we will learn later on that the patient's family and Freud's family were known to each other socially as well, though with what degree of intimacy remains uncertain. That personal knowledge, however, is certainly germane to the patient's already flowering transference during the preliminary session. The omissions about the lady are to be understood largely as compositional or tactical economies on the part of Freud – he will use this material later.

But there is one further ellipsis that cannot be so accounted for. Freud closes his notes of the session as follows: "After I had told him my terms, he said he must consult his mother. The next day he came back and accepted them." Any late-twentieth-century reading of this case cannot overlook the virtual absence from it of Lorenz's mother. As we will learn in due course, she controlled the finances of her almost 30-year-old son, although he actually possessed independent means. Freud's omission is, I believe, purposeful, consistent, and systematic, for the same relative exclusion is to be found in his four other major case histories. In each of them, the role of the mother is minimized, while the relation of the patient to his or her paternal parent occupies the center of dramatic and intellectual interest. This contraction or narrowness of focus, one might add, is not merely idiosyncratic on Freud's part, though it does figure in a pronounced way in much of his writing. It was characteristic of his culture as well, and one of the more strongly marked features of both the major novels and major autobiographies of nineteenth-century culture is the consistency with which they place the relation of father and child (particularly, of course, father and son) at the center of the human universe of development, passion and choice, and how relatively infrequently the relation of mother and child (with a few notable exceptions) occupies that paramount position. One can say that one of the themes of nineteenth-century literary culture has to do with the conflict surrounding this tendency to a suppression of the mother. In this as in so much else Freud is to be understood as occupying a place of special, contradictory importance. While sharing the interests and emphases of his culture, and by focusing so sharply and almost exclusively on the role of the father in his case histories, he nonetheless was the chief figure in undoing this deformation and demystifying this occluded nexus of cultural circumstances – for at the same time it was his theories that placed the mother back where she had in fact always been, at the absolute center of the infant's universe, and as the more important of the two primal sources in the external world of most children's normal developmental lives. This kind of contradiction, as I say, is of an order that one must become acculturated to in dealing with Freud as a singular figure in the history of the modern world. Its consequences for the coherence of the case in question, as we will see, are considerable.

Having therefore consulted with his mother, the patient returned on the following day and, as we have already seen, accepted Freud's terms. Among them was the basic rule – namely, that which has come to be known as free association – which Freud explained to Lorenz, and to which he in turn pledged himself to adhere. What then followed must be one of the most extraordinary first analytic sessions ever to have occurred. The patient began to speak in what we might think of as overdrive.

He first told Freud about a friend of his "of whom he had an extraordinarily high opinion." Whenever Lorenz was tormented by some "criminal impulse," he went to this friend, asked whether he despised him, was reassured that on the contrary he, Lorenz, was a person of "irreproachable conduct" and that he had always been too severe in his self-judgements. This situation, he flew on, repeated in significant ways another relation he had maintained some fifteen years before. His confessor–friend on this earlier occasion had been a 19-year-old student (four or five years Lorenz's senior) who had taken a liking to him and raised his "self-esteem" to such a degree that the influence-prone adolescent "appeared to himself to be a genius." This older youth had subsequently become his tutor, at which point he suddenly began to treat his younger friend "as though he were an idiot." After some time Lorenz realized that his tutor and sometime friend "was interested in one of his sisters," and he realized as well that the whole relation had been staged by the older youth "in order to gain admission into the house." This episode, he characteristically, sincerely, hyperbolically, and mistakenly remarked, "was the first great blow in his life."

Although the patient at once went on without interruption to another subject, we must at this juncture make a brief pause. His first two separable communications to Freud, in what Freud himself thought of and called the first analytic session, were in the way of full-blown transference utterances. He has had, since he was an adolescent, two friends who have served a similar function for him. Whenever, as it frequently happened, he experienced some unfounded and inexplicable impulse to do something horrible, he would consult these friends to be reassured that he was not a monster or a criminal. These friends invariably tell him that he is habitually too severe in his judgements of himself. (They are to be understood as re-externalized fragments of archaic psychic reality.) He is seeking in Freud a third such figure and has indeed found in him something like one. At the same time, the friend mentioned second in order, but who was in point of fact first in time, was no authentic friend in the proving, for he exploited the needs and the credulity of young Lorenz to further his own selfish aims and then threw him over with contempt and callous lack of feeling. He betrayed the trusting youth, and manipulated the relation of dependency to further his personal sexual ambitions. These two first transferential utterances are, I believe, usefully considered as one, and together they express the patient's ambivalence toward Freud. Exceptionally trustful, he is at the same time extremely fearful of being betrayed *again*; each of his thoughts or impulses seems to be immediately connected to another that reverses it.

At the same time we should direct some attention to the forms of these initial communications, for they too are prototypical of the style of utterance of this patient and of the case as a whole. It is difficult to class or categorize the kind of account that he presents over and over again to Freud. He is not trying to tell some long, involved, complex story; his experience does not appear to him as a narrative or novel. Instead he speaks in anecdotes, recalls events of such magnitude or duration that they can as a rule be summarized in a few sentences. He speaks in fragments of narrative, but neither perceives nor suggests some larger kind of fictional structure as deeply informing his own existence. This conclusion is supported by what follows at once, for having made these remarks about his two confessor–friends, Lorenz "then proceeded without any apparent transition" to tell Freud about his memories of infantile and childhood sexuality. His recollections in this connection range from his fourth to his ninth years and chiefly involve two governesses who were employed in his family. They are familiar enough material to students of nineteenth-century literature and nineteenth-century middle-class domestic life. Both of them involve intensely stimulating scenes of seeing and touching, and they left the patient, as he says, "with a burning and tormenting curiosity to see the female body." By body, he is referring primarily to both the genitals and the buttocks. He had these experiences with his governesses in bed and at the Baths. On none of which does Freud have anything immediately to say. He is certainly not surprised or shocked by what he has heard; nor, despite his abandonment of the seduction theory, is he in any way disposed to discredit the accuracy or truthfulness of the account of this patient. On the contrary, he gives full credit to these recollections of early experiences, and observes that "it will hardly be disputed that they may be described as having been considerable both in themselves and in their consequences." But, he continues, such a state of affairs "has been the same with the other cases of obsessional neurosis that I have had the opportunity of analyzing. Such cases, unlike those of hysteria, invariably possess the characteristic of premature sexual activity." And indeed obsessional neuroses "make it much more obvious than hysterias that the factors which go to form a psychoneurosis are to be found in the patient's *infantile* sexual life and not his present one." At the same time, however, the patient is unusually forthcoming with this material, and the reader cannot avoid the suspicion that he is also producing the kind of material that he believes Freud wants and expects him to produce. As a result, one would also have to account for an element of transference-colored determinations in these communications as well.

He then goes on – Freud is at this moment in 1909 directly reconstructing in recollection an account in the first person, made

from notes written down in 1907 on the evening of the same day as the
session – to say that "When I was six years old I already suffered from
erections, and I know that once I went to my mother to complain
about them. ... I had some misgivings to get over, for I had a feeling
that there was some connection between this subject and my ideas
and inquisitiveness, and at that time I used to have the morbid idea
*that my parents knew my thoughts; I explained this to myself by
supposing that I had spoken them out loud, without having heard myself
do it.* I look on this as the beginning of my illness." He also at once
went on to say that at this time there were a number of girls "who
pleased me very much, and I had a very strong wish *to see them naked.*
But in wishing this I had *an uncanny feeling, as though something must
happen if I thought such things, and as though I must do all sorts of things
to prevent it.*" When Freud then asked him to give an example of such
fears, he replied that "*my father* might die" and then confessed that
thoughts of his father's death had occupied his mind from an early age
and had greatly depressed him. It was at this moment that it was
Freud's turn to be finally surprised, for he then learned "with
astonishment" that Lorenz's father "with whom his obsessional fears
were, after all, occupied *now*, had died several years previously."
Indeed, as we shall soon learn, Lorenz's father had been dead for nine
years when the analysis began.

We must read this group of utterances as we have taken those that
preceded it. They must be read as simultaneously made syntheses
that refer both to the patient's past and to his present and immediate
situation. Thus, at the age of 6 he confided to his mother about his
troubling erections with the kind of trustfulness that he is now
confiding to Freud. At the same time, he could remember that he
believed that his parents could read his thoughts – that is to say, part
of his ego had remained externalized. Yet by the same token this is
also precisely what he is saying to Freud; he is telling the
psychoanalyst that he believes that his bad thoughts can be read by
him. And he is in addition terrified by his thoughts, so stricken with
fear that he has not been able to admit to Freud that his father has
been dead for nine years, and has been speaking about him as if he
were alive in the present. In sum, from then until now he has been
suffering from a single source of trouble: he is tormented by his own
thoughts, is aghast at the prospect of what may occur in his own mind,
and is utterly undone by the supposition that ideas and impulses
perceived by him internally may somehow lead to very bad external
consequences. How the connection between internal thoughts and
external results is to be made goes entirely unstipulated.

Immediately thereafter Freud proposes the following series of
interpretations. To begin with, these events recollected from

Lorenz's sixth or seventh year, and described in this first hour of treatment, were not "as he supposed, the beginning of his illness, but were already the illness itself. It was a complete obsessional neurosis, wanting in no essential element, at once the nucleus and the prototype of the later disorder – an elementary organism … the study of which could alone enable us to obtain a grasp of the complicated organism of his subsequent illness." In other words, what Lorenz disclosed in this first hour was the recollection of a childhood neurosis which was already complete, but was at the same time both the nucleus and prototype of another neurosis that was more complicated (but no more complete). The dynamics of what has now become inferrable to Freud are as follows: the child was "under the domination of a component of the sexual instinct, the desire to look," the intense, recurrent wish to see females naked. This wish was not yet entirely ego-alien, so its recurrence had not become fully characterized by the quality of compulsion. Nevertheless, opposition to the wish was already active in the form of a "distressing affect" that regularly accompanied it. "A conflict was evidently in progress in the mind of this young libertine." Along with the recurrent wish, "and intimately connected with it," was a recurrent fear – every time the wish appeared the patient was afraid that something dreadful would happen. That something dreadful was already "clothed in the characteristic indeterminateness" which was henceforward to be an "invariable feature of every manifestation" of the patient's neurosis, as it is of obsessional neuroses as a rule if not in their totality.

Nevertheless, Freud continues, in a child it is not "hard to discover what it is that is veiled behind an indeterminateness of this kind." Freud's exposition of what it is that is behind is put in the form of a grand, universal empirical hypothesis.

> If the patient can once be induced to give a particular instance in place of the vague generalities which characterize an obsessional neurosis, it may be confidently assumed that the instance is the original and actual thing that has tried to hide itself behind the generalizations.

This is a confident assumption indeed, as is Freud's demonstration of his hypothesis, which consists of this reconstruction.

> Our present patient's obsessive fear, therefore, when restored to its original meaning, would run as follows: 'If I have this wish to see a woman naked, my father will be bound to die'.

Freud's hypothesis reveals that what is hidden is itself a covert hypothesis, a statement which contains notions about causality, the status of ideas in relation to the external world, and further back yet something about the "original meaning" of ideas and the logical, rhetorical, and stylistic forms in which those ideas will find expression. That is to say, Freud's emphasis, even in this first session of the analysis, is beginning to fall on different, smaller, more condensed and more local units of structure and expression than the categories of narrative and narrative-like accounts and systems that characterize his work in his other major case histories.

But Freud is not yet done with this first hour, and he begins to launch into a summary of what he has found: it is a series of binary contraries or oppositions, what he calls "the full muster" of the "inventory" of the neurosis. These are, in brief, "an erotic instinct and a revolt against it"; or a wish, and, struggling against it, "a fear which is already compulsive"; an affect that is distressing and, accompanying it, "an impulsion toward the performance of defensive acts." Yet something else still remains to be accounted for, and this is the patient's childhood delusion that his parents knew his thoughts because he spoke them aloud without being able to hear himself do it. Freud's explanation of this delusion is that it is itself a childish attempt to explain by intuition its inklings "of those remarkable mental processes which we describe as unconscious" and which constitute the substance and essence of psychoanalytic investigation. Freud's hypothetical reconstruction of this experience is slightly self-reflexive: "If I speak my thoughts out loud without hearing them," is what he infers the 6-year-old as having said unconsciously to himself. And he completes and translates this "if" clause by saying that it "sounds like a projection into the external world of our own hypothesis that he had thoughts without knowing anything about them; it sounds like an endopsychic perception of what has been repressed." The child's delusion is hence analogous to and a partial demonstration of the psychoanalytic hypothesis; it is also in the present context a piece of active transference material; and, as Freud phrases it, it is in addition something of a linguistic puzzle, since it runs around itself; and how one moves from an "endopsychic perception" of what has been repressed to a "projection into the external world" of the psychoanalytic hypothesis is a transition that is negotiated or gotten past precisely by the surpassingly clever circularity of the formulations made here by Freud.

He is aware that he has not really gotten to the place that he has just asserted we have arrived at together, for he at once adds, "This elementary neurosis of childhood already involved a problem and an apparent absurdity. ... What can have been the meaning of the child's idea that if he had this lascivious wish his father was bound to die.

Was it sheer nonsense? Or are there means of understanding the words and of perceiving them as a necessary consequence of earlier events and premises." The questions then are essentially mental, intepretative, and hermeneutical. The neurosis is put forward in this context as a verbal text or riddle that requires interpretation, and the establishing of coherence and meaning entail the understanding of anterior states of mind as much as they do the establishment of a coherent narrative account. These statements amount to a series of rhetorical questions to which Freud unmistakably believes he has the answers. And with these questions of meaning and interpretation, addressed to the reader and not to his patient, he brings his account of the first hour towards its conclusion. It contains at least six sub-units which pretend to be or strive towards narrative coherence or intelligibility, and each of them fails to reach such a state. These units are nonetheless exceptionally dense in meaning, although that meaning is at this moment being almost entirely supplied by Freud. Our emphasis at this point upon the problems (or problematics) of narrative and meaning in the construction of either a fictional or real world are, it will be seen, not out of place, because in the next two hours the patient will try to tell Freud the story that brought him to the psychoanalyst's office, and we will see what kind of narrative he is capable of representing.

IV

On Thursday, October 3, Lorenz arrived, having nerved himself up to tell Freud about "the experience which was the immediate occasion of my coming to you." Indeed, he said, he was not sure he could do it, "for there was much in himself that he would have to overcome if he was to relate this experience of his." That experience had taken place during August. Lorenz was a reserve officer in the army and was on maneuvers in Galicia. One day, on a short march, he noticed during a halt that he had lost his pince-nez. He had a wire dispatched to his opticians in Vienna to send him another pair by the next post. During this same halt, however, he got into a conversation with a captain of whom he had "a kind of dread ... *for he was obviously fond of cruelty.*" He was, it seems, particularly in favor of corporal punishment, and the patient had previously argued with him in disagreement. On this occasion they struck up conversation again, and the captain "told me he had read of a specially horrible punishment used in the East." At this point, Freud recalls, "the patient broke off, got up from the sofa, and begged me to spare him a recital of the details." Freud was concerned over the agitated state that Lorenz was clearly in, spoke reassuringly to him about his own (Freud's) distate for cruelty, but affirmed as well the impossibility of the request. "The overcoming of resistances," he said, "was a law of the treatment, and on no consideration could it be dispensed with." Having thus expressed himself with suitably Mosaic severity, he went on to make a concession to the patient; Freud would go so far as to play a kind of psychoanalytic Twenty Questions with Lorenz, and would try to "guess the full meaning of any hints he gave me." He quickly guesses, with some help from Lorenz, that the torture consists of rats boring their way into the anus of a bound criminal.

At all the more important moments of this fragmentary account, Freud noted, the patient's "face took on a very strange, composite expression," which Freud could only interpret "as one of *horror at pleasure of his own of which he himself was unaware.*" And he proceeded with the greatest difficulty that "At that moment the idea flashed through my mind *that this was happening to a person who was very dear to me.*" The person to whom this was being done (he was not himself administering the torture), he replied to prompting, was simultaneously "the lady whom he admired" and his father who had been dead for nine years. The patient broke into his own confession to reassure Freud "that these thoughts were entirely foreign and repugnant to him," and to tell him that he had dealt with these horrible mental occurences with a defensive measure that he called a "sanction," which was in fact a verbal formula for warding off or distancing, denying and repudiating the thoughts. Before we consider any further what Freud called the "nonsensical" character of these fears, we should remark that it does not take profound insight to ascertain that this fragmented recollection-fantasy-anecdote is an elaboration and variation of the obsessional neurosis developed at the age of 6. The desire to see followed by the fear that something bad was going to happen that had to be prevented (namely, the death of his father) has been replaced by the loss of the pince-nez and the effort to replace them followed at once by the horrifying fantasy of anal torture and penetration of those most dear to him, which must be concurrently and immediately undone.

But the weird character of this episode – if that is the word for it – had just begun. For the patient then went on to try to recall what subsequently occurred. The events, or more precisely pseudo-events, concerned the cruel captain again, the delivery of the new pince-nez, a trifling sum of money due at the post office, a couple of short, garbled messages, all of these then cooked up into a hodge-podge of unintelligible fears, commands, prohibitions, sanctions, and so on that involved paying 3.80 kronen to one Lieutenant A. The patient almost at once was lost in a maelstrom of thoughts, vows, rituals, formulae, quasi-logical word and narratological games, none of which made any sense, even to him at the time. These intense, obsessive cogitations, plans, counterplans and counter-counterplans resemble a kind of extended Minsk–Pinsk business, or an Abbott and Costello routine, or the course of occurrences in a Marx brothers' movie, although there was nothing funny about it at all to the person within whom this elaboration was fulminating like some kind of rabid psychic infection. By the time he is halfway through with his recital, the end of the second hour had been reached and Freud steps in to comment revealingly on his reconstructed summary.

> It would not surprise me to hear that at this point the reader had ceased to be able to follow. For even the detailed account which the patient gave me of the external events of these days and of his reactions to them was full of self-contradictions and sounded hopelessly confused. It was only when he told the story for the third time that I could get him to realize its obscurities and could lay bare the errors of memory and the displacements in which he had become involved ... at the end of this second session the patient behaved as though he were dazed and bewildered. He repeatedly addressed me as "Captain," probably because at the beginning of the hour I had told him that I myself was not fond of cruelty like Captain N., and that I had no intention of tormenting him unnecessarily.

In other words, Freud has made the patient repeat this much of his account of the precipitating episode three times, and it still remains obscure, not to say absurd. The episode itself is Gogolian in detail; it also reminds one of some of Dostoevsky's early descriptions of the bizarre behavior of small bureaucrats; and it is Kafka-like in tone. In fact, as we shall see, the narrative really cannot be straightened out in the sense of revealing some hidden inner truth. Moreover, the behavior of the patient is more than slightly delirious as well, although when he calls Freud "Captain" it might be observed he is referring to him as well, etymologically, as headman, or shrink as it is referred to nowadays.

On Friday, October 4, 1907, Lorenz "completed his very characteristic story of his efforts at fulfilling his obsessional vow," that is, somehow to pay 3.80 kronen to the wrong person, Lieutenant A. Incessantly tormented, feeling as if "he were in a dream," he is beset without relief by inward "arguments and counterarguments." He must go to a railway station at P—, which is about an hour's drive from the "village in which A. was stationed"; the post office he must get to is at Z—, and he must also catch that day an evening train from P—

to Vienna. One needs a map to make any sense of these feverish deliberations, and for the German edition of 1924 the Stracheys drew one. Unfortunately, however, the map they drew up from Freud's account was itself, as they admit, "totally inconsistent" with "some of the peculiar data" of the case history. In other words, Freud's account itself is so bewildering and murky that their first efforts at clarification were entirely overthrown; and for the English edition of 1955 an entirely new map had to be drawn. This map is consistent with the material of Freud's account, but is entirely useless for advancing any understanding of the case. Agonizingly enmeshed in his compulsive cogitations and empty ratiocinations, Lorenz finally stumbled onto the train for Vienna, and after enduring infinite agonies of doubt at each stop, finally "struggled through from station to station" and reached the capital city. His purpose was to seek out his friend – Freud's precursor – get his advice and then return to Galicia to do heaven knows what. In a state that defies description he arrived late at night and found his friend, stammered out to him whatever he could bring himself to, and was in turn finally calmed down. The next morning, his friend began to try to make some sense of Lorenz's utterances, and these corrections helped Freud to understand some of the garblings and deformations of Lorenz's pathetic efforts at narrative construction. Yet as Freud himself remarks, each time that he (Freud) makes a correction in the chronicle, straightens out some deformation or clears up some contradiction in the account, the patient's "behavior becomes even more senseless and unintelligible than before."

It continued so after Lorenz's meeting in Vienna with his friend. The delirium returned upon him with full force, and into it he now wove a determination to consult a doctor. He conceived that the physician he would seek out would give him a certificate that would allow him, under the pretext that it was good for his health, to return to the scene of the maneuvers and carry out some such action of payment and restitution as his obsession insisted upon. As chance, or something other than chance, brought it about, one of Freud's books "happened to fall into his hands just at that moment" and "directed his choice to me. There was no question of getting a certificate from me, however; all that he asked of me was, very reasonably, to be freed of his obsessions." Freud was confident that he could be of help in this connection, and he began his work, as we have already seen, by trying to make sense of the narrative-fragments that the patient told him, "straightening out the various distortions in them" and transforming them into coherent narrative-like constructions. But it soon becomes evident that this is not working with Lorenz in anything like the way it worked with Dora and with many of Freud's other patients. Lorenz's recollections cannot be straightened out in the sense that they will in their corrected, amended form bring us close to the truth of what actually occurred and what is equally actually being hidden. For it is not the case that these narratives are simply crippled by pathology, and that with appropriate therapeutic measures the pathology can be edited out of them and that we will then have before us a coherent, integral, truthful, and actuality-revealing story. These narratives are, in addition, not merely partly pathology. Nor do they contain in the ordinary sense the "truth" of the case or the meaning of the experience. They are pathology through and through. They are full of narrative activity, and, like some Kafka stories, they are going nowhere at the same time. Their narrative logic and structure resemble that of post-modernist or late modernist fiction – the narrative itself is organic to the pathology. It has no "correct" or so to speak healthy form. Straightening out the narrative deformations and ellipses does not alleviate the pathology or lead to a cure – it only leads to something "more senseless and unintelligible than before." Indeed, Freud himself becomes part of the patient's delirium, and it is indeed this genuinely fortuitous confluence that finally leads the patient to Freud.

Freud, however, was not one to give up easily on his notion of deconstructing and then reconstructing his patient's narrative efforts, and he prefaced his account of the fourth hour of the analysis, which took place on Saturday, October 5, with a number of statements. First, he asks the reader not to "expect to hear at once what light I have to throw upon the patient's strange and senseless obsessions about the rats." The reason that he cannot has to do with "the true technique of psychoanalysis," which "requires the physician to suppress his curiosity and leaves the patient complete freedom in choosing the order in which topics shall succeed each other during the treatment." For "true" technique we should read "new" technique. In his first report on this case to the Vienna Psychoanalytic Society on November 6, Freud remarked that "the technique of psychoanalysis has changed to the extent that the psychoanalyst no longer seeks to elicit material in which he is interested, but permits the patient to follow his natural and spontaneous trains of thought." This is to put the matter in idealized form. Freud is less directional and insistent with the Rat Man than he was with Dora, but he is still as we shall see decidely interventionist and forceful in his therapeutic behavior, and the present case occupies something of a halfway point on the way towards modern classical analysis. Accordingly, he began the fourth session by asking Lorenz "And how do you intend to proceed today?"

Lorenz characteristically begins by trying to tell Freud yet another story, an account of something that he considers "most important and which has tormented me from the very first." He then tells Freud "at great length" about the death of his father from emphysema nine years in the past. The family, including Lorenz, was keeping watch over the mortally ill man. One night Lorenz was reassured by the attending physician that he could safely get some rest. At half-past eleven he had lain down for an hour's sleep and had been woken at one o'clock to be told that his father had died. He had reproached himself for not being present at his father's death, but at first, at least, "the reproach had not tormented him." What was strange, however, was that he was unable to realize "the fact of his father's death." Whenever he heard a good joke, he would say to himself, "I must tell Father that." "When there was a knock at the door, he would think: 'Here comes Father,' and when he would walk into a room he would expect to find his father in it. And although he had never forgotten that his father was dead, the prospect of seeing a ghostly apparition of this kind had no terrors for him; on the contrary, he had greatly desired it." Matters continued on like this for some year and a half. At that time, an aunt of Lorenz's died; this made it necessary for him to pay a visit of condolence at her house, and following this event he suddenly was stricken anew by the recollection of his "neglect" at the death of his father; the recollection began "to torment him terribly, so that he had come to treat himself as a criminal." Moreover, from "that time forward he had extended the structure of his obsessional thoughts so as to include the next world." And in addition, another "immediate consequence" of this development had been that he had become seriously incapacitated from working.[6] His neurosis in its adult development had now fully broken out, and one of its forms was to extend itself in whatever manifestation it happened to take into a bizarre thought system, which could, for example, both reach into the next world and treat his innocent self as a criminal at the same time. That stage had been attained seven and one-half years before the present tense of the case, and Lorenz reported to Freud that during that period "the only thing that had kept him going ... had been the consolation given him by his friend, who had always brushed his self-reproaches aside on the ground that they were grossly exaggerated."

Freud had given the title "Initiation into the Nature of the Treatment" to this section of the text, and we understand why he did so from what follows next. He takes the opportunity of Lorenz's last remark to deliver a short lecture to the patient in order to give him "a first glance at the underlying principles of psychoanalytic therapy." Such a lecture helps us to understand the state of psychoanalytic therapy as practiced by Freud at the time, and helps us also to a closer, qualified understanding of the remarks he delivered himself of at the weekly meeting of the Vienna group. Freud began to speak to Lorenz – in connection with his intractable, tormenting self-reproaches and feelings of criminality – about the meaning of an inappropriate relation between an affect and "its ideational content," in this instance between the intensity of the self-reproach and the occasion for it. He is in fact talking about what he had already called "the displacement of affect" that is characteristic of obsessional neuroses. The logic of common sense, the logic exercised by Lorenz's friend, when confronted with such a "misalliance" will assert that the affect is conspicuously disproportionate and that the influence of criminality is hence patently false. Psychoanalysis, however, reverses the logic of everyday life (as does the logic of psychopathology) and says "No. The affect is justified. The sense of guilt is not in itself open to further criticism. But it belongs to some other content which is unknown (*unconscious*), and which requires to be looked for. ... Moreover, this fact of there being a false connection is the only way of accounting for the powerlessness of logical processes to combat the tormenting idea." This bit of cleverness on Freud's part gave rise at once to further bewilderment, for how in those circumstances could Lorenz admit that "his self-reproach of being a criminal toward his father was justified" when he knew perfectly well that he had never committed anything like a crime against him. On that note of bafflement, the fourth session came to an end.

The next session continued the work of its predecessor and resumed the extended dialogue between patient and analyst. Freud began by trying to explain what "therapeutic effect" the discovery "of the unknown [ideational] content to which the self-reproach was really attached" might have and why. This remark in turn induced him to bring in some distinctions between "*the conscious and the unconscious*" and to stress the circumstance that what existed in an unconscious state was "relatively unchangeable." Freud then pointed to the antiquities that stood about his consulting room: "their burial had been their preservation," he remarked, and "the destruction of Pompeii was only beginning now that it had been dug up." *Mutatis mutandis*, he went on, the same paradox applied to the analysand – people made every effort to save Pompeii, yet by the same token "were anxious to be rid of tormenting ideas like his" – which digging up, unearthing, and rooting out would certainly eventuate in. The patient continued to question and doubt; surely, he affirmed, self-reproaches such as his "could only arise from a breach of a person's inner moral principles," and this was only possible, he pressed on, "where a *disintegration of the personality* was already present," namely in an individual person who felt as broken up into discontinuous pieces of a self as he did. Was there a possibility, he plaintively and rhetorically asked Freud, "of his effecting a re-integration of his personality?" Freud answered by saying that he "was in complete agreement with this notion of a splitting of his personality." The patient had only to bring into alignment and assimilation this new contrast between a "moral self and an evil one" with the notions of the conscious and the unconscious that Freud had already mentioned. Lorenz responded by saying that although he considered himself a "moral person, he could quite definitely remember having done things in his *childhood* which came from his other self." Of course, said Freud; the unconscious *was* the infantile. The "other" self is the infantile self; it was "that part of the self which had become separated off from it in infancy, which had not shared the later stages of its development, and which had in consequence become *repressed*." And it was "the derivatives of this repressed unconscious that were responsible for the involuntary thoughts which constituted his illness." When the patient expressed some further doubts about "whether it was possible to undo modifications of such long standing" and of such an outlandish nature – for example, how could one "refute" his absurd ideas about the next world – Freud was reassuring on this score as well. However severe his neurosis might be, Lorenz's youth was on his side, as was "the intactness of his personality." In this connection, Freud continued, by way of concluding the hour, "I said a word or two upon the good opinion I had formed of him, and this gave him visible pleasure."

This session had something of the pep talk about it, as well as continuing the process of indoctrination that Freud had begun explicitly in the antecedent hour. In all events it seems likely to have strengthened the already powerful transference elements that were distinct in the case from the outset. Moreover, in reading Freud's account of this hour, one gets the sense that the two principals are somehow contriving to speak past one another. When Lorenz states that he feels that his personality is already in a state of disintegration, he is *not*, I believe, referring to the circumstance that he has an unconscious mind whose workings and contents are unknown to him. What he is bringing forward, I surmise, is an intuition that there are splittings in his ego, that his sense of wholeness as a person and his psychic center of gravity have broken down and been displaced, that he no longer feels that he is an integral human being who is in essential command of a continuously functioning ego. Freud responds by agreeing, as if Lorenz meant by disintegration the separation of conscious and unconscious, the mature and the repressed infantile components of the self. But this agreement actually finesses the point that Lorenz is, correctly, making; in addition it permits Freud to slip in a remark to the reverse effect, that

Lorenz's personality is essentially intact. Hence what Freud has done here is to say that he agrees with the patient and then hand him an interpretation which totally turns around the implications of what the patient at first said. And not merely turns them around. I have the sense that Freud had already gotten a distinct mental impression that this patient will have to be dealt with in very simple ways; that he (Freud) will get through to him only in quite small segments of communicative units, and that anything complex is almost certain to be swallowed up in the storms of inchoate mentation that for the larger part constitute Lorenz's inner life. Therefore, he has taken Lorenz's insightful utterance about himself in the most elementary possible sense, even if that sense involves some fudging of point and truth on the analyst's part. He has also added for good measure a couple of pats on the back, a detail which again brings to the forefront the immense differences between this case and that of Dora, and of Freud's behavior in both instances.

The sixth and next session began with the patient unconsciously repeating much of the material that had already occurred during the first hour. He first said to Freud that he had to "tell me an event in his childhood." He then reiterated the business about his belief when he was 6 or 7 that his parents could read his thoughts, and then followed this remark by a variation on the second part of his childhood syndrome. "When he was twelve years old he had been in love with a little girl." Although he had not felt the love to be sensual, "she had not shown him as much affection as he had desired. And thereupon the idea had come to him that she would be kind to him if some misfortune were to befall him; and as an instance of such a misfortune his father's death had forced itself upon his mind." He had of course at once repudiated the idea with great force. "And even now," Freud comments, "he could not admit the possibility that what had arisen in this way could have been a 'wish'." It could have been no more, Lorenz said, than "a train of thought." At this point, Freud makes a decision to press hard on the patient. If it were not a wish, he objects, why had he bothered to repudiate it? Getting no satisfactory answer, he presses still further: Lorenz is treating the phrase "his [or my] father might die" as if it actually involved *lèse-majesté* or high treason. The great therapist of speech and language now has Lorenz in chancery. On the one hand, Lorenz is treating phrases and expressions as if they were identical with acts. And on the other, he is not taking those phrases and expressions seriously enough, for they are also in some important measure real things: they are not mere verbal fortuities. Freud continues to press Lorenz with further examples, and Lorenz is shaken but does not submit. At which juncture Freud breaks off the argument "with the remark that I felt sure this had not been the first occurrence of his idea of his father's dying; it had evidently occurred at an earlier date, and some day we should have to trace back its history." The Master himself has already forgotten that this wish occurred in the very first hour of the analysis.[7]

Lorenz's response to this remark is to repeat the whole thing once more in still another variation. He suddenly recalls that "a precisely similar thought had flashed through his mind a second time, six months before his father's death." He was already in love with his lady, but financial obstacles "made it impossible to think of an alliance with her." At that moment the idea struck him that *"his father's death might make him rich enough to marry her."* His repudiation on this occasion took the form of an immediate wish "that his father might leave him nothing at all, so that he might have no compensation for his terrible loss." And, still more, the same idea, though in mitigated form, had occurred to him on the day before his father's death.

> He had then thought: "Now I may be going to lose what I love most"; and then had come the contradiction: "No, there is someone else whose loss would be even more painful to you."

And he responded to these thoughts as well with surprise and instant denial. At which point Freud intervenes with yet another "fresh piece of theory." "I told him," he writes, that "every fear corresponded to a former wish which was now repressed." Freud is preparing the ground, in other words, for the notion of ambivalence, and remarks "that it was precisely such intense love as his that was the precondition of the repressed hatred. In the case of people to whom he felt indifferent he would certainly have no difficulty in maintaining side by side inclinations to a moderate liking and to an equally moderate dislike." Freud goes on at considerable length in this way and acknowledges that it will be difficult to discover the source of this feeling and to determine why it remains indestructible. But he is unambiguously clear in his promptings that the source of all these feelings is to be found in the patient's childhood.

To which Lorenz, not surprisingly, replies that it all sounds "quite plausible," but that he didn't believe a word of it. (In a footnote, Freud observes that he is not surprised either. Discussions such as this never aim "to create conviction. ... A sense of conviction is only attained after the patient has himself worked over the reclaimed material, and so long as he is not fully convinced the material must be considered as unexhausted.") Lorenz then proceeded in a fairly incoherent way to protest again the love and friendship he had felt for his father and the intimacy that had always existed between them. He followed this by saying that although he loved his lady very much, he did not really feel sexual impulses towards her at all. "Altogether," he said, "in his childhood his sensual impulses had been much stronger than during his puberty." At which point, Freud figuratively sprang forward again, for Lorenz had now, he remarked, produced both the answers they were searching for and the "third great characteristic of the unconscious" – the first two, we recall, Freud had explained to his patient, were its infantile and repressed markings. The third, which also had to be "the source from which his hostility to his father derived its indestructibility was evidently something in the nature of *sensual desires*, and in that connection he must have felt his father as in some way or other an *interference*." This remark too is by way of a third or fourth repetition, though Freud obligingly and hopefully offers it as if it represented a step forward. But after some further to-ing and fro-ing he does move onward to make what the reader has been led to expect, namely a construction. He is forced to conclude, he remarks interpretatively, that this wish to get rid of his father as an interference "must have originated at a time when circumstances had been very different – at a time, perhaps, when he had not loved his father more than the person whom he desired sensually, or when he was incapable of making a clear decision. It must have been in his very early childhood, therefore, before he had reached the age of six and before the date at which his memory became continuous: and things must have remained in the same state ever since." The construction consists of two parts: first, Freud displaces the significant date backwards into the period obscured by infantile and early childhood amnesia; and second, in the most delicate, oblique and indirect manner he introduces the figure of the Oedipal mother and hence the massive unresolved conflict that is at the center of the hitherto untractable neurosis.

The next session, which was the seventh and last on which Freud was to report in something resembling consecutive detail, began with the patient reiterating his disbelief in the idea that he could ever have entertained such a wish against his father as Freud had imputed to him. At the same time he at once contradicted this denial by declaring that "it would only be right if his thoughts were the death of him, for he deserved nothing less." He then, without much transition, went on to recount what he called a "criminal act" that he committed before he was 8 years old. He had a brother 18 months younger than he, of whom he was both extremely fond and extremely envious, since the brother was stronger and better-looking than he and consequently the general favorite. The incident happened before Lorenz was 8, for he was not yet going to school – which in his instance had begun at that age. The boys were playing with toy guns; Lorenz loaded his with a toy ramrod, told his brother to look up the barrel and pulled the trigger. The brother was not hurt at all, but Lorenz had "meant to hurt him very much indeed. Afterwards I was quite beside myself, and threw myself on the ground and asked myself how ever I could have done such a thing. But I *did* do it." Freud at once returns to his single-minded current strategy. "If he had preserved the recollection of an action so foreign to him as this," he remarks to his patient, how could he "deny the possibility of something similar, which he had forgotten now entirely, having happened at a still earlier age in relation to his father."

Lorenz's response to this provocative nudge was wholly characteristic. He launched into an account of "other vindictive impulses" that he felt, "this time toward the lady he admired so much." She could not love easily; indeed she did not love him. When he had sometime in the past become convinced of that negative circumstance he had elaborated a generally incoherent fantasy which involved his marrying someone else, thereby taking revenge on his lady, and then causing his wife in the fantasy, whom he did not love at all, to die. At which point he recognized again in himself "the quality of *cowardice* that was so horrible to him." As Lorenz was going on in this way, Freud improved the occasion by addressing his patient with another short lecture.

> I pointed out to him that he ought logically to consider himself as in no way responsible for any of these traits in his character; for all of these reprehensible impulses originated from his infancy, and were only derivatives of his infantile character surviving in his unconscious; and he must know that moral responsibility could not be applied to children. It was only by a process of development, I added, that a man, with his moral responsibility, grew up out of the sum of his infantile predispositions.

And although in a footnote Freud immediately added that "I only produced these arguments so as once more to demonstrate to myself their inefficacy," one may with plausibility entertain some doubts about such comments. In these remarks to Lorenz, Freud is quite consciously speaking as an educator and liberator; he is about as far as it is possible to conceive from the prosecuting attorney and demonic discoverer of truth that he was in the case of Dora. His good-natured preaching is more than an exercise in "inefficacy"; it is also an act of genuine support and kindness towards a patient of whom he is fond and whom he wants to help.

With the addition of one or two further small points, this brings us to the end of the seventh hour, and to the end of Freud's chronological and quasi-narrative account. He closes the section with the following remark: "This is as much of the present case history as I am able to report in a detailed and consecutive manner. It coincides roughly with the expository portion of the treatment; this lasted in all for more than eleven months." Leaving to one side the apparently unconscious and unintended ambiguity of that last clause, we still have to confront a distinctly odd or curious kind of statement. Why is Freud unable to report any further on the case "in a detailed and consecutive manner"? Were the subsequent hours even less coherent or consecutive than the eight sessions that he has reproduced for his readers? The surviving sections of the original record do not encourage this belief. And besides, how coherent is the "expository portion of the treatment" that he has reconstructed for us? In what sense is it expository or an exposition? What or how does it expound? It is certainly not a consecutive narrative, such as we find some of Freud's other patients producing – however imperfect and defective those stories may be. It is rather a series of mini-anecdotes connected in no apparently meaningful order. It contains one wildly complicated and grotesque episode – the "story" of the pince-nez, the rat punishment, and the obsessional convolutions of miscarried efforts to pay 3.80 kronen to Lieutenant A – which is itself a species of inchoate non-accounts. And it contains in overwhelming entanglements and tireless variations a single theme or subject, the patient's relation to his dead father and his inability to confront it. As Freud says in two places later on: (1) "We may regard the repression of his infantile hatred of his father as the event which brought his whole subsequent career under the dominion of the neurosis" (238); and (2) Lorenz's "attempt to deny the reality of his father's death is the basis of his whole neurosis." (300) Although these statements appear incongruent, that circumstance begins to dissipate if we understand statement (2) as a restatement or sub-version of (1), or as a practically inevitable consequence of it. These two statements contain, I believe, what Freud decided almost at once was the essence of the case: it was a decision in which he never wavered, and he never wearied of pressing home his conviction of its pertinence. These pages contain as well the opening phases of what we can understand in novelistic terms as the construction of a study of character, and Freud uses all the devices familiar to a habitual reader of nineteenth-century fiction to represent character in both external or behavioral appearances and internal movements of thought and feeling, including such movements as the character himself is unaware of and does not or cannot know. What we do not have, however, is a coherent exposition in the narrative form that Freud seemed originally to aim for, and this circumstance as much as anything else, suggests at least one of his reasons for breaking off the hour-by-hour account at this moment and embarking upon different strategies of exposition, for that is precisely what he now does.

There may be another reason as well. For in the next hour Freud, feeling that the patient was inadequately forthcoming about his lady, that she still "remains most mysterious" to his understanding, and that such resistance must be frontally attacked and broken down, "requested" that the patient "bring a photograph of the lady with him – i.e., to give up his reticence about her." From the patient's point of view such "requests" are without exception read as orders, demands, requirements, or threats, and Lorenz responded with a kind of transference storm of struggle and resistance, while at the same time producing the psychic material that Freud was to work on next. It is no accident, either, I suggest, that in the next section Freud also deals with further material that was produced by another action of his that most analysts today would not think of undertaking. One day Lorenz showed up and said he was hungry; Freud ordered that he be served a meal. This "unorthodox" response on his part produced another hurricane of transferential behavior from Lorenz. It is at least possible that by this time Freud was aware that such behavior on his part was not conducive to sustaining the analytic neutrality and distance that he was developing as a clinical theory and teaching to his followers, and so it is not surprising that he does not report in the case history on these vigorous interventions.

V

What he does do in the next three sections of the essay – which conclude the "Extracts from the Case History" and the first half of the case history as a whole – is to produce three essays of differing length on three different subjects. The first of these, Section E, is called "Some Obsessional Ideas and Their Explanation" and is an extension of the kind of character study that he has been writing in the immediately preceding pages. It consists of a set of connected clusters of illustrations of character rather than a continuous narrative. The problems with obsessional ideas, he remarks again, is that they typically seem senseless, gratuitous, incomprehensible, and crazy. How is one to render them into sense and meaning? The solution that first offers itself is to bring the obsessional ideas into some "temporal relationship with the patient's experiences, that is to say, by enquiring when a particular obsessional idea made its first appearance." The first example he produces is intended to elucidate Lorenz's frequent suicidal impulses.

He had once ... lost some weeks of study owing to his lady's absence: she had gone away to nurse her grandmother, who was seriously ill. Just as he was in the middle of a very hard piece of work the idea had occurred to him: "If you received a command to take your examination this term at the first possible opportunity, you might manage to obey it. But if you were commanded to cut your throat, what then?" He had at once become aware that this command had already been given, and was hurrying to the cupboard to fetch his razor when he thought: "No, it's not so simple as that, you must [first] go and kill the old woman." Upon that, he had fallen to the ground, beside himself with horror.

This sounds like Raskolnikov on the Ringstrasse, but Freud has a simple enough construal of this decidedly odd bit of behavior. The patient was angry at the old lady for causing the lady he loved to be absent. This anger was really rage because it remained unconscious and hence, by the same incremental logic, experienced as murderous rage, which was in turn followed by the severe response of his unforgiving super-ego that he kill himself as a punishment for such "savage and murderous passions." But the whole internal and unconscious transaction passed into consciousness in reverse order – which Freud helps us to understand by interpolating that "first" into the conscious command that came out last.

A similar self-destructive impulse had to do with Lorenz's obsession on one occasion to make himself rapidly and immediately slimmer – because he suddenly believed that he was too fat [or "*dick*" in German]. This notion led to maniacal behavior in blazing midsummer heat and on one occasion to his almost jumping off a cliff. But it too was explained in the same way. His lady, once again, had been stopping at the same resort; but she was in the company of an "English [really American] cousin," of whom the patient was intensely jealous and whose name was Richard. Once more his senseless and self-despoiling activity arose as a reaction "to a tremendous feeling of rage, which was inaccessible to the patient's consciousness and was directed against someone who had cropped up as an interference with the course of his love." In other words, we are playing the same single note again, and the patient is experiencing in relation to the woman he loves just what he also experienced in relation to his father (and mother, it is implied but mysteriously not said) in infancy.

Freud then generally adduces a number of obsessions and manias that Lorenz experienced, such as an obsession to protect his lady against imaginary dangers or an obsession to understand, which was expressed by his compulsively asking anyone who had just said something to repeat himself. All of these express the absolutizing tendency of the unconscious; and all of them are, themselves, principally defenses against anger, hostility, rage, and aggression. "A battle between love and hate was raging in the lover's breast," and the defenses are erected against the hate. But they also and at the same time *represent* that struggle of opposing impulses and gradually become themselves parts of the pathology. The hypothesis that is entailed in this connection is that mental life is largely composed of conflicting or opposing impulses; and a corollary of this hypothesis is that ambivalence is an equally fundamental attribute of psychic existence. In addition, however, these examples, as well as others, demonstrate that symptom-formation is different in obsessional neuroses than it is in hysteria. In the former, compulsive behavior is usually constructed in successive stages, in which one stage neutralizes or tries to "undo" an earlier one. By contrast, in hysteria symptoms are usually built up by inventing a piece of behavior that is "a compromise ... which enables both the opposing tendencies to find expression simultaneously." Hysteria, in other words, is both symbolic and often a parody of symbolism, while obsessive neuroses undertake to express themselves through "some sort of logical connection (often in defiance of all logic)," and hence become parodies of the logical processes.

No better illustration of such ambivalent propensities could be found than Lorenz's verbal behavior. During the course of his adult neurosis, he experienced a revival of religious feelings and took to making up prayers for himself that sometimes lasted for over an hour. The reason for this increasing engrossment of time was that his prayers kept turning into their opposite. For example, "if he said, 'May God protect him', an evil spirit would hurriedly insert a 'not'." Like a character in Dostoevsky again, he was beset by verbal demons, miniature seizures of apparently gratuitous spite. To protect himself against himself, he erected further defenses upon these breached defenses, and giving up his prayers, he replaced them "by a shorter formula concocted out of the initial letters or syllables of various prayers. He then recited this formula so quickly that nothing could slip into it." Bedevilled by his thoughts, what he had repressed was precisely the devil in him. At no point was he able rightly to "appreciate the depth of his negative impulses." Although he was occasionally aware of an urge to do some mischief to his mysterious lady, by and large in his fantasies about her "he only recognized his affection" and denied or repressed "his thirst for revenge" at her frequently expressed indifference to him. His denial, which is another kind of splitting off of part of the self or ego, is another of his dominant traits of character or habitually deployed modes of defense.

It is the same defense that he used all his life in conceiving of his relation to his father as well.

The next section (F), called "The Precipitating Cause of the Illness," is unusually rich, opaque and contradictory. By "precipitating cause" Freud means the event in adult life which was the occasion of the outbreak of the most developed form of the neurosis – for he has said long ago that Lorenz as a child already had a full-blown, yet simultaneously nuclear, obsessive neurosis. He also means that what Lorenz and he have already previously agreed upon as the precipitating event – the death of Lorenz's aunt, after his father died, and the visit of condolence that Lorenz paid to her house – is not the real precipitating cause, as the reader has until now been led to believe, but that some other event is. The "cause" presented itself characteristically "quite casually" during one session and without Lorenz's awareness "that he had brought forward anything of importance" or that he had suddenly remembered something that had not previously been present to his consciousness. These circumstances lead Freud to a digression on the different defenses commonly to be found in hysteria and obsessional neuroses.

In hysteria it is the rule that both the precipitating recent causes of the illness and the infantile experiences that are the preconditions for the transformation of experiences, ideas, and emotions into symptoms undergo repression and are hence overtaken by amnesia. In obsessional neuroses, on the contrary, the infantile preconditions may or may not be overtaken, completely or in part, by amnesia, but "the immediate occasions of the illness are, on the contrary, retained in the memory. The trauma, instead of being forgotten, is deprived of its affective cathexis." What remains in consciousness is a colorless, undervalued, and minimally signifying "ideational content," whose appropriate, original affect has been displaced elsewhere. To differentiate between these two kinds of defenses, there is on the surface "nothing to rely upon but the patient's assurance that he has a feeling in the one case of having always known the thing and in the other of having long forgotten it." Which leads Freud to add in a footnote that in an obsessional neurosis there are "two kinds of knowledge, and it is just as reasonable to hold that the patient 'knows' his traumas as that he does *not* 'know' them. For he knows them in that he has not forgotten them, and he does not know them in that he is unaware of their significance." Which leads him once again to suspect that cognitive and epistemological questions and puzzles are closer to what is going on in obsessional neuroses than they are in other forms of psychic impairment.

Having said this, Freud then proceeds to make an extended detour. He recounts an amusing story from a case "many years ago" that gave him his first insight into those self-reproaches displaced onto wrong causes that are characteristic of obsessional disorders. The case was of "a government official [who] was troubled by innumerable scruples." One of them was that he paid Freud in florin notes that "were invariably clean and smooth." When Freud remarked on this, the bureaucrat (who can be found in any one of a dozen nineteenth-century works of fiction) informed him that the notes were by no means newly drawn from the State treasury; instead, he explained, "it was a matter of conscience to him ... not to hand any one dirty paper florins." They were full of germs and could do harm to someone. Therefore, "he had ironed them out at home." When it came to his sexual life, however, quite another group of rules and directions obtained. He was quite relaxed about this part of his life. He played "the part of a dear old uncle in a number of respectable families"; in this role, he took young girls off for a day's excursion in the country and arranged things so that they would miss the last train back to the city. When this happened he would take two rooms in some hotel, and then, he said, "when the girl has gone to bed I go in to her and masturbate her with my fingers." To which the younger Freud rejoined, "But aren't you afraid of doing her some harm, fiddling about in her genitals with your dirty hand?" At this, the official flared up: "'Harm? Why, what harm should it do her? It hasn't done a single one of them harm yet, and they've all of them enjoyed it. Some of them are married now, and it hasn't done them any harm at all.' – He took my remonstrance in very bad part, and never appeared again." Freud goes on to remark that he "could only account for the contrast between his fastidiousness with the paper florins and his unscrupulousness in abusing the girls entrusted to him by supposing that the self-reproachful affect has become *displaced*. ... The displacement ... ensured his deriving a considerable advantage from his illness."

Freud tells this yarn with unmistakable pleasure; it is already, one can assume, part of the nascent history of a new discipline. (It is also one of the few genuinely funny stories in an uncommonly unfunny profession.) Yet the anecdote represents no real advance in the text itself. It is a repetition of what we have already learned about the primary dynamic process of this neurosis, namely displacement of affect. To be sure it does introduce the themes of anality, money, and dirt in relation to obsessions that will soon be discussed at length in the present text. Most of all, however, it serves to postpone for several pages Freud's recounting of the "precipitating cause" of Lorenz's illness. He comes at this matter in so crab-like a way, I suggest, because he has difficulty in telling it. And the difficulty at least in part has to do with how much of the story he has to leave out, censor, suppress, or distort for a variety of reasons. The story is told with considerable vagueness and some obscurity. And it introduces, briefly and for what is really the first substantial time, the patient's mother.

We learn, by way of introductory detail, that "she was brought up in a wealthy family with which she was distantly connected. This family carried on a large industrial concern." The family were in fact wealthy Viennese Jews; in the notes they are named Rubensky; and Lorenz's mother was that familiar cultural phenomenon, a poor relation, a kind of continental Fanny Price. Lorenz's father, "at the time of his marriage, had been taken into the business, and had thus by the marriage made himself a fairly comfortable position." What is implied, but not quite stated, in the text (though it *is* explicit in the notes) is that Lorenz's mother and father were both originally of "very humble circumstances"; in short, they were poor; they were not, however, unconnected. They were both related to the Rubenskys, and, what we also learn from the notes alone, they were connected by virtue of their being first cousins (287). Moreover, Lorenz had known two other things of antecedent importance to the precipitating event. First, his parents' "marriage was an extremely happy one." But second, he also learned that his father, "some time before making his mother's acquaintance, had made advances to a pretty but penniless girl of humble birth." What we additionally learn from the original record, was that Lorenz was also convinced by some remark of his mother that "her connection with Rubensky was worth more than a dowry, that his father had married her and abandoned his love for his material advantage." Although this information does not directly contradict the assertions made about the parents' happy marriage, it is not in unmitigated agreement or congruence with it either.

So much by way of introduction. The patient's father died in 1899. Some time thereafter, probably in 1902 or 1903,

> the patient's mother told him one day that she had been discussing his future with his rich relations, and that one of her [his mother's] cousins had declared himself ready to let him marry one of his daughters when his education was completed; a business connection with the firm would offer him a brilliant opening in his profession. This family plan stirred up in him a conflict as to whether he should remain faithful to the lady he loved in spite of her poverty, or whether he should follow in his father's footsteps and marry the lovely, rich, and well-connected girl who had been assigned to him.

This is all very well until we recall that Lorenz's mother and father were cousins, the girl being proposed as a wife is a cousin as well, and (we learn from Freud's original notes) that the patient's lady, Gisela by name, was also a cousin of his! Although this sounds like some plot hatched by Wilkie Collins, it really does not reduce to narrative sense, nor does Freud make any effort at such a reduction. Perhaps the best we can do is to repeat the admonition voiced more than once in *War and Peace* (and bearing upon the classical history of the English and European novel) that "Cousinhood's a dangerous relation."

But we cannot permit matters to rest here. We must call attention once again to Freud's determination – as opposed to his procedure in the case of Dora and elsewhere – not to bring full narrative consequentiality to bear on this, forgive the expression, rat's nest of familial relations. He follows a very different procedure; in fact, he suppresses the material; and so far as I can tell he is wise to have done so. For the information about the various cousins that is reproduced in the original record provides no means, to my knowledge, of constructing a coherent narrative. Nor is it likely that such a construction would do much good. Lorenz does not think in large, linear and parallel groupings of narratological sequences. Indeed, what we get from such a set of passages on the "precipitating cause" as we have just rehearsed is one further repetition in permutated form of what we have already encountered. In this instance Lorenz's mother is acting as his father had acted twice before, as an *interference* between himself and his object of love. His father had behaved in this way in both the archaic infantile and childhood past and in the patient's late adolescence, when Lorenz had first declared his love for his poor cousin, now his lady, Gisela. His mother had behaved that way in the proposal some years later of the family-arranged marriage; and Gisela had behaved that way herself in refusing on at least two, and possibly more, occasions Lorenz's advances of marriage to her. And, as we shall see in a moment, Freud is going to be construed as behaving in such a way too. Hence the fundamental repertoire of Lorenz's behavior undergoes an expansion: the consideration that the cause of the inexpressible rage that he experiences in one situation after another, and which he cannot feel or express directly but must displace into various obsessive symptoms, is now combined with the possibility that one of his primal ways of relating to other persons of both sexes is as entities who actively interfere with his deepest wishes and desires. Moreover, this mode of relating is so profound and pervasive that it has consumed an extraordinary portion of his almost thirty years of sentient existence.

But before we get to this point, Freud has interpreted for Lorenz how the latter had resolved the conflict between his love for his lady and the wishes of his mother and his family; both of which latter,

Freud explained, represented to Lorenz "the persisting influence of his father's wishes." Lorenz did so by falling ill; "or, to put it more correctly, by falling ill he avoided the task of resolving it in real life." This avoidance was successfully attained, since the chief result of his illness was an obstinate incapacity for work, which allowed him to postpone the completion of his education for years. "But," Freud continues, "the results of such an illness are never unintentional; what appears to be the *consequence* of the illness is in reality the *cause* or *motive* of falling ill." QED. Once again cause and consequence change hands and are interchangeable, and we are once more in the presence of a familiar kind of displacement.

One further turn and we are done with this peculiar section. Lorenz of course at first refused to accept Freud's elucidation of the marriage business. There followed "an obscure and difficult period in treatment," full of severe resistances, recriminations, and interpretations on the part of the patient. This period came to an end when a phenomenon of the transference was brought forward. One day Lorenz met a young girl on the stairs of Freud's house whom he immediately "promoted" into being Freud's 12-year-old daughter, Anna; he also then imagined that the reason that Freud was "so kind and incredibly patient with him was that I wanted him for a son-in-law." Such a conjecture involved both wildly inflating Freud's financial and social position and at the same time putting him as, inevitably, another obstacle between Lorenz and the lady he loved. This bitter transferential skirmish came to its appropriate termination in a dream whose significance even Lorenz (again much unlike Dora) could not elude.

> He dreamt that *he saw my daughter in front of him; she had two patches of dung instead of eyes.* No one who understands the language of dreams will find much difficulty in translating this one: it declared that *he was marrying my* daughter not for her "beaux yeux" but for her money.

Once again, Lorenz has reproduced Freud's construction of his primordial means of responding to others in his life. In this connection, however, we may note two pertinent matters. Although the production of this kind of presentation as part of the transference appears to us today as unavoidable and wholly appropriate, there is as well something almost comically inappropriate about this whole episode. For entirely unknown to the reader of the case, and present only in the notes, is the circumstance that about two months into the analysis Lorenz meets and then begins to have a successful affair with a young dressmaker. I think one ought to be quite direct about this.

He behaves as a well-placed young Viennese of his time and station did. She is his kept mistress; he has affection for her; there is never any question that their relation is going to go anywhere. He exercises the privilege of buying her sexual favors in return for treating her with some decency and conveying gifts and money in her direction. Freud is in his notes studiously reticent in his comments on this matter, but there are one or two moments (as well as the sense one gets of his attitude towards the situation as a whole) that make it unmistakable that he is all in favor of this development. He notes how potent with the dressmaker Lorenz reports himself to be, and there is no reason to believe that Freud doubts this. He is in fact in favor of his patient's stunted sexual life changing in the direction of greater activity. And indeed at one moment (311) when Lorenz reports that he had been in bed with his girl, that she had lain on her stomach and that "her genital hairs were visible from behind," Freud responded by saying "that it was a pity that women nowadays gave no care to them and spoke of them as unlovely." Analytic neutrality indeed! Yet what is of further moment, to be sure, is that all of this, and much more, is not reported in the case history at all. Nor can one imagine how it easily could be.

Finally, there is the fact that in the transference dream which ends this section, Lorenz once again produces his essential representation of others and his essential habits of relating to them. And yet this reproduction entails a new dream and interesting new details. In portraying a character in this way, Freud is doing something that immediately recalls such nineteenth-century novelists as Dickens or Dostoevsky. Dickens, for example, had the superlative ability to create, as everyone has always noticed, unforgettable characters. One of the unforgettable things about such characters is that they seem on the one hand very simple, yet present themselves in ways which while preserving that apparent simplicity nevertheless continually vary and seem (and indeed are) profound. Dickens does this, generally, by finding certain idiosyncratic utterances of written speech that belong singularly to this character; moreover, these forms are capable of apparently inexhaustible new presentations. It is almost as if Dickens had discovered what we think of today as certain particular deep structures out of which to generate the apparently limitless utterances of one of his great characters. Freud has done something similar with Lorenz, and with obsessional neuroses. He has discovered one or two structures or forms of relation deep in Lorenz's life, and it is upon these that he focuses all his analytic attention. At the same time these structures, or units of relations, are apparently capable of generating a theoretically numberless variety of dreams, fantasies, obsessions, defenses, and ideas, and, while being all of them variations of a few rather elemental groups of relations, are able continuously to bring forth original and striking material. It is an extraordinary achievement on Freud's part to have been able to catch and record this process, and there is no evidence in the text to suggest that he was aware that this is what he was in point of fact doing.

VI

In the final, and longest, section of the first part of the case, "The Father Complex and the Solution of the Rat Idea," we see Freud writing in his mode of superlative complexity. We cannot do him justice here; constraints of space require increasingly severe compression of the material.

To be extremely brief, the discussion of the precipitating cause of the illness prompts Freud to delineate two paths that lead Lorenz back to his early childhood. Both have to do with his relation to his father; the first is through *identification* with him as both child and late adolescent; the second is in *struggle or conflict* with him over objects of erotic choice. The postulation of this reciprocal duality leads Freud to begin to tell the story of Lorenz's father, who seems to have been a most attractive man – all of Lorenz's aborted stories tend to get transmuted into stories that belong primarily to other people; that repeated tendency is part of the pathos of his largely circular or non-linear existence. Indeed one can only, Freud implies, comprehend the nature of Lorenz's thwarted sexuality through the story of his father's life. It is primarily through the part played by his father as opposition and impediment in the "sphere of sexuality" that Lorenz's "prematurely developed erotic life" (and prematurely cut off from development as well) is to be understood. To demonstrate this argument he produces three illustrations of Lorenz's adult sexual behavior. All occurred after the death of his father. The first took place several years after that event on the occasion of Lorenz's first experiencing, at the age of 26, "the pleasurable sensations of copulation." During that experience, "an idea sprang into his mind: 'This is glorious. One might murder one's father for this!'" Freud remarks that this was "at once an echo and elucidation of the obsessional ideas of his childhood." The Diderot of *Rameau's Nephew* would of course have agreed.

The other two moments have to do with Lorenz's masturbatory behavior. Childhood masturbation was in complete amnesia for him, and he did not practice it to any extent during adolescence, or until his twenty-first year, that is, until shortly after his father died. The onset of the impulsion created great shame in him, and he soon "foreswore the habit." The impulsion thereafter reappeared only upon rare and exceptional occasions. It was provoked, for example, by "especially fine moments," epiphany-like accesses of feelings of exaltation or uplift, which contained as well, Freud quickly pointed out, two elements, "a prohibition, and the defiance of a command" – thus adducing once more, implicitly, the theme of anal eroticism. And it reappeared in yet another commutated shape in Lorenz's repeated nocturnal behavior while he was trying to study for his examinations. This ritual involved opening the door of his flat between midnight and one o'clock, "as if he expected a visit from his father at the hour when ghosts are abroad." (This is the first of what will be many allusions to *Hamlet*.) It was followed by the patient's returning into his flat and taking out his penis before a looking glass. And it should be abundantly evident by now, Freud writes, that "in this single unintelligible obsessional act, he gave expression to the two sides of his relation with his father."

These indications, plus "other data of a similar kind," led Freud in the tenth session of the analysis to adduce a construction. He inferred that when Lorenz was a very small child (certainly before he was 6) he had been found guilty of some masturbatory act by his father and had been severely punished for it. This castigation had put an end to the childhood masturbation but had also "left behind it an ineradicable grudge against his father and had established him for all time in his role of an interferer with the patient's sexual enjoyment."

To Freud's "great astonishment," Lorenz then told him of an episode from his very early childhood that he himself did not remember at all, but that his mother had adverted to repeatedly throughout his life. It is one of the more touching moments in a case history of considerable poignancy. When Lorenz was between 3 and 4 years old

> he had done something naughty, for which his father had given him a beating. The little boy had flown into a terrible rage and had hurled abuse at his father even while he was under his blows. But as he knew no bad language, he had called him all the names of common objects that he could think of, and had screamed: 'You lamp! You towel! You plate!' and so on. His father, shaken by such an outburst of elemental fury, had stopped beating him, and had declared: 'The child will either be a great man or a great criminal!'

Although he had no recollection whatever of the event, Lorenz believed that it had made a permanent impression on his "own character. From that time forward he was a coward – out of fear of the violence of his own rage." He also learned from his mother that the offense for which he had been punished was that he had *bitten* someone. The event could not help but make an impression on Freud as well, since the scene retold to him by Lorenz resonates with symmetry and power with a famous scene from Freud's own childhood. In addition, the disclosure of the scene itself, plus the circumstance of the biting, breaks the case open along several lines at once.

The lines of branching along which the case divides are three in number: they involve (1) the interpretation of the ur-scene itself, (2) the effect of Freud's construction upon the subsequent course of the analysis, and (3) the interpretation of the obsession with rats opened up by the detail that it was Lorenz who had in the far-off and forgotten past perpetrated the first act of biting. I cannot discuss these branchings in sufficient detail and can only make some schematic observations about how Freud proceeds. He proceeds first by a simple strategy of composition and confines or encapsulates his entire discussion of the construction and scene from childhood to an enormous footnote. He discusses the effects of this moment in the analysis on the transference in a vivid but extremely cursory way. And he spends the largest part of this section in a dazzling exegesis of the "Rat idea." In my discussion I will retain the order in which Freud takes up these matters but will reverse the proportions of space that he devotes to them.[8]

Freud's discussion of the reconstructed – and never actually remembered – scene from Lorenz's early childhood proceeds by way of his theory of infantile sexuality and touches on problems left permanently unresolved in the wake of the abandoned seduction theory. Constructions, revelations, inferred scenes of this kind regularly crop up in the course of psychoanalysis, he remarks; often enough they "evade final elucidation," and the analyst must "leave it undecided whether the scene in question actually took place or not." Moreover, it is imperative to "recognize that more than one version of the scene (each often differing greatly from the other) may be detected in the patient's unconscious phantasies." The question then turns upon – as it did in the episode in which Freud disclaimed his own seduction theory – matters of historical interpretation. Such matters are perforce problematical. And this is in turn the case by reason both of the nature of historical events and of the way in which both personal and transpersonal histories undergo formation.

If we do not wish to go astray in our judgment of their historical reality, we must above all bear in mind that people's "childhood memories" are only consolidated at a later period, usually the age of puberty; and that this involves a complicated process of remodelling, analogous in every way to the process by which a nation constructs legends about its early history ... in his phantasies about his infancy the individual as he grows up *endeavors to efface the recollection of his autoerotic activities*; and this he does by exalting their memory traces to the level of object-love, just as a real historian will view the past in the light of the present. This explains why these phantasies abound in seductions and assaults, where the facts will have been confined to autoerotic activities and the caresses or punishments that stimulated them. Furthermore, it becomes clear that in constructing phantasies about his childhood the individual *sexualizes his memories* ... though in doing this he is probably following upon the traces of a really existing connection.

Such a passage serves to suggest how complex, equilibrated, and many-sided Freud's sense of history was; and it serves to remind us as well how much of the seduction theory was left residually behind even when, as in the largest number of instances, no actual seduction is to be finally settled upon as having been committed. There is always some element of the metahistorical in all psychoanalytic dealings with the clinically and culturally historical pasts.

And even in the present instance, where Freud has independent evidence that bears upon the prehistoric past of his patient, the matter remains referentially undecidable. For "the statement made by the patient's mother leaves the way open to various possibilities." Adults have their own reasons in abundance for censoring and editing the past, especially where their children are concerned. Nevertheless, there is no way of deciding whether or not such a process is to be detected in the instance of Lorenz's mother – which in an at least partially metahistorical situation is what one expects. At which point, Freud switches gears again:

A deeper interpretation of the patient's dreams in relation to this episode revealed the clearest traces of the presence in his mind of *an imaginative production of a positively epic character.* [my italics] In this his sexual desires for his mother and sister and his sister's premature death were linked up with the young hero's chastisement at his father's hand.

The epic character of these fantasies is something that remains permanently a private possession of Freud's mind. The material for the epic is presumably, at least in part, scattered about in the original notes, but it remains undeciphered, an arcanum. There is indeed much matter there about one of the patient's sisters, less about other sisters, and something about his brother, but Freud resolutely keeps almost all of it out of the case history, does very little with it interpretatively in the notes, and does not develop the "epic" character which he had imputed to it. For having said the foregoing, he at once switches gears again.

> It was impossible to unravel this tissue of fantasy thread by thread; the therapeutic success of the treatment was precisely what stood in the way of this. The patient recovered, and his ordinary life began to assert its claims: there were many tasks before him, which he had neglected far too long, and which were incompatible with the continuation of the treatment. ... The scientific results of psychoanalysis are at present only a by-product of its therapeutic aims, and for that reason it is often just in those cases where treatment fails that most discoveries are made.

In his reference to threads and unravelling, we know at least *which* epic Freud is thinking of – though as far as I know he never before or after used the figure of Penelope in analogy to that of the analyst. Hence, no epic narrative will be found emerging from this case, though, if we take Freud's word, it remains concealed contingently within it. Freud then goes on to state by indirection that this case is the opposite of the case of Dora on almost every ground – therapeutically, heuristically, and in the role pursued by himself, the analyst. It is also his way of making amends for the case of Dora, for rationalizing some of the things that went on in it, and for his trying to suggest allusively the differences in him that are to be detected after an interval of almost a decade – the first decade one might call it of actual psychoanalytic practice. And having implied all that in his most characteristically compressed style, he then goes on to append one final paragraph to the footnote, which functions as a kind of graceful bowing out from the subject. That paragraph merely says that this constructed and retold scene from Lorenz's childhood is altogether typical of "*the nuclear complex of the neuroses*" and occurs in all of us "irrespective of how greatly or how little real experiences have contributed toward them." At the same time "real events are usually to a large extent responsible for bringing" such pieces of psychic history about – in particular, they are responsible for the parts assigned to the father as opponent and "interferer" with the sexual activities of sons. Even when he is trying to get away from a subject, Freud cannot do so without introducing a note of intractable equivocation – which sustains the subject in extension, although he himself has compositionally affected his disappearance from it.

As for the transference, that too was qualitatively affected by the emergence of this prehistoric scene. Lorenz was shaken for the first time in his steadfast denials that he had ever expressed the kind of fury at his father that the material adduced in the analysis strongly suggested. But he was less shaken than Freud expected him to be. For, unlike his predecessor, Dora, his "capacity for being illogical" kept urging him to discount the evidential value of the scene because "he himself could not remember" it. As a consequence, Freud writes "it was only along the painful road of transference that he was able to reach a conviction" that was commensurate with the material that he himself brought forward. And a little later Freud describes the transference as "this school of suffering, [in which] the patient won the sense of conviction which he had lacked." Such statements inevitably recall to the student of literature very similar phrases from Keats's letters, and there can be no question that for Freud the full experience of the transference in psychoanalysis was the equivalent of Keats's "vale of soul-making" – how else except through such pain and suffering are we to school an intelligence and make it into a soul. But Lorenz did not behave like Keats or like a character aware of the dignified circumstance that his sufferings are themselves the means by which we traverse the tragic vale of soul-making, the world of our ineluctable, humanizing experience. On the contrary, the material brought out by the prehistoric scene released in him the most powerful urgings in the negative sector of the transference:

> he began heaping the grossest and filthiest abuse upon me and my family, though in his deliberate actions he never treated me with anything but the greatest respect. His demeanor as he repeated these insults to me was that of a man in despair. "How can a gentleman like you, sir," he used to ask, "let yourself be abused in this way by a low, good-for-nothing fellow like me? You ought to turn me out: that's all I deserve." While he talked like this, he would get up from the sofa and roam about the room ... he was avoiding my proximity for fear of my giving him a beating. If he stayed on the sofa he behaved like someone in desperate terror trying to save himself from castigations of terrific violence; he would bury his head in his hands, cover his face with his arm, jump up suddenly and rush away, his features distorted with pain, and so on.[9]

And although the language that Freud uses may invoke the sense of high tragedy that John Keats brought to his contemplation of universal human experience, the behavior of Lorenz cannot but remind us of the grotesque tragi-comedy of characters from Dostoevsky – it is germane to our sense of Freud's cultural project that it include this range of reference to such informing moments of deliberate literary representation throughout the nineteenth century.

Moreover, we should briefly note that what Lorenz wins through to is a "conviction" of the rightness and necessity of Freud's construction. Freud himself does not even claim that his construction is *true*: such a claim would be unwarranted. What he does assert is that Lorenz came to be persuaded of the truth of it – for psychoanalysis, it may be, no more is possible, not to say necessary.

These two occurrences, Freud's construction of the prehistoric scene plus the sudden animation of negative transference responses, were accompanied by a third – which was a monstrous outpouring of associations to the rat fantasy and related subjects that Lorenz had hitherto withheld. It is not too much to suggest that this deluge of material was produced, mixed-metaphorically, as a kind of faecal hemorrhage. What is involved is not a single coherent story but a welter of mini- or sub-stories, many of them not belonging to the patient. All of them have to be disentangled bit-by-bit, but they are not put together again by Freud to make a single hetereogeneous whole in the sense that modern narratological theory ascribes to the conception of wholeness. The clarification proceeds largely by a set of verbal games, puns, and bridges and by a series of non-verbal but nonetheless equally symbolic associations. There are word plays on rats: *Ratten* (rats), *Raten* (installments), *Spielratte* (gambler), and *heiraten* (to marry). These verbal movements are themselves interwoven with the immense range of symbolic significances that can be ascribed in dreams, stories, myths, fairy-tales, and ordinary life to the image of the rat – as biter, as that which burrows and penetrates and eats, as penis, as carrier of disease, as hidden faecal mass, as worm, and as baby. All of these seem abstract and quasi-mechanical, yet in the actual working out fit piece by concrete piece into the fragmentary history of Lorenz's life. Again and again, what is recurred to is Lorenz's unacceptable, repressed, and denied rage at his father, his lady (and his mother), all of whom in one way or another have pre-empted his story. He has no story to speak of, apart from his covert rage, and when this rage has been translated into the languages described in the foregoing sentences his delirium about rats disappears. When and how this process actually occurred is not recorded in either the case history or the surviving notes. But there is no reason to doubt that it did take place.

VII

The second part of the case history, which is much shorter than the first, had the title "Theoretical" added by Freud in 1924. It is partly that, but it is also partly a summary of what has gone before in Part I, partly additional remarks and adduction of clinical material, and partly something altogether different again. This difference becomes more apparent in the later stages of the section.

In Section (A), "Some General Characteristics of Obsessional Structures," Freud tries to narrow the aperture of his concentration upon "obsessional thinking" as a group of purely psychic phenomena and to pay more attention to their "phenomenology." For example, he tries to demonstrate once again that the secondary defenses which the patient constructs and enlists to oppose his obsessional ideas are not "purely reasonable considerations – but, as it were, hybrids between the two species of thinking; they accept certain of the premises of the obsession they are combating, and thus, while using the weapons of reason, are established upon a basis of pathological thought." Freud calls these hybrid productions "*deliria*," and the chief point about them is how closely they resemble the patient's unfailingly incoherent efforts at story-like narrative. They are themselves an element of the pathology that is being at the same time fought against. This peculiar characteristic of being at the same time alien or foreign to the ego and yet a component of the ego's functioning as well reveals itself most particularly in the endless word plays, commands, prohibitions, and other verbal activities that are prominent attributes of this condition. Each such production, Freud remarks, is "like a mutilated telegraph message," whose "actual text" may appear in a dream, in a speech in a dream, or in a succession of apparently permutated but essentially repetitious obsessional ideas or acts. He provides a number of examples of such metaphorical transformations, including various plays on words and anagrams (which are expanded upon at much greater length in his notes), and concludes that such a use of "the defensive forces ... by the repressed ones ... is also a good example of the rule that in time the thing which is meant to be warded off invariably finds its way into the very means which is being used for warding it off." This thinking by contradictions, or dialectically, leads a kind of shadow existence in the pathology as well, and each successive fragment of the neurosis provides a kind of sub-text to be analyzed in terms of such a dialectical play.

Freud goes on to state that the study of the "*psychological* significance of obsessional thinking ... would be of extraordinary value ... and would do more to clarify our ideas upon the nature of the conscious and the unconscious than any study of hysteria or the phenomena of hypnosis." In other words, Freud is asserting his belief that the study of obsessional thinking will lead to fundamental discoveries about the nature of thought itself, although he doesn't himself stipulate what those discoveries might be, apart from generally intimating that study of thought on the borderline between conscious and unconscious processes will assist us to understand better the ways in which we construct reality. Which leads Freud on to Section (B), "Some Psychological Peculiarities of Obsessional Neurotics: Their Attitude towards Reality, Superstition and Death." He deals first with Lorenz's typically contradictory attitude towards superstitions, for there existed in him the co-presence simultaneously of superstitious and not superstitious beliefs. In this connection, he regularly employed such "sleight of hand" mental manipulations as the unacknowledged use of his peripheral vision to convince himself that he experienced premonition of important events – which of course he did not. He was at once an unconscious con-man of himself and like some popular novelist of the time, deeply preoccupied "with the inexplicable coincidences of everyday life with which we are so familiar." And Freud makes a perfunctory explanatory pass at suggesting the infantile roots of each such pair of oppositions – the opposition consisting chiefly though not exclusively in the idiosyncratic mixture of the normal and the pathological in each of these mental operations.

In this context, Freud turns recursively to the distinction he had made earlier between hysteria and obsessional neuroses. In the former, the defense of repression leads to amnesia and hence the severance or deformation of narrative conjunctions and coherences. In the latter, the defense of displacement or withdrawal of affect leads to the "severance of causal connections." Now causal and narrative sequences are often closely related, but they are not identical.

The need for new causal hypotheses to replace those that have been displaced is connected in turn, and by reversal, with the obsessional symptom of continual uncertainty or *doubt*. The purpose of doubt as an unconscious defense is twofold: general and obsessive doubt helps us to avoid both the certainties and the actual uncertainties of the real world; and it allows us as well to keep that real world at bay. Compulsive speculation about the great imponderables of existence, such as "paternity, length of life, life after death, and memory" – the topics of childhood speculation in addition – leads to speculation about thinking itself, and to efforts to evoke or imagine other possible worlds, an undertaking that the Rat Man is continually preoccupied with and that Freud is able to take note of but not to order into a conventional narrative representation. In this particular connection – more precisely in terms of speculation about the uncertain status of one's father as opposed to one's biological mother – Freud notes that "a great advance was made in civilization when men decided to put their inferences upon a level with the testimony of their senses and to make the step from matriarchy to patriarchy." This terse conjecture on the history of civilization suggests that in Freud's mind, the bodily evidence of the senses, and our belief in them, is both anterior and inferior to the spiritual evidence of the intellect and humanity's belief in the operations of logic and inference – which he associates with patriarchal order and identification on behalf of civilized persons with the father. And it is somewhere in around here that the attentive reader may begin to suspect that Freud is rapidly losing interest in the Rat Man himself, and in the case, and is embarking unknown to himself on yet another interpretation or minor case history. Indeed, a large portion of the remainder of the essay consists of this scarcely covert undertaking. Freud, I imagine, has been thinking about this matter ever since he learned of the incident of Lorenz's going to the door between twelve and one o'clock at night in expectation of the appearance of his dead father – who could only appear of course as an apparition or ghost. This conjunction of circumstances can bring only one character to mind, namely Hamlet, and the last part of the case history of the Rat Man is an interpretation of Hamlet's character that is complementary to Freud's famous passages about him in *The Interpretation of Dreams*. I will only touch upon Freud's interpretative remarks to suggest the depth to which he is carried by this current of associations.

In the earlier work, Freud regarded Hamlet as falling within the categories of hysteria, and brought him forth along with Oedipus as one of the two cardinal representations of the fundamental crisis of childhood existence, which had not yet been given the name by which it ultimately came to be known. On this occasion, however, he augments his interpretation of Hamlet by regarding him, obliquely, as suffering from an obsessional neurosis as well. Thus to Lorenz's neurotic compulsion to doubt there is added doubt on matters of universally grave concern, paternity, mortality, life after death – all those matters that preoccupy and sometimes divert Hamlet's already blunted purpose. These are rapidly followed by such concerns – or themes – as the incapacity of Lorenz (and Hamlet) to come "to a decision" on important matters, and the concomitant effort to "postpone every decision" – a description of one side of the vastly overdetermined problem of Hamlet's delay; by the "fantasies of revenge" which beset both characters in different degrees; by their "obsession for understanding" and their paralyzing ambivalence toward the principal objects of their affections.[10] This ambivalence leads in its turn in both to "a partial paralysis of the will" and to the simultaneous domination in them of the processes of "*compulsion* and *doubt*" over the executive powers of action that are appropriate to grown men in their respective cultures. All of these stimulate Freud (241) to quote Hamlet in a footnote, and it is thereafter difficult to believe that he is unaware of what he is doing – he is both completing or adding to his earlier interpretation of *Hamlet* and taking leave of the Rat Man, whose story is no longer being sought after, but whose character is being reinvoked by this quasi-unacknowledged rereading of Shakespeare.

The generalized compulsion to doubt is in both characters a displaced and powerful impulse to act, and in both "by a sort of *regression*, preparatory acts become substituted for the final decision, thinking replaces acting, and, instead of the substitutive act, some thought preliminary to it asserts itself with all the force of compulsion." Such obsessive thinking in both is one expression of the vicissitudes that the "epistemophilic instinct" or drive has undergone in obsessional neurotics; it also issues, among other things, in the symptomatic behavior of brooding. The "act of thinking itself" becomes sexualized in both, and the mental detective work, feverish ratiocination, and compulsive playing with words of both Hamlet and Lorenz are different manifestations of closely related psychic formations. The displacement of impulses to action into the realm of thought leads in such cases only to more thought, but thought which is undertaken "with an expenditure of energy which (as regards both quality and quantity) is normally reserved for actions alone." Hence another reading of Hamlet's delay. And when Hamlet does try for the first time to act, he does so in a context that bears upon the present case in a sense that is almost too good to be true. Closeted with his mother, accusing her of being disloyal to his dead father, Hamlet thinks that his surrogate father (and self), Claudius, is hidden behind the arras, and mistakenly stabs Polonius, crying "How now! a rat? Dead, for a ducat, dead!" It is hard to believe that both Freud *and* Lorenz were altogether unaware of such a convergence, and indeed in Lorenz's "rat currency," when he says, "For each copulation, a rat," the two are brought into virtually explicit juxtaposition. Moreover, both works have graveyard scenes as well as ghostly fathers in them; Hamlet's disgust has its counterpart in Lorenz's childhood coprophilia and adult fastidiousness – and so it goes; the comparisons and analogues have really only just begun, and it is prudent on my part to end them here with no more than this suggestion of their ramifications.

Freud brings the entire case history to a close by apologizing for the incompleteness of his account, and by recording his impression that his patient had "as it were, disintegrated into three personalities." One of these is altogether unconscious, and the other two are preconscious entities between which his consciousness "could oscillate." His unconscious personality was made up of his repressed childhood sexual impulses, and "might be described," Freud writes, "as passionate and evil impulses" – these correspond roughly to the id in the later structural theory. His two other personalities also anticipate the later theory, but they are conceived of in an interestingly different way. In one of them, his so-called "normal state," he is said by Freud to be "kind, cheerful, and sensible – an enlightened and superior kind of person." This is the ego, and we can see that the ego in this general description is the child of the enlightenment and the secular nineteenth century, a creation of reason, progress, and middle-class virtues. In his "third psychological organization," however, Lorenz "paid homage to superstition and asceticism." This precursor of the super-ego was composed "chiefly of reaction-formations against his repressed wishes, and it was easy to foresee that it would have swallowed up the normal personality if the illness had lasted much longer." It is also no accident, it seems to me, that one can make out in this scheme a version of general nineteenth-century anthropological and evolutionary accounts of the stages of the development of thought and civilization. What is of further note, however, is that Freud ends with this additional turn of enquiry into the nature of character and of possible worlds evoked by the different scenarios that different kinds of character require. Moreover, he avoids any further reference to coherent narrative accounts and narrative structures in this successful resolution of a wholly psychical disturbance – a structural deformation of the processes of thought. Lorenz came to Freud compulsively verbalizing but verbalizing unintelligibly as well. His projected narratives were uniformly opaque and disjointed and often senseless and absurd. Rather than seeking therapeutic alleviation in some grand, novelistic design, Freud intuitively and brilliantly concentrated on small, often non-narrative units of thought and memory. He repeatedly prompted Lorenz to speak directly about small matters and come to the point on minor segments of experience rather than trying to construct large story-like structures of thought. In doing so, and in succeeding, he revealed a number of important non-narratological agencies through which both psychoanalysis and the classic nineteenth- and twentieth-century novels represent and construct their hypothetical accounts of the world. They do so through such devices as character study, the evocation of a series of alternative, possible worlds and by fitting together as best they can extended fields of reference that are both internal and external at the same time. The case of the Rat Man does not have the grand narrative sweep of the case of Dora or the Proustian character of the multivalent, multi-layered set of narratives of the case of the Wolf

Man. It represents, however, the actual process of the psychoanalytic study and construction of character in all its extensiveness, and it does that, despite its exceptional self-censorship and necessary self-limitation, in exemplary style.[11]

VIII

Is this, then, the final outcome of this exceptional piece of writing that goes off in several directions at once? First, it is an unsurpassed reconstructed account of an actual piece of psychoanalysis, in all its fragmented, partly coherent, partly less than coherent, permanently open-ended character, a character in which closure is theoretically possible but rarely achieved. Second, it is an account, we now can see, in which an enormous amount of relevant material has to be excluded (as demonstrated in Freud's now available set of original notes) in order to make primordial intelligibility possible. Third, it is non-literary in the sense that its areas of significance are not organized along the lines circumscribed by nineteenth- or early-twentieth-century expectations of narrative structure – including modernist expectations. But fourth, it is literary in a number of alternative senses, such as Freud's extended and unstated new interpretation of Hamlet's character, which occupies most of the last section of the case history – and in other senses already mentioned as well.[12]

It is literary in still one further sense, for it does finally issue in a written narrative in a highly refracted though fairly important and interesting way. To demonstrate that refraction we are required to make one final brief detour. That excursion takes us around the Austro-Hungarian Empire once more and beyond, to Germany and England. In Munich, at about the time of the Rat Man's analysis with Freud, a brilliant young psychiatrist of about the same age as Lorenz was working as an assistant at Kraepelin's famous clinic. This young man's name was Otto Gross, and he was at the time, among much else, an ardent but by no means uncritical follower of Freud and the new psychoanalytic discipline. The ardency was expressed in his self-taught style of practicing analysis on others. He was, Ernest Jones reports, "my first instructor in the technique of psychoanalysis," and it was "in many ways an unorthodox demonstration." Gross frequented and/or lived in Schwabing, the artistic and bohemian quarter of Munich, and he was usually to be found at a table in a café that was open around the clock practicing non-stop analysis upon whoever happened to sit down with him. Despite the unorthodoxy of the setting and procedure, Jones remained permanently astonished at the intuitive perspicacity of Gross's ability to divine the thoughts of others. Jones was, he wrote many years later, "never to see" such penetration again, "nor is it a matter that lends itself to description."[13] The "by no means uncritical" part of Gross's discipleship is articulated with sufficient clarity in this letter of September 25, 1907, from Jung to Freud.

> Dr. Gross tells me that he puts a quick stop to the transference by turning people into sexual immoralists. He says the transference to the analyst and its persistent fixation are mere monogamy symbols and are as such symptomatic of repression. The truly healthy state for the neurotic is sexual immorality. Hence he associates you with Nietzsche.

The son of Hans Gross, who was the founder in central Europe of the modern technology of criminal investigation, Otto was brought up in a household in which the patriarchal ideal of the family seems to have been taken almost to the point of lunacy. He responded more or less in kind, in an endless chain of acts of reversal, revenge, and destruction of himself and others, and occasionally of liberation as well. Although he was a vegetarian and abstained from alcohol of any kind, he was also addicted to both cocaine and opium. He was an arch-priest of the erotic and of free self-expression, and on at least one occasion helped a frustrated young woman to kill herself. He had many love affairs himself, two of the more important ones being with two of the three von Richthofen sisters. He first had an affair with Else von Richthofen Jaffe, the eldest of the sisters, and she also bore him a son while she was married to Edgar Jaffe. He then (or at the same time – the chronology is very murky) also had an affair with Frieda von Richthofen Weekley; this relation seems to have begun in about 1907; its date of termination remains unclear. Both he and Frieda claimed subsequently to have liberated the other into the world of erotic fulfillment. In whichever direction the arrow of agency is finally pointed seems scarcely to matter: each of them had enough determination and will to experience and self-expression for at least two and possibly many more.

The subsequent parts of the story have to be followed along two separate threads of narrative. In the first place, Gross got himself involved with both Freud and Jung and the case of the Rat Man. That triple involvement is clearly present in a letter that Freud wrote to Jung on April 19, 1908, just before the First International Psychoanalytic Congress that was to take place at Salzburg. Freud is looking forward to seeing Jung:

> we shall also have to talk about Otto Gross; he urgently needs your

medical help; what a pity, such a gifted, resolute man. He is addicted to cocaine and probably in the early phase of toxic cocaine paranoia. I feel great sympathy for his wife: one of the few Teutonic women I have ever liked. ... I am having great difficulty with my paper, because a real, complete case cannot be narrated but only described. ... And I have no case that is completed and can be viewed as a whole.

In his response to this communication, Jung informed Freud that Gross took large quantities of opium in addition to the cocaine. Freud had planned to take Gross on as a patient, but after the Congress, Jung took Gross in charge and returned to Switzerland with him for a course of therapy. Frau Gross, Freud reported, in some slight bewilderment, seemed for her part "to be seriously smitten" with Ernest Jones. "It looks," Freud characteristically worried, "as if this were going to end badly."

On May 14, 1908, Jung reported to Freud that Gross was suffering from a "definite obsessional neurosis." In his answering letter, Freud concurred with Jung, and recalled his meeting Gross at the Congress in Salzburg. He recalled as well what Gross said to him:

His earliest childhood memory (communicated in Salzburg) is of his father warning a visitor: Watch out, he *bites*! He remembered this in connection with my Rat Man story.

A number of things emerge from this nexus. First, it is clear that Gross identified himself with the son in Freud's dramatic analysis of a father-son relation – and that this identification is syntonic with Gross's general program of repudiating Western civilization. Second, however, as the anecdote comes filtered to us through the epistolary consciousness of Freud, something else is trailing along with the story of the Rat Man. That something else is almost certainly a secondary recollection of the famous incident from David Copperfield's early life. *David Copperfield*, we should recall, was one of Freud's favorite novels; he had early on identified with the young David himself; and in this passage of condensation we can make out once again as well Freud's counter-transferential identification with Lorenz. At any rate, what is beyond any possibility of doubt is Otto Gross's knowledge of and feeling for both Freud and the case of the Rat Man.

The rest of the story of Gross and psychoanalysis can, for our purposes, be shortly summarized. Jung undertook heroic measures of therapy with him, and at the beginning had high hopes for improvement. Freud seconded those efforts, and was committed to the belief that successful therapy of "such a fine man, with such a good mind ... must be regarded as a benefit to society." Within a month, however, Jung was admitting failure. Gross, he wrote, was an eternal 6-year-old. The diagnosis of obsessional neurosis was changed to that of dementia praecox - later to be renamed as schizophrenia. And Gross had taken French leave of Jung, "jumped over the garden wall" at Burghölzli, and disappeared in the direction of Munich. Freud sympathized with his colleague, but there was little that remained to be done or said, short of his offering additional sympathy to all concerned. Neither Freud nor Jung, however, wavered in their respect for Gross's intellect or insight.

In this connection, Gross is affiliated in still one more context with this case. On June 3, 1909 Freud wrote to Jung that he had the day before

> received a book by Otto Gross: *On Psychopathic Inferiorities [Über psychopathizsche Minderwertigkeiten]*. I haven't studied it yet, but obviously it's another outstanding work, full of bold syntheses and overflowing with ideas. And again two different ways of indicating emphasis ... which makes an exquisitely paranoid impression. Too bad, the man has a good mind! To tell the truth, I don't know if I shall be able to understand the book. A good deal of it is too high-flown for me. ... On the other hand, I suddenly feel like writing the Salzburg rat man, and if you like I can give you the piece for the second number [of the *Yearbook*, of which Jung was the editor].

It seems no accident that this associative collocation has occurred, and no doubt Gross's implication in this case has ramifications that extend far beyond what I have here merely adverted to. I shall confine myself to following only one more of these. Gross's book had been sent to Freud not by Gross himself but by his famous

> old man, who, in response to my letter of thanks and appreciation, asked me to write to Otto, telling him how much I had liked the book and that I should like to discuss certain parts of it with him. Then, after meeting with him, I was to write the father my opinion. This I firmly declined to do, citing the results of your examination. I have too much respect for Otto Gross.

Apart from Freud's familiar integrity, this letter reminds us once again of where his identifications in the analysis of Lorenz were mobilized and how they were consolidated. Jung's identifications were in this episode more labile. For although Gross figured prominently in Jung's famous essay, "The Significance of the Father in the Destiny of the Individual (1909), so prominently indeed that Jung concedes something like co-authorship to him, by 1911 Jung had lost all feeling for him, and was calling Gross "a complete nut." He was probably right by then; things kept going steadily downhill for Gross, and he died in Berlin in 1920 from multiple causes, including drugs, undernourishment and exposure.[14]

The second thread of narrative has to do with Gross, Frieda and D. H. Lawrence. It is not an altogether unbroken thread chronologically, but it is clear enough for our purposes. According to a recollection of Else Jaffe, her sister, Frieda von Richthofen Weekley, first met Otto Gross through her (Else) in about 1907. At that earlier time, Frau Jaffe wrote in 1960, Frieda lived

> in the inner turmoil caused by the impact of what we called Freudian theories on our feelings and thoughts. (About 1907.) I say *our*, because it was through me that Frieda knew that "remarkable disciple of Freud" she mentions at the beginning of her book *Not I, But the Wind* ... we shared the happenings of that period.[15]

Frau Jaffe's guarded words are interpretable in a number of ways, but they do not entirely tally with her sister's account. Frieda Weekley first met D. H. Lawrence in April 1912, and the passage in question is as follows:

> I had just met a remarkable disciple of Freud and was full of undigested theories. This friend did a lot for me. I was living like a somnambulist in a conventional set life and he awakened the consciousness of my own proper self. ... Fanatically I believed that if only sex were "free" the world would straightaway turn into a paradise. I suffered and struggled at outs with society, and felt absolutely isolated. ... And then Lawrence came. It was an April day in 1912. ... He said he had finished with his attempts at knowing women. I was amazed at the way he fiercely denounced them. I had never before heard anything like it. ... We talked about Oedipus and understanding leaped through the worlds.[16]

The *just* in the first sentence of the foregoing passage does not exactly square the dates 1907 and 1912; moreover, the letters from Gross to Frieda Weekley that survive are undated, though Martin Green states that some were written in 1907 and 1908 and guesses that some are from as late as 1910.

Our sense of clarity is not improved if we consult further authorities. Harry T. Moore, for example, writes:

Just how much Lawrence knew of Freud at this time, and of Freud's theories about the Oedipus complex, is difficult to determine. Frieda told Frederick J. Hoffman in 1942, "Lawrence knew about Freud before he wrote the final draft of *Sons and Lovers*. I don't know whether he had read Freud or heard about him before we met in 1912. But I was a great Freud admirer; we had long arguments and Lawrence's conclusion was more or less that Freud looked on sex too much from the doctor's point of view."[17]

This makes Lawrence sound very much like Otto Gross, and in her subsequent written response to Moore's book, Frieda Lawrence underscores this affinity with new and further emphasis:

> I had a great friend, a young Austrian doctor who had been a pupil of Freud's and had worked with him. Consequently he had been much influenced by Freud, and through him I was much impressed too. So Lawrence through this friend and me had an almost direct contact with these then new ideas.
>
>   He got most of his ideas in this living way, never so much from books, but mostly he used himself as his own guinea-pig.[18]

The passage of many years and Frieda Lawrence's general swampiness have blurred some details even further: Gross was a pupil of Freud's in the sense that he read him and practiced a kind of analysis; he certainly never worked with Freud. But the balance of the statement seems to stand up; Frieda Weekley learned most of whatever she knew about Freud from Gross, and she passed on what she had taken in at the time to the young D. H. Lawrence. The effects of those transactions on the final version taken by *Sons and Lovers* (1913) have been evident for some time; and in any event it was not until 1914, when Lawrence met and became friendly with David Eder and Barbara Low that he may be said to have come into direct personal touch with people who had an intimate and professional acquaintance with psychoanalysis. As for Lawrence's ultimate understanding of Freud, that may be gathered from his two doctrinal works of 1921 and 1922, *Psychoanalysis and the Unconscious* and *Fantasia of the Unconscious*. There is little evidence in either book that Lawrence had read Freud to any great profit, and indeed such a remark hits wide of what was by then Lawrence's great purpose – and it hits wide as well of how his genius developed.

In 1913, however, matters were detectably different. Lawrence's major work was just beginning. He was not yet astream in that full career of genius in which he had to protect himself against influences such as Freud in order to be fully himself as a mind and writer. Yet even then the influence can be seen as partly deflected and reformed within the organizing sensibility of the young writer. In one of his letters, Otto Gross had written to Frieda Weekley:

> Now is a moment like no other ever before. Through a practical method, a technique of research, we can look into the very essence of spiritual life. And who has eyes to see can now see in this newly opened perspective the future itself at work. In this direction my road is free; the enormous shadow of Freud lies no longer over my path.[19]

In such a passage Gross seems to be saying that he is using his own version of Freud's discoveries and method to go beyond Freud, to free himself from the constraining authority of orthodoxy, and to find the road along which modern humanity's emancipation and salvation is to be pursued. And so, I conjecture, did the D. H. Lawrence of 1912 and 1913 feel about both Freud and Gross – about both of whom he had heard plenty from Frieda Weekley. Indeed at the time Lawrence must have felt something of an identification with Gross, Frieda Weekley's previous lover, and there is a moment in *Twilight in Italy* at which this identification is made playfully clear. Lawrence is recalling his walking trip of 1913 through Switzerland to Italy. During that journey he had tea with two genteel old ladies, who asked him whether he was Austrian.

> I said I was from Graz; that my father was a doctor in Graz, and that I was walking for my pleasure through the countries of Europe.
> I said this because I knew a doctor from Graz who was always wandering about, and because I did not want to be myself, an Englishman, to these two old ladies. I wanted to be something else. So we exchanged confidences.[20]

Playful or not, the identification is palpable. As I have already said, the effect of what Lawrence had learned about Freud can be perceived in a general way throughout *Sons and Lovers*. But I believe that Lawrence had also learned or heard something about the case of the Rat Man. Otto Gross had heard Freud's four-hour verbal presentation of the case at Salzburg in 1908, while he was still probably having an affair with Frieda Weekley. He had, as we have seen, identified himself with Lorenz to Freud – and it is difficult to believe that Frieda Weekley had not learned something of the case from him, as well as from others. In any event, Freud's "Notes Upon a Case of Obsessional Neurosis," appropriately transmogrified, turns up in Lawrence's first important short story, "The Prussian Officer."

"The Prussian Officer" was written in Bavaria in the spring of 1913, one year after D. H. Lawrence and Frieda Weekley had gone off together. Although there are a number of contemporary topical allusions in the story, and although it makes glancing references to what Lawrence had learned about the military career of Frieda von Richthofen's father, who had been one of Bismarck's junior officers before and during the Franco-Prussian war of 1870,[21] my purpose here is to suggest how certain details of the case of the Rat Man find either a significant place or lodgement by analogy in the narrative structure of this remarkable story.

The narrative is set in the countryside, during hot weather (a blistering couple of spring days in the story, August in the case history), while a troop of infantry are on maneuvers. The two main characters in the story are the Prussian officer himself, who is, as in the case history, a cruel Captain, and his young orderly, who although he is not a reserve officer (as Lorenz was), has only "three months" left to serve, "when his time would be up." The relation between the Captain and his nameless servitor is immediately revealed to be intense, extremely ambivalent, inarticulate, and explosive. The two cannot bear to look one another in the face. The Captain "very rarely looked direct at his orderly, but kept his face averted, as if to avoid seeing him." And the "orderly was afraid of really meeting his master. His subconsciousness remembered those steely blue eyes and the harsh brows, and did not intend to meet him again." The motif of looking/not looking, which is so prominent in the case history, may turn up in the story fortuitously, but there can be nothing accidental about the provenance of the word "subconscious" – it was, and remains, the conventional imprecise translation of Freud's word for unconscious.

Relations between the Captain and his orderly are rapidly elaborated as antagonistic, savage and covertly homosexual, castrating and Oedipal – they are so in the sense that the superordinate and subordinate roles filled by each are ineluctably taken to the farthest point of uncompromisable extremity. For example, the orderly has a deep scar on his left thumb, the result of an accident with a wood axe. The Captain cannot endure the sight of that thumb and its scar: "he had to use all his will-power to avoid seeing the scarred thumb. He wanted to get hold of it and —. A hot flame ran through his blood." That — is there for the reader to fill in for himself, as well as to dramatize a repressed segment, or blank, a hiatus in the Captain's consciousness. Its meaning, however, cannot be mistaken, although the Captain cannot by the same token acknowledge to himself that he is in the grip of uncontrollable passions so powerful that "all his blood seemed to be corroding."

The first central scene of the story arrives abruptly, when the orderly, dumb and blind himself with inarticulateable resistance and passion, cannot answer a question put by the Captain to him while the orderly is serving dinner.

> He felt blind. Instead of answering, he turned dazedly to the door. As he was crouching to set down the dishes, he was pitched forward by a kick from behind. The pots went in a stream down the stairs, he clung to the pillar of the banisters. And as he was rising he was kicked heavily again and again, so that he clung sickly to the post for some moments.

This anal assault is, I suggest, a condensation (and superb imaginative adaptation) of both the account of the rat torture (including the pot) and the childhood beating scene – which in the case history are the two great mirroring and mutually reflecting moments of dramatic intensity. And that it is in the story a kind of anal rape is made clear by subsequent details in the text; not only are the orderly's thighs blackened with bruises, but also he feels as if he were "disembowelled" by this dreadful attack. Later on, he can hardly sit on a horse because of "the pain of keeping his seat," and at the end, after he is dead, "The doctors saw the bruises on his legs, behind, and were silent."

After he is so cruelly assailed, the ego of the orderly – like that of Lorenz – begins to come apart: "he went away, feeling as if he himself were coming to pieces, disintegrated." He tries to compel his mind away from his present predicament, makes every effort "not to be forced into consciousness." Indeed his mind, Lawrence marvellously writes, was "too tearingly active in the incoherent race of delirium to observe" either itself or the world about it. This inchoate, inarticulate race of delirium is not unlike the conscious, tumultuous deliria of fantasies, magical formulae, and verbal hemorrhaging of the Rat Man.

But instead of falling at once into a labyrinth of obsessional and finally crazy defenses against his rage, as Lorenz did, the orderly takes a direct and fatal Oedipal revenge upon his sadistic assailant. While he is serving the Captain lunch, at a halt in a clearing in the woods, something snaps in the orderly, and he springs upon his adversary.

> The spur of the officer caught in a tree root, he went down backwards with a crash, the middle of his back thudding sickeningly against a sharp-edged tree base, the pot flying away.

And in a second the orderly, with serious earnest young face, and underlip between his teeth, had got his knee in the officer's chest and was pressing the chin backward over the farther edge of the tree-stump, pressing, with all his heart behind in a passion of relief, the tension of the wrists exquisite with relief. ... He did not relax one hair's breadth, but, all the force of all his blood exulting in his thrust, he shoved back the head of the other man, till there was a little "cluck" and a crunching sensation.

After this rape and castration in reverse and in retaliation – including a displacement upwards – has been consummated, the orderly lapses into terminal delirium. His ego literally goes into a state of decomposition. He surfaces momentarily to hear "something knocking." It is a bird in a tree, which "like a mouse ... slid down the bare trunk." Other birds "crept like swift, erratic mice, running here and there among the beech-mast." But the orderly is in a state of spiritual dissolution: "He did not know where he was or what he was." He sees a woman passing by but "He had no language with which to speak to her. She was the bright, solid unreality."[22] The end finally comes as the orderly breaks up into a group of psychic fragments, dislocated, shattered pieces of ego, flashes of extreme experience that are bound to remind us of moments in the case history.

He lay still, in a kind of dream of anguish. His thirst seemed to have separated itself from him, and to stand apart, a simple demand. Then the pain he felt was another single self. Then there was the clog of his body, another separate thing. He was divided among all kinds of separate things. There was some strange, agonised connection between them, but they were drawing farther apart. Then they would all split.

Here is one way, I submit, that a young genius makes creative use of another, older genius. It is no case for the anxiety of influence, and the dead Captain had no map of misreading rolled up in his belted field case either. Lawrence had not, I am convinced, read the case history in German. He had, I strongly suspect, heard some account of it from Frieda Weekley, who had almost certainly learned about it from Otto Gross, who had in turn heard Freud's four-hour discourse in Salzburg in 1908 and who had probably read the work when it was published the next year as well. Despite the distortions that are unavoidable in such a chain of transmission as I have suggested, and despite his own defensiveness, Lawrence was alive to some of the truths that Freud discovered in his great case, and put them to expeditious and lasting creative use. And if Freud could not himself find an appropriate or workable narrative form for this extraordinary case history, we can say that it did at last, and in some part, find a narrative home in this wonderful early story.

Let us leave the last of these many words with Frieda Lawrence. In *Not I, But the Wind* she has this to say about the story.

> The strange struggle of those two opposite natures, the officer and his servant, seems to me particularly significant for Lawrence. He wrote it before the war but as if he had sensed it. The unhappy, conscious man, the superior in authority envying the other man his simple, satisfied nature. I felt as if he himself was both these people.
>
> They seemed to me to represent the split in his soul, the split between the conscious and the unconscious man.

The Freud of 1913 would have endorsed that last sentence about D. H. Lawrence, as the Freud of 1909 had endorsed it about his patient, who, we must recall, did not survive the war that Lawrence, as well as others, had already sensed.

Notes

1   Ernest Jones, *Free Associations: Memories of a Psycho-Analyst* (New York, 1959), p. 166.
2   *The Standard Edition of the Complete Psychological Works of Sigmund Freud*, Vol. I, p. 223; this is from Draftk, "The Neuroses of Defense (A Christmas Fairy Tale)" that Freud included in letter 39 to Fliess, dated January 1, 1896.
3   This expectation, we learn from Abram Kardiner, changed only after World War I, when Freud had to accommodate himself to both an increased influx of Americans seeking him out and an increased efflux of inflated Austrian currency. See *My Analysis with Freud* (New York, 1977), p. 18.
4   Freud wrote simply "reproach" or "*Vorwurf*" in the original. Strachey translates this as self-reproach, and he might have put the noun in the plural form as well, since the self-condemnatory processes in obsessional neuroses are almost invariably multiple.
5   There is some question as to whether these character traits are not themselves part of a specific cultural–historical context that no longer exists as and where it once did, and whether people with such pronounced idiosyncrasies of personality appear today in psychoanalyst's offices – and exist in the middle classes of western society at large – with the frequency that they did almost 100 years ago. Changes in both toilet-training procedures among the middle classes of Western society and in the technology of dealing with infantile excretory materials – diaper services and then disposable diapers – seem to enforce the impression of a general relaxation in this erotogenic zone which had been for several centuries at least a combat zone as well.
6   This protestation is partly rationalization, for we are to learn later on as well that the patient "had on the whole been idle at his work during his father's lifetime." (204) It seems likely that the patient's life-long neurosis had prevented him from

ever working at very much; what is interesting about this matter, among other things, is that Freud shows almost no interest in it at all.

7   In this mishap over narrative Freud was not alone. The narrative account of this case is so chaotic and un-story-like or non-narratological that almost everyone commits some similar blunder. In all the many psychoanalytic commentaries on this case history that I have read, there is hardly a single article or essay of any length that does not contain at least one error of fact in recounting or recon-structing the history of the Rat Man. There may be more than one reason for this occurrence. Unlike Freud, most psychoanalysts are not very good readers; to put the matter less invidiously, they are better listeners than they are readers.

8   For the most obvious reasons. His interpretation of the meaning of the "Rat Idea" cannot be improved upon, although it has been augmented; and his other two discussions have attracted very little notice.

9   For some odd behavior behind the head of the couch on the part of Freud, see H. D., *Tribute to Freud* (New York, 1956), p. 21.

10   The term "ambivalence" was to be coined by Bleuler in the year following the publication of this case history.

11   As I have observed earlier, Freud does not deal with the immense amount of material produced by Lorenz and noted down in the original record that has to do with Lorenz's sisters and his mother, and other members of the family as well. Nor does he deal in any detail with Lorenz's dreams or with large numbers of his verbal tricks, games, gibberings, and nonsensicalities. Had he tried to do so, he would have been lost. The material as "reproduced" in the original record simply does not give itself to coherent, sequential interpretation or even, often, to consistent chronological ordering. In recognizing these circumstances and avoiding the apparently insoluble complexities thrown up by them, Freud per-formed a great service for his patient, his readers, and for psychoanalysis itself. In this case, rich and dense and obscure as it may be, he was really shaving with Ockham's razor. Among the results of such self-restraint are the still unexplored richnesses and unresolved mysteries and refractorinesses of the case that is, among his major writings, the most difficult to read and the most resistant to serial interpretative schematization. The case is an immense tribute to his clini-cal acumen and skill and to his exceptional clinical tact, virtues for which he has recently rarely been praised or even recognized.

12   One sense has heretofore gone unmentioned: Freud originally thought of calling the account of the Rat Man "Aphorisms relating to Obsessional Neurosis," the title suggesting again the heavily punctuated structural syntax of the study. See W. McGuire (ed.), *The Freud/Jung Letters*, trans. R. Manheim and R. F. C. Hull (Princeton, 1974) pp. 145, 159.

13   Jones, *Free Associations*, pp. 173 f.

14   The fullest account of Gross in English is to be found in Martin Green, *The Von Richthofen Sisters: The Triumphant and Tragic Modes of Love* (New York, 1974), pp. 32–100. Parts of this reconstruction are perforce speculative, a circumstance which Green himself admits.

15   E. W. Tedlock (ed.), *Frieda Lawrence: Memoirs and Correspondence* (London, 1961), pp. 425 f.

16   Frieda Lawrence, *Not I, But the Wind* [1934] (Carbondale, 1974), pp. 3 f.

17   Harry T. Moore, *The Intelligent Heart* (London, 1955), pp. 131 f.

18   *Frieda Lawrence: Memoirs and Correspondence*, p. 140; the passages come from a short piece responding to Moore's biography that appeared in the *New Republic*, February 28, 1955, and, with some editorial changes, in the *New Statesman*, August 13, 1955. See *Memoirs and Correspondence*, p. 429.

19   *Frieda Lawrence: Memoirs and Correspondence*, p. 88.

20   D. H. Lawrence, *Twilight in Italy* [1916] (London, 1934), pp. 269 f; I am indebted for this allusion to Martin Green, *The Von Richthofen Sisters*, p. 60.

21   See Moore, *The Intelligent Heart*, pp. 114 f, 147 ff.

22   Earlier in the story it is revealed that the orderly has a girl or sweetheart; when the Captain learns of it he bitterly resents it, and indeed is himself sexually envious and jealous of his inferior's youthful, spontaneous animality.

5 Psychoanalytic Theory and Cultural Change

I

To bring together psychoanalytic theory and cultural change, as I shall set out to do, is to evoke at once certain familiar juxtapositions and unsettled considerations. Such an undertaking brings forward the relation, for example, of the unconscious to history and to social change. These notions almost instantly set off in turn ideas about the role played by the individual psyche, or the psychology of individual persons, in history and vice versa, the connection between historical circumstances and individual psychology – the psychology, for example, of notable actors in one or another historical drama. The continued existence of a sub-discipline that calls itself psychohistory suggests something of the persistent interest exerted by such imputed connections, correlations, and causalities. Among the many questions elicited by this series of terms, and what they exemplify, is one that I should like to choose as a theme for discussion. And I shall first bring it forward in its simplest interrogative form: Does the psyche itself have a history? Can we ascribe a significant historical existence to unconscious mental structures, and can we write some parts of that history? Does cultural change affect us in the sense that it is registered by inferrable and describable alterations in the institutions of our unconscious minds?

These questions are of an interest that is both antecedent to and that passes beyond the sphere of theoretical conjecture. They touch on matters that affect each of us: in changes in the modern family, for example, and in the ways such changes have manifested themselves in the contemporary personality – in character development and neurosis. Finally, they invite us to speculate on the origins and attributes of the much-discussed if very loosely defined and understood "narcissistic personality" and its relations to the culture as a whole.

If we consult Freud himself, and indeed we must, as the starting-point in such a discussion, we quickly find ourselves in a familiar bewilderment bred out of the profusion and complexity of the relevant materials as they distribute themselves throughout his work. As a cultivated European of the late nineteenth century, Freud was soaked in the past, in works written in the past and transmitted through accretions of tradition. Moreover, history tends to appear in

Freud's work as the inveterate recurrence of things, incidents or mental happenings from the past in the present. That recurrence was typically an obtrusion, a repetition in disguised or transmogrified shape of something from the past that somehow had not been successfully accommodated to its condition as part of the past – as something that had happened and was, in that measure, over and done with. Freud's specially favored mode of explanation was almost always historical. For Freud the privileged explanation of an event tends regularly to be a coherent account of its historical existence, and the innermost meaning of a phenomenon is likely to be inseparable from a hypothetical demonstration of how it came to be. Like Darwin's theory of evolution, to which it owes a good deal in a very general way, psychoanalytic theory's explanatory powers are largely historical or retrospective; they are not on the whole, or in an interesting sense, predictive. Indeed Freud's own inclination to be partial to genetic explanations and forms of discourse has led one modern critic to accuse him of "originology," an intellectual heresy that he shares with other pre-eminent members of his historical culture.

At the same time, Freud's own explicit dealings on a large scale with historical problems tended to take the form, as he himself acknowledged, of mythologies, of "scientific myths," to be sure, but myths nonetheless.[1] Moreover, Freud regarded the unconscious in its more distant regions and in its primal workings as outside of time. To be rendered as part of the dynamic unconscious means, at one pitch of discourse, to be taken out of time and history. Inaccessible to the normal processes of time and hence resistant to change, the repressed unconscious becomes a piece of ahistoric history. And in Freud's habitual use of expressions and figures of speech from archaeology, history and its prefixtural variant forms are regularly knit together.

There is one context, of course, in which Freud does attend to history in more familiar or what may be thought of as more normative senses of the term. This has to do with his manner of conceiving of the life of each individual person, or each individual representative of the human species or race, for that is how he thinks of us. The lives of each of us comprise a history, whether that history be articulated in a full narrative account or array of accounts or remain fragmentary, incomplete or latent. Beginning before birth and ending in early childhood, each life has a prehistory, which is relatively recoverable or reconstructable. Each life's history, furthermore, is punctuated with what appear to be supra-historical, or perhaps cultural, episodes and elements. For example, no life is without its personal experiences of myth, epic, romance, and tragedy. We are all of noble birth, we have all lost our royal parents, we all go through an internal personal drama of grandiose sexual and aggressive ambitions and catastrophic retribution for those illicit, immitigable aspirations. These exemplary and recurrent themes of experience belong for Freud to the species as much as they do to each of us. The inflection of that experience in each separate individual, Freud often remarks, generally recapitulates the processes undergone by larger cultural entities. Yet what helps in part to animate these processes as history is that each one of us actually sustains in his own person that which the species, our ancestors, or a character we will read about is said to have passed through. And what also helps to animate them as history is that each one of us can testify to goings-on in the past that appear to us to have the warrant of actuality: but the shape of that testimony is invariably a conjectural reconstruction, a fabrication, something we have made, a history.

Freud writes this history many times and in a variety of forms. Sometimes he composes stories, as in his case histories. On other occasions he writes institutional history, as when, for example, he deals with the growth across time of the ego. Each time Freud reconstrued his theories, he devised a new historical report of them. And he did so not only because he had built up his explanations as they changed from year to year, but also because those explanations themselves were fundamentally historical. They are so in the sense that they are theoretical figurations of human development. Each grown human being is the outcome of a series of complex processes of development. These circumstances are in some important parts biologically programmed, but they are also open to modifications, arrestments, and diversions at many points along the way. The theory strongly implies a telos – a designated goal or end. That telos or goal is what for want of any other terms one calls normal maturity. The theory in its evolving versions undertakes to illuminate both how this development is attained and the uncountable ways in which it may miscarry. It also undertakes to explain the disadvantages and deficits that regularly attach to developmental processes that have gone astray, and it undertakes as well to explain the occasional immense value that may accompany abnormal, incomplete, or aberrant development – most notably, of course, in figures of singular creative cultural powers. And psychoanalytic therapy is itself founded in part upon such considerations. It is resolutely historical; it cannot be carried forward into the future without remembering the past; its interpretations and reconstructions are all in the service of a yet-to-be realized developmental telos – although that telos is by no means inflexibly specified.

I believe that these broad observations about individual psychic development apply as well to Freud's notions of the development of the psyche in human culture – and he as much as says so in a number of places. To the question, then, "Does the psyche itself have a history?", we have answered Yes. But this affirmative response is so generalized and inclusive that it is almost useless. I propose therefore to revise and narrow the question and ask instead, Does the psyche have a modern history? We will again refer to Freud, though on this matter, I believe, he offers us a less than direct answer.

One of the ways in which we can resume the discussion is to consult Freud's final and fullest representations of his theory of the mind. Significantly, he began to publish works containing this revisionary scheme after the end of World War I. These writings contain new descriptions of the structural workings of the mind, a newly revised theory of the instincts, and new dispositions of mental forces as these were ascribed to their organization in newly classified unconscious psychic formations. In one of these agencies, the super-ego, the nexus of unconscious psychic processes and cultural phenomena is explicitly put forward.

Freud had made some preliminary observations about the super-ego – which he initially called the ego ideal – in his 1914 essay "On Narcissism: an Introduction"; he discussed this agency briefly again in "Mourning and Melancholia" (1917) and at some further length in *Group Psychology and the Analysis of the Ego* (1921). It was, however, in his account of certain of the "higher functions" of the mind in *The Ego and the Id* (1923) that he first developed this conception at length; thereafter it was a permanent occupant of one of the centers of his attention. The ego ideal, Freud had first speculated, is the later substitute, constructed by each individual to take the place of the "lost narcissism" of infancy and early childhood, when each of us "was his own ideal." In order to assure that "the narcissistic satisfaction from the ego ideal" is sustained, Freud postulated a "special psychical agency" whose task was to watch the ego and measure it in comparison to the ideal. These functions or characteristics, Freud reflects, are associated with what is commonly known as "conscience," and this internal watchman or monitor is in turn connected with the mind's self-critical faculty and its sense of guilt. Hence from the very outset, Freud's discussion of this agency was placed in a context in which some of the most primordial and some of the most advanced mental functions were brought together, juxtaposed in such a way as to elicit their latent contradictoriness.

In *The Ego and the Id*, before discussing the super-ego, Freud laid down a number of new conceptual preconditions. First, he proposed a revised conception of the ego; in this conception a part of the ego, "and Heaven knows how important a part," he wrote, was now to be thought of as unconscious. Second, he redivided the mind into two primary agencies, the id and the ego; in this scheme the ego "is that part of the id which has been modified by the direct influence of the external world" through the mediums of perception and consciousness. If the ego is a partly unconscious agency formed originally by gradual differentiation from the id, it is also an agency some of whose higher functions remain unconscious as well. It remains very strange, Freud remarks, that "there are people in whom the faculties of self-criticism and conscience – mental faculties that is, that rank as extremely high ones – are unconscious and unconsciously produce effects of the greatest importance." Such discoveries, he goes on, compel us, "in spite of our better critical judgment, to speak of an 'unconscious sense of guilt'," and they compel him as well to assume or postulate "a grade in ..., [or] a differentiation within the ego." What is novel about this entity and calls for explanation is that it is "less firmly connected with consciousness" than, presumably, other and less highly developed functions of the ego. This entity he called the "super-ego."

In order to account for the existence of the super-ego, Freud takes us back to some of our most primitive experiences, our earliest relations with objects. In the first months of life, Freud speculates, "in the individual's primitive oral phase, object-cathexis [the investment of an object with desire] and identification are no doubt indistinguishable from each other." Working backwards now once again, from his experience of melancholic or depressed adult patients, Freud notes that often when someone is required to give up a sexual or love ojbect, the renunciation is achieved by means of an "alteration" of the ego, an alteration "which can only be described as a setting up of the object inside the ego." This occurs by means of a process that Freud calls "introjection," which takes as its model and is "a kind of regression to the mechanism of the oral phase," that is to say to experiences of oral incorporation and their primitive psychic derivatives. Hence there is latently postulated here a gradient of experiential processes which are at first either fused or undifferentiated: incorporation and expulsion are related to introjection and projection, and these are in turn connected with and partly built up into identifications and object choices. (These processes tend to be repeated, with developmental variations, at successive stages of psychic growth.) And if these represent a rough model of how we acquire unconscious psychic objects, then they also represent for Freud a model of how we give them up. It may be, he remarks, that this process of indentification/introjection "is the sole condition under which the id can give up its objects."

In any case, our first and most important identification, the origin of our ego ideal, is our identification with our parents; this identification is "direct and immediate"; it precedes object-cathexes but is reinforced by those further identifications which are in turn the normal outcome of our first object-choices, namely those same parents. In one series of connected acts we simultaneously prepare to give up our objects and appropriate them. We can do so largely because we have begun to distinguish between an internal and an external world. These extremely condensed formulations are Freud's first account of the prehistory of the super-ego, of its precursors and forerunners.

He then proceeds to supply an account of the formation of the recognizable super-ego itself. The "broad, general" outcome of the child's complex relations to both mother and father – as both sexual objects and objects of identification – will be the organization of this institution, which Freud calls "a precipitate in the ego," and that consists "of these two identifications in some way united with each other. This modification of the ego," he continues, "retains its special position." That position is an extremely potent one – it is nothing less than confrontational. The super-ego, Freud writes, confronts the other contents of the ego. And it makes that confrontation inexhaustibly and on two fronts. It is the simultaneous source of both precepts and prohibitions. It tells us that what we must be like (chiefly our fathers) we must also not be like (we may not do everything our fathers do). This double-binding characteristic is itself a consequence of the super-ego's revolutionary origin – its purpose in coming into existence was to repress – in the sense of both overcoming and doing away with – the Oedipus complex. In that situation of crisis "the child's parents, and especially his father, were perceived as the obstacle to his Oedipal wishes; so his infantile ego fortified itself for the carrying out of the repression by erecting this same obstacle within itself." This act of borrowing, this loan of strength, Freud asserts, "was an extraordinarily momentous act." For the differentiation of the super-ego from the ego represents nothing less than "the most important characteristics of the development of both the individual and the species; indeed, by giving permanent expression to the influence of the parents it perpetuates the existence of the factors to which it owes its origin." In other words, let there be civilization. This act of differentiation is for Freud both profoundly revolutionary and profoundly conservative. It sets going the revolutionary human project of culture, yet it prescribes as a prime condition of such an evolution a transmission of culture in the shapes through which each of us aboriginally apprehended it. The primal cultural scene is the disclosure made to each of us that culture is inexpugnably parental.

For Freud the super-ego brings into being the higher and "supra-personal" side of human nature. In it he discerns the origins of religion, morality and the social sense. At the same time, the super-ego is "the heir of the Oedipus complex," and by virtue of this patrimony is "also the expression of the most powerful impulses and most important libidinal vicissitudes of the id." In establishing the super-ego, "the ego has mastered the Oedipus complex and at the same time placed itself in subjection to the id." We are involved in what appears to be irreducible contradiction. Higher and lower converge, for the act of mastery is at once an act of subordination. And in this more-than-paradoxical sense the super-ego, whose origins are ultimately in the external world, comes to represent *vis-à-vis* the ego the realities of the internal world, of the id, of the psyche itself. One of the things that Freud was trying to do, I believe, in this disquieting derivation was to explain how it is that the inner forces opposing instinctual and libidinal impulses seem to have the very character of what it is that they are opposing; how it is that our consciences and our senses of guilt can be as wild, peremptory, savage, and ferocious as the actions and thoughts for which they upbraid and punish us. They are so, Freud suggests, because they are in fact derivatives of the identical forces to which they are antagonistic. Through the inception of the institution of the super-ego, by internalizing through special means particular features of the external world, instinctual-libidinal impulses have been transformed into impulses that are opposed to instinctuality. Or, put differently yet once again, the super-ego is a differentiated part of the ego much of whose force comes from sources in the id (pp. 52f.).

The point which Freud's thinking about the super-ego had reached in *The Ego and the Id* may be very roughly summed up as follows. The super-ego represents a step forward in the evolution through structural differentiation of the ego. It is at once "a special agency in the ego" that also "stand[s] apart" from it and confronts its "other contents." Through processes of internalization called introjection and identification, it enables us to achieve a *renunciation* of our earliest object-choices which is at the same time a *preservation* within us of these "most momentous objects." The super-ego is both heir to the Oedipus complex, and a means by which the past continues to exert mastering power over the ego. It dominates the ego by being a representative of the id and drawing upon its binding force; and it further subjugates the ego by the permanent installation in us of images and representations before whom we will forever feel small, weak, and dependent. "As the child was once under a compulsion to obey its parents, so the ego submits to the categorical imperative of its super-ego." (p. 48) Furthermore, however much the super-ego may in part represent our "higher nature," from the point of view of "instinctual control, of morality" it tends to be "super-moral" and to "become as cruel as only the id can be." The more we check and subdue our aggressiveness toward the external world, the more severe and aggressive do we become in our ego ideals – the more aggressive do we become towards our own egos, indeed ourselves. One additional explanation for this remarkable phenomenon refers back to the origins of the super-ego in which the parents, and principally the father, are taken as the model for identification. "Every such identification," Freud writes, "is in the nature of a desexualization or even of a sublimation." A transformation of this kind entails a defusion of erotic from aggressive instinctual components (which were presumably combined in the original relations to the parental objects), and this defusion permits a release of aggressiveness and is the source of the "general character of harshness and cruelty" of the ego ideal, of its "dictatorial" commands.

In a number of essays written at about the same time as *The Ego and the Id* Freud pursued what he clearly took to be much unfinished business on his part with this agency, and he did so in one important instance in the context of his unfinished business with the puzzling – he calls it "mysterious" – problem of masochism. In "The Economic Problems of Masochism" (1924), he writes, among much else, that one of the primary functions of the ego is to synthesize, to unite and reconcile the various claims of the functions and powers it serves; in this connection it can look to the super-ego as a model, for that institution serves as representative of both the id and the external world. Freud recapitulates the genesis of the super-ego as a representative of the id and of its derivatives, and ascribes much of its harshness, severity, and inexorability to this strand of development. His description of the other strand of development, however, undergoes a sudden expansion. The internalized figures (or imagos) who serve in the super-ego as the agency known as conscience are not only the former libidinal objects of the id – "these same figures belong to the real external world." Their power was first perceived, Freud movingly writes, as "one of the most strongly-felt manifestations of reality." Behind that power, and allied to it, "lie hidden all the influences of the past and of tradition." In virtue of this confluence of disparate exterior realities, the super-ego, heir to and substitute for the Oedipus complex, also represents the real external world and thus "also becomes a model for the endeavors of the ego."

The super-ego goes through a still further development in the changing configuration of our individual ethical sense. In later childhood we experience an "ever-increasing detachment from parents, and their personal significance for the super-ego recedes into the background." To their residual unconscious images "there are then linked the influences of teachers and authorities, self-chosen models and publicly recognized heroes, whose figures need no longer be introjected by an ego which has become more resistant. The last figure in the series that began with the parents is the dark power of Destiny which only the fewest of us are able to look upon as impersonal." Freud has now set forth in outline a complex three-stage sequence. The first stage consists itself of an interlocked series of phases beginning with the earliest experiences of the indifferentiated self/object world and moving through a variety of increasingly organized experiences of both self and object and accompanying psychic processes, this pre-genital, pre-Oedipal phase is followed by the Oedipal experience itself whose outcome is the organized structure itself; and this is succeeded by later experiences of childhood and beyond in which, ideally, the super-ego gradually becomes more impersonal and less parental, more depersonified and more self-chosen, in which figures can apparently be idealized or identified with by the ego without being introjected. In this extended early account of the fortunes of the super-ego, the external human world, the world of culture, of the past and of tradition, and of all the forms in which we can take them into ourselves receive for the first time full play. And the play that they receive is relatively benign, when it is compared to that part of the super-ego which is derived from and remains the representative of the id, of its first libidinal objects and their introjected successor forms. It is these that in their supervisory and punishing operations partly cause the ego to be afraid of the super-ego. These, plus what the super-ego can do by returning our impulses of destructiveness back from the external world and, without transformation, onto the ego, which is now recognized as masochistically inclined in regard to the sadistic tendencies of the super-ego. Furthermore, this helps us to understand in yet another connection the origins of our ethical sense. Its origins are in point of fact disclosed in the recognition that it is unoriginal. Our first "instinctual renunciation is enforced by external powers," and it is "only this" – the combination, I take it, of renunciation, enforcement, and external demand – that creates the ethical sense. This ethical sense "expresses itself in conscience," and its characteristic, iterated demand is "further renunciation of instinct." This particular piece of circular, and incremental, devilry has a great future in Freud's subsequent writings.

II

Throughout the latter part of his career, Freud returned at crucial moments to reconsider the central importance of the super-ego in the psychic economy of our unconscious minds and to rework its place within his evolving theoretical system.

In "The Dissolution of the Oedipus Complex" of 1924, Freud focuses upon bringing into further systematic coherence the disparate elements that cluster about the central, or Oedipal, phase of the formation of the super-ego. The Oedipal crisis is brought towards resolution by the fear of castration – that outcome being in the case of the male child either the punishment for or the precondition of the fulfillment of the fantasies of genital satisfaction entailed in the permutations of the Oedipal situation. Hence a conflict is bound to arise between the boy's "narcissistic interest" in his penis and his libidinal impulses. The normal result of this conflict is that the boy's wishes for phallic integrity eventually subdue his genital cravings. Or, as Freud dryly notes, "the whole process has ... preserved the genital organ" and at the same time "has removed its function." Hence the phase-appropriate onset of what was then called the period of latency. In addition, the partial desexualization and sublimation of the wishes that attach to the Oedipal drama are now transformed into new and renewed impulses of affection with which the child now begins again to regard both parents. Finally, Freud turns to supply a belated account for the analogous experience in girls.

In a short essay of the same year of 1924, "Neurosis and Psychosis," Freud turns again to apply his new theory to another group of occurrences. The classical transference neuroses he now views as a conflict between the ego and the id; psychoses correspond fundamentally to a conflict between the ego and the external world. And in between he postulates a group of disorders that are the resultants of conflicts between the ego and the super-ego – he offers melancholia as a typical example of the infirmity – and these he calls "narcissistic neuroses," in view, one speculates, of the specific aggressive attack made by the institution of the super-ego on our capacities of self-esteem and in view of the general imbalance in the deployment of narcissistic impulses that such a concerted assault implies. He also now envisions the possibility that the ego, in order to avoid a "rupture" with one of its dominating client agencies, may undertake to deform itself "by submitting to encroachments on its own unity and even perhaps by effecting a cleavage or division of itself." These alterations in the structure of the ego would, within the new set of terms, account for "the inconsistencies, eccentricities and follies of men" and would be analogous to what in the original theory of the early 1900s were the sexual perversions, "through the acceptance of which," Freud reminds us, "men spare themselves repressions."

All the same, Freud reserves a certain measure of skepticism about the value of these extended proceedings. And he permits himself to write that "It is true that we cannot tell at once whether we have really gained any new knowledge by this, or have only enriched our store of formulas." This minatory observation has a characteristic edge to it; and it refers I believe to the undertaking of ego psychology. Freud seems, among other things, to be wondering whether this new terminology may be the beginning of psychoanalysis as a formal system and is giving voice to intuitive doubts about the larger value of such a development. The doubts that he has in mind, I imagine, have to do with whether the new theoretical system will have the heuristic powers to which his first theoretical discoveries gave him such rich access. It is an admonition that has notably not been regarded.

In "Some Psychical Consequences of the Anatomical Distinction Between the Sexes" (1925), Freud reviews once more these new formulations in an effort to arrive at a further integrated representation of them. In boys, at least, Freud asserts, the Oedipus complex "is not simply repressed, it is literally smashed to pieces by the shock of threatened castration. ... In normal, or, it is better to say, in ideal cases, the Oedipus Complex exists no longer, even in the unconscious; the super-ego has become its heir." The metaphoric model tacitly being suggested is either the king is dead, long live the king, or the child is father of the man, or both. Moreover, since this development ensures the continued existence of the penis, and hence of the propagation of the species, Freud goes on to say that "the catastrophe of the Oedipus Complex (the abandonment of incest and the institution of conscience and morality) may be regarded as a victory of the race over the individual," and of culture or society as well he might have added.

In the important and difficult book, *Inhibitions, Symptoms and Anxiety* (1926), Feud refers on a number of separate and important occasions to the role of the super-ego in symptom formation – a role which it shares with the ego itself. Freud's major dealings with the super-ego in this work, however, have to do with his new theory of anxiety and his tracing of its evolutionary presence throughout the course of our experiences. He now conceives of anxiety as the response of the organism to a perceived situation of danger. The prototype of this situation is the experience of birth. Anxiety comes into effective existence, however, in the infantile experience of separation from the mother, an occurrence which is reacted to as a loss, a loss of a primal object. This experience of separation and fear is itself divided into three sub-phases: (1) the original biological prototype; (2) the fear of the direct loss of the mother-object; and (3) after the mother has begun to be internalized, as "a loss of object incurred indirectly." (p. 151) These repetitions of experiences and fears of object losses prepare the small child for an alteration in the content of anxiety in the next phase of development. Castration fears during the Oedipal crisis are the next form taken by anxiety, and these are normally transformed as the super-ego is depersonified into moral or social anxiety -- into a generalized unconscious fear of loss of the super-ego as itself an object of love. Finally, there is the universal human experience of the fear of death, which on this scheme Freud conceives of as the fear of being finally abandoned by the super-ego, which we project outward as the neutrally protective powers represented in the idea of fate or destiny itself. I think it should be noted that an inexplicit positive correlated state probably accompanies each of these structural transformations of anxiety. Freud does indeed observe that "mental health very much depends on the super-ego's being normally developed – that is, on its having become sufficiently impersonal." And that has not happened with people who suffer from neuroses; "their super-ego still confronts their ego as a strict father confronts a child; and their morality operates in a primitive fashion in that the ego gets itself punished by the super-ego." (*The Question of Lay Analysis*, 1926, p. 233) It is to be presumed that a similar process of evolution might be observed in culture as well. That is true for Freud in some degree; in some other degree it is less than true; and in another sense entirely it is not true at all.

The degree to which for Freud it is true is suggested in this passage from *The Future of an Illusion* (1927). "It is not true," Freud writes, "that the human mind has undergone no developments since the earliest times and that, in contrast to the advances of science and technology, it is the same today as it was at the beginning of history. We can point out one of these mental advances at once. It is in keeping with the course of human development that external coercion gradually becomes internalized; for a special mental agency, man's super-ego, takes it over. ... Every child presents this process of transformation to us; only by that means does it become a moral and social being." (p. 11) This process is, Freud concludes, "a most precious cultural asset." The degree to which it may be less than true is expressed in his last great work, *Civilization and Its Discontents* (1930). Indeed that treatise seems to have as a principal intention the demonstration in detail of the variety of senses in which it is not true. Of all Freud's work, this essay has been commented upon most widely, so I am spared the effort of recapitulating it in any detail. For present purposes it has to be enough to remark that in this work Freud asks a single major question, "Why is man unhappy?" and that he then proceeds to supply himself and the reader with a super-abundance of answers.

These answers divide into two categories. First, we are unhappy because we "cannot tolerate the amounts of frustration which society imposes ... in the service of its cultural ideals." That frustration expresses itself most fully in civilized humanity's sexual life, which, Freud writes, beginning with the prohibition against an incestuous choice of object, has undergone "the most drastic mutilation." Additional taboos, laws and customs ordaining still further restrictions have followed, and although not all societies are equally severe in the constraints they impose, the society of Western civilization has gone the farthest in restrictively prescribing legalized, permanent heterosexual monogamous genital sexuality as the ideal norm for every grown person. Freud himself admits that this is an extreme picture, and that it is impossible to put into sustained social execution. Indeed, he continues, "only the weaklings have submitted to such an extensive encroachment upon their sexual freedom, and stronger natures have only done so subject to a compensatory condition" – namely, the assurance of a certain measure of personal security and civility. Nevertheless, he concludes, the sexual life of civilized man remains "severely impaired; it sometimes gives the impression of being in process of involution as a function. ... One is probably justified in assuming that its importance as a source of feelings of happiness, and therefore in the fulfillment of our aim in life, has sensibly diminished." (p. 105) Half a century has passed since Freud made these statements. In that interval the sexual life of part of Western culture has begun to undergo a series of qualitative changes, in both attitudes and behavior, that are neither foreseen nor made room for in Freud's assertions. Whether his statement about sexuality's decrease as a source of feelings of happiness holds or must also be modified remains, in my opinion, an arguable question.

The second great source of man's unhappiness is his instinctive aggressiveness. This force expresses itself directly enough in collective, organized human history, but it also makes itself felt in the sacrifices that civilization exacts from each individual's original will to Hobbesian undertakings. The centrality of the aggressive instinct in Freud's later writings can hardly be excessively estimated. It constitutes for the later Freud "the greatest impediment to civilization." (p. 122) And civilization deals with this threat by introjecting and internalizing it in each one of us, by sending that aggressiveness back to where it came from and directing it towards our own egos. "There it is taken over by a portion of the ego, which sets itself over against the rest of the ego as super-ego, and which now, in the form of 'conscience', is ready to put into action against the ego the same harsh aggressiveness that the ego would have liked to satisfy upon other, extraneous individuals. The tension between the harsh super-ego and the ego that is subjected to it, is called by us the sense of guilt; it expresses itself in the need for punishment." Through the progressive internalization of the authority of the super-ego, the "phenomena of conscience ... reach a higher stage." Since "nothing can be hidden from the super-ego, not even thoughts," the presumably substantive distinction between "doing something bad and wishing to do it disappears entirely." In other words, the history of the super-ego on this score is an exemplification of the axiom "doing better and feeling worse."

Moreover, Freud now presses very heavily on the double source or derivation of the sense of guilt. At first instinctual renunciation occurs as a "result of fear of an external authority"; when as one of the outcomes of such renunciations, the super-ego is formed, matters fail to improve, for the super-ego, in addition to insisting upon renunciation, presses for unremitting punishments as well, since the continuance of the repressed and forbidden wishes cannot be concealed from it. And this remains true whether the renounced impulses in question are erotic or aggressive; if it is the second of these, then "every piece of aggression whose satisfaction the subject gives up is taken over by the super-ego and increases the latter's aggressivenesss" against the ego. (p. 129) In either instance, what we have done is to exchange the threat of external unhappiness – the loss of love or the promise of punishment on the part of outward authority – for what Freud calls "a permanent internal unhappiness," the unhappiness brought about by "the tension of the [unconscious] sense of guilt." In addition, Freud observes, referring to Melanie Klein's work, "the severity of the super-ego which a child develops" often fails to correspond with "the severity of treatment he has met with. A child who has been very leniently brought up can acquire a very strict conscience," although it would be incorrect as well to overemphasize the degree of independence involved in this context.

What cannot be overemphasized is Freud's conviction of the primordial importance and "fatal inevitability" (p. 132) of the sense of guilt. For him, it is "the most important problem in the development of civilization," and our loss of happiness through its "heightening" is the "price we pay" for the general "advance of civilization." (p. 134) In addition, since the sense of guilt is "at bottom nothing else but a topographical variety of anxiety," and since anxiety in its "later phases coincides completely with *fear of the superego*," and since the relations of anxiety "to consciousness exhibit ... extraordinary variations," it is very conceivable, Freud writes, "that the sense of guilt produced by civilization ... remains to a large extent unconscious, or appears as a sort of *malaise*, a dissatisfaction, for which people seek other motivations." (pp. 135 f.) One has the sense that an inner door is being shut. No exit.

I am left with an abiding sentiment of contradiction. On the one hand, the intellectual construction itself is massive, logical, and, once one has entered into it, formidably difficult to disengage from, if it is not entirely escape-proof. It is virtually claustral in the way it closes down one alley of possibility after another and leaves progressively decreasing scope for mitigation and alleviation. On the other hand, the psychic reality that it purports to exemplify is itself contradictory in nature. Not only is it grounded in indissolubly opposed impulses; its fundamental character is constituted in conflicting conceptual terms. And it anticipates no ending to either discord, contestations, or contradictions. The super-ego is itself one of the central sites of such antagonisms. It is the most latterly developed of the three primary institutions of the mental apparatus; it consists of portions of the experienced world that have been internalized and differentially transmuted; it remains open to alterations throughout the course of life, and is itself a register in each individual person of cultural development. Yet it is also in Freud's account simultaneously rigid, unbending, inflexible, severe, unforgiving, sadistic, and primitive, and it perseveres in every one of these qualities. It is one of the places at which society and culture penetrate into our unconscious minds and permeate their workings. That penetration and permeation take place, in each of us, not merely by way of our parents themselves but by way of inflection through our parents' super-egos. In his *New Introductory Lectures on Psychoanalysis* (1932), Freud writes, "a child's super-ego is in fact constructed on the model not of its parents but of its parents' super-ego; the contents which fill it are the same, and it becomes the vehicle of tradition and of all the time-resisting judgments of value which have propagated themselves in this manner from generation to generation. ... The past, the tradition of the race and of the people, lives on in the ideologies of the super-ego, and yields only slowly to the influences of the present and to new changes."(p. 67)

Freud has in such passages, I believe, shifted the pitch of discourse and has actively introduced the notion of a collective or transpersonal super-ego; and in *Civilization and Its Discontents* he did, to be sure, assert that "the community, too, evolves a super-ego under whose influence cultural development proceeds." These two formations have many points of agreement; chief among them is that both set up "strict ideal demands, disobedience to which is visited with 'fear of conscience'." Actually the mental processes concerned are "more familiar to us and more accessible to consciousness as they are seen in the group than they can be in the individual man." In that individual person, "when tension arises, it is only the aggressiveness of the super-ego which, in the form of reproaches, makes itself noisily heard; its actual demands [that is to say, its positive precepts, commands and ordinations] often remain unconscious in the background. If we bring them to conscious knowledge, we find that they coincide with the precepts of the prevailing cultural super-ego. At this point the two processes, that of the cultural development of the group and that of the cultural development of the individual, are, as it were, always interlocked. For that reason some of the manifestations and properties of the super-ego can be more easily detected in its behavior in the cultural community than in the separate individual." (pp. 141–2) Freud has issued us with a very general hunting license. The question may be whether, after surveying the desolation he has already wrought across this tract of psychic territory, there is anything left to pursue. The answer, of course, is that I believe there is.

III

In what remains, I intend to follow the subsequent history of the psyche by means of a circuitous route. I want in an extremely cursory and foreshortened way to bring forward three psychoanalytic contributions made by followers of Freud. I will refer to them both as actual contributions and as the registers or expressions of putative changes both in the culture and perhaps in the psyche since the time of the writings of Freud. The contributions were made by Abram Kardiner, Erik Erikson and Heinz Kohut, and they may be suggested in the central piece of terminology chosen by each: Kardiner's notion of "basic personality," Erikson's notion of "identity," and Kohut's notion of the "self." The very names of these conceptions suggest their inner affiliation. Each of these terms represents its author's effort to situate his thinking in a central, informing context. This context represents, to locate it once again, the places of intersection of unconscious mental activities and culture. Each of these conceptions is closer to conscious personal experience than Freud's grand abstract institutions; each also attempts to mediate between those agencies and the actualities of cultural experience. And each of them, in its own manner, is prominently concerned with the historical fate of the super-ego.

Kardiner's pioneering work was done in collaboration with ethnographers and other social scientists. The "basic personality" type, he argued, tended to be specific to certain cultural configurations or institutional constellations, and these two kinds of entities tended additionally to sustain one another. Kardiner's investigations focused upon the examination within one culture or another of the relations between childhood experiences and disciplines as institutions of one order and religion, folklore and social oganizations as institutions of another, though related, order. The hypothesis these analyses were testing out ran to the effect that if the known "conditions of childhood become consolidated and form a basis for subsequent projective use, then we can expect to find some evidence of it in all projective systems" – namely, cultural institutions. And in his two chief works, *The Individual and His Society* (1939) and *The Psychological Frontiers of Society* (1945) Kardiner undertook to explore these correlations. For example, in his study of the Tanalese of Madagascar, he was led to inquire into a peculiarity of this culture, its belief that "no remedy is effectual unless accompanied by some compulsive ritual." Kardiner's explanation for this idiosyncrasy was that actual experience had led the Tanalese to the "conviction that all good things happen after obedience to some arbitrary command. This constellation is created ... by experience beginning at six months, when they are expected to have complete sphincter control and are beaten if they fail, and is followed by similar disciplines during their formative years." Their view of external reality is founded essentially on attitudes of extreme obedience and propitiation. Within the family "the authority of the father is absolute," and status is inflexibly fixed.

Kardiner then introduced a further complicating number of considerations. The Tanalese personality with its peculiar sense of reality was attached to a particular arrangement of institutions and economy – dry cultivation of rice on communally owned land. When the exhaustion of the jungle compelled abandonment of the method of dry cultivation for wet, there was a scramble for the fertile valleys, private ownership replaced communal holdings, family organization broke up as a consequence, and the entire culture began to come apart and collapse. Kardiner's conclusions upon these matters were that in a culture which conceives of reality along the lines of the Tanalese nuclear projective systems, there will be a radical impairment of adaptive capacities. The external world can be dealt with in a very limited number of ways if it is perceived "in accordance with the analogy of an all powerful father and an obedient child. When the father's power gives out, as it did in Tanala, only disorganized aggression and panic could ensue. The individual who deals with the outer world on the basis of obedience can develop no sense of responsibility for his own fate and cannot therefore develop those manipulative powers of which he is capable. The intensity and cruelty of an exacting super-ego is no surrogate for responsibility for oneself."

Kardiner elaborated these findings in his extended analyses of other and very different cultures. He composes, for instance, a most impressive account of the Comanche, which was for a short period a highly successful predatory culture. Through extremely considerate child-rearing the Comanches developed in their braves a character that was uninhibited, courageous, and full of positive self-esteem. Yet Comanche action – warfare, conquest, and plunder – was exercised "exclusively outside the society," and hence the capacity of that society as a whole to develop was severely limited. Comanche society could exist "only as long as there were slaves to steal and cattle to rustle. In other words, this fine ego structure ... was bought at the expense of criminality perpetrated on others and at the cost of the complete collapse of the society once this criminality was incapable of being exercised." It is almost as if Comanche society had no cultural or transindividual super-ego when it came to other groups or societies. Or, as Kardiner pointedly puts it, "in Comanche we have ... a prototype of a society which has developed a high degree of freedom for the individual who is strong and uninhibited but devoted to 'criminal' ends. It can serve as a contrast to those societies which are internally anarchic and externally highly moral." And Kardiner went on to ask with, as he said, complete justification, "what value is this personal freedom of development in a culture which is devoted to criminal ends."

This analysis was followed by a polar contrast, an account of Alorese society in Indonesia, in which infant and child-rearing practices were capricious, inconsistent, chaotic, neglectful, arbitrary, unstable, and cruel. These behaviors led to a personality type characterized by low degrees of organization, aspiration, and idealization. Strong positive attachments to parents were not established, and hence internalizations of parental ideals were poor, as were certain further internal structural consequences of such an absence. Alorese society as a whole was characterized by a basic "general mistrust," in which each individual member felt isolated, and both aggressive and executive ego functions were extremely fragile and fragmentarily developed. Kardiner reminds us that if his theory is correct, then it follows that "repressions do not fall in the same place in all cultures," and that among the Alorese "the earliest relations of the child to the mother prevent the formation of constellations normal to Western man – the strong attachment to the mother, the capacity to idealize her, the capacity to introject her and the formation of strong and organized aggression patterns." And he concludes that "if the super-ego is inadequate and there is no internalization of discipline, we cannot expect the society to have any interest in social justice, in a judicial system, or even in government."

Such reservations seemed to apply to the society he had just dealt with.

The last culture Kardiner examined was a rural, midwestern American community, "Plainville, USA." Kardiner had no difficulty in constructing from James West's accounts the familiar basic personality type of our society, formed in this connection in childhood primarily out of strong attachments by way of idealization and internalization of the parents, especially the mother. This personality was also thwarted sexually in ways that psychoanalysis had for some time made readers familiar with. However, a number of changes also seem to have occurred. Except for the very poor, religion was already (in 1939) in a state of desuetude, and had been replaced as a salvational equivalent – as it had been in the society at large – by "success or social well-being." Indeed, Kardiner observed, "the whole system of deferred gratification had lost its standing as a social expedient." At the same time, the citizens of Plainville seemed to have adequate psychic structure to make adaptations possible to what would become an extremely rapidly changing world. In order to begin to explain some of the complexities of our civilization's internal character, Kardiner undertook a schematic interpretation of its past history.

Medieval cosmology conceived of the world as governed by a "powerful father whose commands" were at the same time "natural law." Under the dual influence of the Reformation and the new natural and mathematical sciences of the seventeenth century that succeeded it, the elements of this constellation underwent a transmutation. Natural law was freed from its contingency on divine will; man's conception of himself and his relations to both the deity and the world shifted, as did the valences and vectors of force within those mental agencies which govern the individual person's sense of responsibility for himself and his sense of authorization to investigate and explore freely both external and internal circumstances. It amounted, in Kardiner's words, to "a new allocation of the superego or conscience mechanisms." This new allocation had its due influence on social and personal realities, on notions of the deity, on economic formations (which of course also influenced these allocations in turn), and on changing class and status groupings. But, according to Kardiner, the most direct and important consequence of these summatory changes was an "alteration of the whole superego system."

Moreover, this alteration was not altogether an unmixed blessing. In such a transformation of the "systems of self-validation in Western society," although the "value of power and enjoyment were greatly augmented," the "psychological burdens placed on the individual" were concomitantly augmented as well. The increased internalization of conscience that marked those changes associated with the Reformation were directed largely towards those "impulses which [fall] under disciplinary bans in childhood – chiefly the pleasure drives." The same intensified internalization of conscience also created a situation in which conscience "could wield far more despotic power than was ever done" by the older ecclesiastical institutions. Hence the "psychological burdens of Western man were intensified" at the same time as the aggrandizing internalized conscience provided new freedoms from external constraints along certain lines of self-expression and activity in the world. And in due course of time the anxiety of salvation would be replaced by the secular "anxiety as judged by self-esteem," a yet further alteration of the locus of conscience.

From Kardiner's cross-cultural studies there emerges the hypothesis that certain things that "we were induced to regard as parts of human nature – the capacity for idealization of the parents, the capacity to introject the parents and thus lay a firm basis for super-ego formation, so essential to the stability of a culture ... these essential features in the development of a conscience can be strangulated in infancy." And from his historical excursion there re-emerges the hypothesis that the disposition of forces within the super-ego may within a single culture change across historical time. Hence it is possible to imagine and discover societies or cultures in which there is an actual super-ego deficit; and hence it is also possible to demonstrate within the course of development of one complex society and culture alterations within the unconscious.

This reading of Kardiner's major work leads to the inference that it ended with the covert stipulation that two further books be written. Their titles would almost certainly have had to be *Childhood and Society* and *Young Man Luther*. I make such a remark not to minimize the substance of Erikson's contribution but to suggest its consequent place in an overdetermined sequence of developments (to which I cannot here do anything that resembles justice). Erikson is the most cheerful of ego psychologists, and to the buoyancy of his native temperament he has added the incurable optimism of his adopted culture.

Identity as used by Erikson in the context of ego psychology means something very like "the self" in one of its several psychoanalytic bearings – the inner representation of the ego as it is invested with narcissistic impulses. Erikson first used the term, however, in the form of "ego identity," which he both associated with and distinguished from both the super-ego and the ego ideal. Erikson conceived of the super-ego as "a more archaic, more thoroughly internalized and more unconscious representative of man's unborn proclivity toward the development of a primitive, categorical conscience." The ego ideal, however, in Erikson's own redesignation of it, "seems to be more flexibly and consciously bound to the ideals of the particular historical era as absorbed in childhood." And the third step in this hierarchy is ego identity or identity, which would "in comparison be even closer to changing social reality in that it would test, select, and integrate self-images derived from the psychosocial crises of childhood in the light of the ideological climate of youth." (*Identity: Youth and Crisis*, pp. 208 ff.) As that last clause suggests, Erikson tends to use the term in ways that include all three of the differentiated phases. What I think he essentially means by the conception is contained in the following passage: "a process 'located' *in the core of the individual* and yet also *in the core of his communal culture*, a process which establishes, in fact, the identity of those two identities." In other words, the locus of meeting of individual psyche and culture once again.

Erikson's strengths, it is to be noted, are not those of abstract conceptualization or consecutive theoretical power. He is a master of the vignette and of the telling detail; his best historical works are amplified and elaborated resonations of quite specific historical moments or episodes: Luther's fit in the choir, or The Event in Gandhi's life, the mill strike at Ahmedabad. We can see those considerable gifts at work in Erikson's writings on Luther, as he develops in rich and intimate detail some of the matters that Kardiner had abstractly adverted to. The Renaissance, Erikson writes, was in large measure a series of revolutions made to regain power and reclaim pleasure from "the Church's systematic and terroristic exploitation of man's proclivity for a negative conscience." (Negative conscience equals "sense of guilt" or tension between ego and super-ego, such terms now becoming, in these quarters, the functional equivalents of dirty words.) The Catholic Church in Luther's time tried to exercise an "absolute power of negative external conscience: negative in that it was based on a sense of sin, and external in that it was defined and redefined by a punitive agency" exclusively in charge of morality and the enforcement of sanctions against disobedience. The Renaissance "gave man a vacation from his negative conscience," and thus freed the ego "to gather strength for manifold activity." The provincial Luther was overtly no Renaissance man at all; yet, Erikson suggests, he had prepared himself "to do the dirty work of the Renaissance, by applying some of the individualistic principles immanent in the Renaissance to the Church's still highly fortified homeground – the conscience of ordinary man." His life's work, which was, we should not forget, "dirty work," was located upon "the unconquered frontier" of this largely negative "tragic conscience." "Luther's work orginated," Erikson goes on, "in the hypertrophy of the negative conscience inherent in our whole Judaeo-Christian heritage."

Erikson then reaches for a characteristically well-turned and reverberant conclusion: "We must accept this universal, if weird frontier of the negative conscience as the circumscribed *locus* of Luther's work. If we do, we will be able to see that the tools he used were those of the Renaissance: fervent return to the original texts; determined anthropocentrism ...; and the affirmation of his own organ of genius and craftmanship, namely, the voice of the vernacular." (*Young Man Luther*, pp. 193 ff.) Erikson's culture heroes tend to speak in such distinctive voices; they are most of them rebellious idealists of a complex sort, whose lives and works have enlarged our humanity, largely at the expense of the weakening of the archaic super-ego.

Yet the matter is by no means historically that straightforwardly simple. Erikson's focusing upon problems of ego identity and cultural identity and the concomitant effort to weaken or neutralize "the autocracy of the infantile super-ego" arose in some degree out of his clinical experience. The shift in emphasis expressed by his work, he states, has been "dictated by historical accident – i.e., by the revolutions that are taking place in our lifetime, affecting our personal fortunes as well as the symptoms presented and the unconscious demands made on us by our patients ... the patient of today suffers most under the problem of what he should believe in and who he should – or, indeed, might – be or become; while the patient of early psychoanalysis suffered most under inhibitions which prevented him from being what and who he thought he knew he was." Freud discovered in his patients a deep upset in their "sexual economy owing to the manifold hypocrisies and sexual repressions imposed" on them. Freud's theory explained "the symptoms characteristic of its own period"; in our time, however, "the study of identity ... becomes as strategic ... as the study of sexuality was in Freud's time." (*Childhood and Society*, pp. 279 ff.) In this characteristic passage, Erikson is apparently associating or aligning problems of identity with problems of character disorder. Both seem to represent something of a way-station on the way from the structural or transference neuroses that were the principal subjects of Freud's researches to the disorders of narcissism and of the narcissistic personality that have in recent years come to engross the forefront of psychoanalytic preoccupation.

These latter phenomena have been joined with a third theoretical formulation, the psychoanalytic notion of the self. Although this conception has itself an interesting history in the various branches of psychoanalytic thought, it has been associated most extensively with the work of Heinz Kohut and his two most substantial contributions, *The Analysis of the Self* (1971) and *The Restoration of the Self* (1977). I can do no more than point to his major theses. The presenting symptomatology of patients suffering from narcissistic personality disorders tends to be "ill defined." Originally vague complaints soon focus, however, on "pervasive feelings of emptiness" and impressions on the part of the patient that he "is not fully real"; tendencies towards feeling "vaguely depressed" regularly occur along with convictions of being "drained of energy" and having no "zest" for work or other activities; these co-exist with extreme vulnerability to shiftings in self-esteem, and heightened sensitivity to the interest – or lack thereof – of others in him. The patient's experience of himself tends to be fragmentary and discontinuous, and based once again, in a simplified sense, on an unstable and precarious sustainment of self-esteem. A patient will typically complain of "a pervasive feeling that he was not fully alive (though he was not depressed); of painful tension states which lay on the borderline of physical and psychological experience; and of a tendency toward brooding worrisomeness about his physical and mental functions." Vertical splittings in the ego will separate sectors of overt exhibitionistic claims and grandiose behaviors from central sectors of depleted self-esteem, inclinations towards shame, and profound needs for approval. Disturbances of self-acceptance accompany feelings of general "inner uncertainty and purposelessness concerning widespread sectors of ... life." It seems on the face of it as if these people are actually suffering from what was once called unhappiness.

What these symptoms reveal, Kohut concludes, after some decades of clinical experience, are a number of underlying deficits. These deficits largely have to do with the inadequate formation at a series of points of development of the super-ego. For example, what is ordinarily missing in the early lives of such patients is the massive, but phase-appropriate experience of both infatuation with and disappointment in the Oedipal parents, an experience that leads "ultimately to the idealization of the super-ego, a developmental and maturational step which is of great importance in protecting the personality against the danger of narcissistic regression." That is to say, there has not occurred in such patients "the building up of those aspects of the super-ego which direct toward the ego the commands and prohibitions, the praise, scolding and punishment that the parent has formerly directed toward the child." Such patients lack, in other words an adequate "nuclear super-ego" upon which later structures may be built up. What in their experiences these patients have suffered is in general fathers whom they have been unable to idealize, in large measure because, according to Kohut's testimony, the fathers themselves have been disturbed in their own self-esteem so that they have been unable to tolerate the role of idealized figures that children (sons of course in particular) demand and require of their parents if they are in fact to achieve the large-scale internalizations of structure that form a super-ego. And behind this experience Kohut's later theoretical account postulates an anterior extended phase of an unempathic mother, a mother who has been unable to function as a primitive self-object, an empathic "mirror for the child's healthy exhibitionism" and sexual ambitions. These two generalized experiences of failure – of the mother as primary mirror and basis of the self as a self-object, and the father as a primary self-object in the form of an idealized object – combine in a number of permutations to produce the disorders known as narcissistic personalities. These impairments are characterized by insufficient psychic structures which are themselves connected with inadequate experiences of internalization, identification, and idealization. Such persons are, in Kohut's words, "not predominantly swayed by guilt," that is to say by pressures exerted by the super-ego; on the contrary, their "predominant tendency," in this connection, is to be "overwhelmed by shame "

These patients seem to form a most striking contrast to the men and women that walked in off the Berggasse these many decades ago. Whatever their afflictions, these predecessors did not seem to suffer from the deficits of internal structure that Kohut and others claim to have observed in their patients of recent years.

These perceived changes in what appears to be the dominant pathology – or to put it more technically, the dominant structures of unconscious defense – of those members of the middle class who choose to resort to psychoanalytic treatment have suggested a number of areas of possible exploration. What seems to come into sharpest focus in these patients is not a representation of a "psychic apparatus trying to deal with drives and structural conflicts," but an unconscious struggling to maintain its primitive cohesion, a self moved by the anxiety that it may in fact be distintegrating. These young patients have been raised in families in which distance rather than excessive closeness seems to have characterized the relations between parents and children. The older structural neuroses were in part the result of deprivations and negative excesses that arose out of such circumstances as the belief in, and even the reality of, the integrity of the family as a unit, out of a social life that was densely concentrated upon the home, and out of the relatively "clear-cut definition of the roles of father and mother." Where the surrounding immediate world of the middle-class child "used to be experienced as threateningly close," it now tends "more and more" to be perceived "as threateningly distant." Children who in the past tended to be "*over*stimulated by the emotional ... life of their parents ... are now often *under*stimulated." Where previously childhood erotic life was connected with Oedipal rivalries, parental inhibitions and severe internal conflicts, "many children now seek the effect of erotic stimulation in order to relieve loneliness," and fill an emotional blankness or absence. In the past, structural neuroses with their emphases upon repressions, inhibitions and guilts in the form of a punishing and excessive super-ego arose out of a matrix in which "the pathogenic effect of parents suffering [themselves] from structural disorders was especially great because, within the confines of the closely knit family situation, the parents' opportunity to act out their conflicts with their children was especially great." Today smaller families, a relative increase of absense of parents from the middle-class home, and the increasing importance of peer groups as formative influences in idealization and internalization all tend to a situation moving in a relatively polar direction from that typified by the classical situation just referred to.

These changes have come about gradually and in the course of generations. They have been produced by myriad circumstances and express themselves in behavioral, social, and cultural forms that are too numerous and too complex for me to do more than continue to advert to allusively. They have to do most generally with changing relations of authority within the family, between men and women in their different roles, between parents and children, and children and their decreasing number of siblings. They have to do as well with the continued destabilized relations within, between and among such institutions of authority as the family, schools, and religion and with the general dispersion of authority away from and out of these former centers of command, interdiction, and guidance and the apparent non-existence as yet of evolutionary replacements for them. To say more than this at such a preliminary point of historical research would be to vulgarize by prematurity the very problematic that the present argument brings forward.

It was in 1881, more than 100 years ago, that the meetings between Josef Breuer and Anna O. that led to so much began to take place. It was Freud himself who made so much of those meetings, and his dealings with them led him on to make a number of fundamental discoveries about the mind. Among them was his theory that the unconscious mind will tend to form itself into a limited variety of structures or agencies. Today we can see that the particular configurations of those agencies as Freud first perceived and then

theoretically constructed them were appropriate to and expressive of
the deep character structure of late high Victorian bourgeois culture –
even, perhaps, as it was beginning to come apart. In particular the
excessive and punitive powers of the super-ego in that theory and
character were prototypical of that culture and of its leading
awareness of itself. I have tried very briefly to sketch how in the
course of time that character has changed, how a piece of unconscious
structure itself has been permeated and informed in its defensive
configurations by cultural changes, and I have tried to enlist some
developments in psychoanalytic observation and theory itself as the
primary evidence in this account. I have tried to show how a character
that was ridden by guilt, rent by conflict, and simultaneously
overstimulated and overinhibited has in its ascendancy begun to give
place to an unconscious (and not so entirely unconscious) psyche
characterized by "inner emptiness, isolation, and unfulfillment." No
one in full possession of his senses could long for a return of the
agency of the super-ego in the forms and intensities of its earlier
historic manifestations. Yet no one fully alive today can fail to
perceive that the exchanges and bargains that constitute cultural
development do not amount to a rational progress either. As
psychoanalysis as a unique cultural and therapeutic discipline begins
to envisage the completion of its first century of existence and looks
forward to beginning its second, it seems to me that the tasks
confronting it in the culture that it has arisen from, taken hold in, and
that it critically expresses, are at least as grave and as severe in
magnitude as the tasks that first confronted it 100 years ago.

Note

1   It does not help matters terribly much that he also suggested that "every
    science come[s] in the end to a kind of mythology."

6 Some Cultural Precursors of Psychic Change

There exists a critical practice that is normally followed, and that I am going to follow on the present occasion, but that we normally also do not draw attention to. Why is it that we customarily look to art, to literature, to cultural developments and scientific theory as the indicators in advance of large changes in fundamental attitudes, as the first notices of alterations in collective sensibility? I assume that there is a general agreement on the theoretical principles of determination and overdetermination in human affairs, and in particular on that part of those affairs which may be described as mental – and I am in agreement with this settled group of assumptions. At the same time, the activities that constitute art, literature, and cultural and scientific theorizing appear when they are compared with such realms of activity as economics, politics, or family life, to be relatively free and less directly dependent upon specific social circumstances. What I am suggesting is that in shifting the direction of the arrow of determinate analysis we are by no means abandoning the principle of determination or overdetermination. Whether we think of these activities in an interior sense as comparatively conflict-free functions of the ego, or, less doubtfully perhaps, in an exterior sense as the quasi-autonomous domain of the superstructure *vis-à-vis* the base, is not at this juncture of compelling importance. What is at issue is our recognition of the differential quality of determinateness in these realms and the uses to which those differences and that recognition may be put.

In the dim, indeed the virtually sub-aqueous, light cast by these scandalously foreshortened theoretical remarks, I should like to turn to my subject, or to the way into it. I should like to direct our regard to what I take to be an often overlooked contradiction or set of contradictions in the dominant character type in nineteenth-century middle-class or bourgeois society and culture. This character type has been habitually, and properly, associated with the historical life of industrial capitalism in its early expansive and even heroic phase; and the contradictions within it may be seen to fall within the ambiguities inscribed by the activities associated with acquisitive behavior and the social and economic institutions that legitimized and promoted such behavior. On the one hand this character-type was thought to be highly governed by certain normative rules and values that derived directly from economic rationality. Hence this character-type regulated much of his life by rational calculation, and in particular by the kind of calculation which relied upon the supposed consequences of what the unremitting practice of the virtues of thrift, frugality, and industry might have upon one's individual existence. These virtues were to be realized largely in the quality of devotion to work or vocation that was internalized within this character-type, but they extended to more general deferrals of gratification in other regions as well. They entailed sobriety of thought, dress, and demeanor, moderation of impulse and speech, and temperation of behavior that often transformed itself into demands for temperance that were nothing short of intemperate. This character-type also believed in, and believed it practiced, self-discipline; and the purpose of such self-discipline was not merely the socially desirable subordination of unruly and disorderly impulses, but the still higher purpose of self-improvement, which, it was believed, should be carried on throughout life and literally unto death. At the center of this type stood the personal virtues of probity and integrity of character, and of rectitude and moral uprightness in one's dealings with the world, other people, and one's self. It was from these austere virtues that the behaviors of rational economic calculation were understood to issue; and it was to these same severities that the successful results of such behaviors returned, to confirm them and to reinforce one's conviction of their lawfulness. On one side, thus, this character-type represented itself in the world through ordinances (issued to itself and to that world) that were ascetic and self-denying; and these ordinances, indeed, constituted the heart of its claim to a high spirituality. This spirituality, of course, is the mainspring of Weber's unsurpassed account of the Protestant Ethic.

On the other hand, this same character-type, when regarded from another perspective, seemed to be constituted out of very different elements. This other perspective might be supplied by a different social location, or it might be supplied by a shifting of internal focus within the dominant character-type itself. The same acquisitive behaviors were now construed as bearing a negative valence. Rational calculation was in fact an institution for the methodical expression of aggressiveness. The thrifty, frugal, and industrious middle-class merchant or bourgeois manufacturer or financier was at the same time greedy and rapacious. Deferral of gratification was by no means incompatible with a wide variety of appetitive practices, and the middle classes of the period were represented as often in pleasure-seeking and pleasure-taking activities as they were in their dedication to work. The claims to high spirituality were a permutated and incompletely sublimated form of materialism; self-discipline was regularly put into the service of personal aggrandisement; sobriety did not extinguish the love of comfort and luxury and the desire for consumption; self-improvement co-existed comfortably with a wide spectrum of hypocritical personal attitudes and institutional practices, and appeals made on behalf of probity and integrity of character did not simply cancel out the existence of a moral double standard. The member of the bourgeoisie was not simply ascetic; he was equally sensual, and was referred to conventionally as *l'homme moyen sensuel*. And his ordinances of self-denial, however often they were issued, were regularly accompanied in the mass by an extravagant and vulgar display of objects and acquisitions both inanimate and animate.

I do not raise these opposing accounts to impute singular truth to either of them. I raise them as what they were – covert and unacknowledged contradictions of character and of the structure of individual self-hood that are connected in very deep and complex ways with the historical character of the society in which they were played out and with its large contradictions. They refract those contradictions, they express them and they react back on them, although they are not, it seems to me, finally reducible to them. It was, in my view, possible to live with these contradictions, to adapt to or deal with them, to overlook or avoid them, or to go on with the business of living as if they didn't exist, so long as it was still possible to believe in the existence of some sort of transcendant value or moral authority that was, in certain senses, outside of one's self. Whenever this belief seemed imperilled, the contradictions rose towards the surface; when the belief became impossible, they erupted.

In the writings of the great Victorian moralists, literary and social critics and cultural sages, this drama of contradictions was played out in extraordinary detail, complexity, and consequentness, as it was in other idioms in the works of the great nineteenth-century bourgeois novelists and their successors, the central creative figures of twentieth-century modernism (I will not have time here to deal with or even touch upon this corresponding line of development). The writings of the chief Victorian critics form a coherent, complex, and yet sequential set of discourses. In them we can see prefigured, for what was indeed the first time, much of what has come today, a century later, to be enacted on a much larger cultural scale.

The first and most exemplary figure in this cultural drama was Thomas Carlyle. Born in 1795 and raised in the tradition of Scottish Calvinism, Carlyle attended Edinburgh University where he was exposed to the chilly winds of eighteenth-century rationalism and skepticism. Recalling these experiences in his spiritual autobiography, *Sartor Resartus*, he writes, "The hungry young ... / looked up to their spiritual Nurses; and, for food, were bidden eat the east-wind ... Often we would condole over the hard destiny of the Young in this era: how, after all our toil, we were to be turned-out into the world, with beards on our chins indeed, but with few other attributes of manhood; no existing thing that we were trained to Act on, nothing that we could so much as Believe." The young Carlyle's deconversion took the form of a personal crisis that became emblematic for the era. Thrown back upon his isolated self, the Universe, he writes, in a memorable passage, "was all void of Life, of Purpose, of Volition, even of Hostility: it was one huge, dead, immeasurable Steam-engine, rolling on in its dead indifference, to grind me limb from limb." With the loss of belief in a celestial salvation, of an afterlife to be paid for by suffering here on earth, he asked himself the fatal question, "Why am I not happy?" The question was fatal because, of course, in this context it has no answer. As he recovered from his crisis (which I cannot discuss in any detail) Carlyle formulated a number of central insights. First, in a world deserted by a traditional transcendant authority, the question of individual happiness and self-realization becomes a central problematic.

Man's Unhappiness, as I construe, comes of his Greatness; it is because there is an Infinite in him, which with all his cunning he cannot quite bury under the Finite. Will the whole Finance Ministers and Upholsterers and Confectioners of modern Europe undertake, in joint-stock company, to make one Shoeblack happy? They cannot accomplish it, above an hour or two; for the Shoeblack also has a Soul quite other than his Stomach; and would require, if you consider it, for his permanent satisfaction and saturation, simply this allotment, no more, and no less: *God's infinite Universe altogether to himself*, therein to enjoy infinitely, and fill every wish as fast as it rose. Oceans of Hochheimer, a Throat like that of Ophiuchus: speak not of them; to the infinite Shoeblack they are as nothing. No sooner is your ocean filled, than he grumbles that it might have been of better vintage. Try him with half of a Universe, of an Omnipotence, he sets to quarrelling with the proprietor of the other half, and declares himself the most maltreated of men. – Always there is a black spot in our sunshine: it is even as I said, the *Shadow of Ourselves*.

It is this direct claim upon life, Carlyle argued, that had to be renounced, before life, properly speaking, could begin again. And hand in hand with this self-renunciation, Carlyle discovered a new transcendant value. He discovered it in conduct, in action. "Doubt of any sort," he wrote, quoting Goethe, "cannot be removed except by Action." And the form of action that he invested with special moral authority was work – indeed he called it the Gospel of Work.

I too could now say to myself: Be no longer a Chaos, but a World ... Produce! Produce! Were it but the pitifullest infinitesimal fraction of a Product, produce it, in God's name! 'Tis the utmost thou hast in thee: out with it, then. Up, up! Whatsoever thy hand findeth to do, do it with thy whole might. Work while it is called Today; for the Night cometh, wherein no man can work.

Even in a world given over to Mammon, there is hope, so long as one is earnest about something. "Idleness," he writes, "is worst, Idleness alone is without hope: work earnestly at anything, you will by degrees learn to work at almost all things. There is endless hope in work, were it even work at making money." These insights and formulations were immensely influential, insofar as one can say that the written utterances of one man influence others. They were syntonic with a number of the central impelling forces of society at that time, and were indeed in part articulate expressions of those forces. Yet they did not hold permanently for Carlyle. The capitalism of the period did not bring forth the heroic figures that he thought it would; nor did it produce the new "religious mythus" that he believed, in large measure correctly as I think, human beings required. It did not, in other words transcend itself; it did not produce the "natural supernaturalism" that Carlyle believed the modern world had to invent for itself. It produced economic and social crises; it produced wealth and continued to distribute that wealth with sinful inequity. And as it did so, Carlyle's critical asperity went sour; the anti-intellectual tendencies that were always powerfully latent in him rose to expression, and the high spirituality of the middle-class values that he put in idiosyncratic and powerful form gave way to an illiberal authoritarianism that was as hostile to bourgeois individuality as it was to almost anything else. He had reached a dead end.

The second great figure in this discourse is John Stuart Mill, who, starting out at a point remote from Carlyle, went through a similar situation and crisis and arrived at similar conclusions. Mill had been deliberately raised by his father to have no religious beliefs and to have no experience of religious sentiments. Yet at the age of 15, John Stuart Mill underwent an experience of conversion. He read the works of Jeremy Bentham, his father's philosophical master, and found religion in among other things the "greatest happiness principle." From that moment, he writes, "I had what truly might be called an object in life; to be a reformer of the world. My conception of my own happiness was entirely identified with this object." For five years he lived with this faith, but in 1826 at the age of 20, he found himself out of sorts and in a state of incipient depression.

In this frame of mind it occurred to me to put the question directly to myself: "Suppose that all your objects in life were realized; that all the changes in institutions and opinions which you are looking forward to, could be completely effected at this very instant: would this be a great joy and happiness to you?" And an irrepressible self-consciousness distinctly answered, 'No!' At this my heart sank within me: the whole foundation on which my life was constructed fell down. All my happiness was to have been found in the continual pursuit of this end. The end had ceased to charm, and how could there ever again be any interest in the means? I seemed to have nothing left to live for.

Mill's crisis was prolonged, profound and quasi-suicidal. His passage out of it is described in his *Autobiography* in considerable and illuminating detail. When he emerged on the other side, he felt that his experiences of this period had left two very marked effects on his opinions and character.

In the first place, they led me to adopt a theory of life, very unlike that on which I had before acted, and having much in common with what at that time I certainly had never heard of, the anti self-consciousness theory of Carlyle. I never, indeed, wavered in the conviction that happiness is the test of all rules of conduct, and the end of life. But I now thought that this end was only to be attained by not making it the direct end. Those only are happy (I thought) who have their minds fixed on some object other than their own happiness; on the happiness of others, on the improvement of mankind, even on some art or pursuit, followed not as a means, but as itself an ideal end. Aiming thus at something else, they find happiness by the way. The enjoyments of life (such was now my theory) are sufficient to make it a pleasant thing, when they are taken en passant, without being made a principal object. Once make them so, and they are immediately felt to be insufficient. They will not bear a scrutinizing examination. Ask yourself whether you are happy, and you cease to be so. The only chance is to treat, not happiness, but some end external to it, as the purpose of life. Let your self-consciousness, your scrutiny, your self-interro-gation, exhaust themselves on that; and if otherwise fortunately circumstanced you will inhale happiness with the air you breathe, without dwelling on it or thinking about it, without either forestalling it in imagination, or putting it to flight by fatal questioning. This theory now became the basis of my philosophy of life.[1]

The second important result of these experiences, Mill said, was that they led him for the first time to give "its proper place among the prime necessities of human well-being, to the internal culture of the individual." What he meant by this first became clear to him when he read the poetry of Wordsworth at this time and found there what he called "the very culture of the feelings." Yet what one feels in Mill and what makes the reading of his autobiography so poignant an experience is the sense that it communicates of transcendance lost never to be regained. This may not be the worst thing in the world, and to have gone on to become John Stuart Mill, the saint of rationalism, and much else, is nothing to sneeze at. Nevertheless, his book, and indeed his life (apart from his work, which he pursued with Carlylean dedication) is characterized by pervasive emotions of loss, of absence, of the unrecoverable.

To mention Wordsworth, culture, and loss brings us inevitably to the third figure in this extended cultural discourse. Matthew Arnold begins with the conviction that traditional moral and religious authority are moribund. He begins as well with the insight that Carlyle's central project had failed and that this central project had been in fact to import the ideals of the French Revolution into England. For Carlyle those ideals were largely captured in the phrase, "the career open to talents," or as a sub-doctrine in the Gospel of Work, "the tools to those that can use them." The overriding moral authority behind the middle-class claims to social and political hegemony were to be found in the ideal of society reorganized as a meritocracy – an open hierarchy in which individual talents could freely express themselves and find their appropriate place and rewards. For Arnold, as for Carlyle, and I am quoting Arnold, the French Revolution remained "the greatest, the most animating event in history," and it remained so precisely by virtue of the "force, truth and universality of the ideas which it took for its law, and from the passion with which it could inspire a multitude for these ideas, a unique and still living power." It had changed the world, and yet it had failed as well. For the exacerbating circumstance that all these exceptionally creative figures had to face was that even in the wake of the French Revolution and of reform in England, mind and power remained radically alienated from one another. Confronted by a society in which, as he described it, "our upper class is materialized, our middle class [is] vulgarized, and our lower class is brutalized," Arnold chose a less direct route than that pursued by Carlyle or Mill. He put together a remarkable discourse that was controlled by a number of connected and sometimes interchangeable terms: these were criticism, culture, literature or poetry, and humane letters or education. And it was in the arena composed by these activities that he tried to reinscribe transcendant value. In criticism he saw a disinterested and free play of the mind upon all things, an activity whose purpose was to see the object as in itself it really is, in which the mind as a rule takes up an adversary position towards the social and cultural situation in which it finds itself, while yet remaining at the same time in the ultimate service of that society and culture. The culture that he proposed was not the culture in which he lived. It too was an ideal practice whose final aim was that "of all great spiritual disciplines ... man's perfection or salvation." Through getting to know the best that has been thought and said, in cultivating our inwardness and responsiveness to great and high thoughts and books, we would be doing our best to, in the end, make "reason and the will of God prevail." Literature was, he repeatedly remarked, "a criticism of life," and poetry was the highest form of that utterance.

> The future of poetry is immense, because in poetry where it is worthy of its high destinies, our race, as time goes on, will find an ever surer and surer stay. There is not a creed which is not shaken, not an accredited dogma which is not shown to be questionable, not a received tradition which does not threaten to dissolve. Our religion has materialized itself in the fact, in the supposed fact; it has attached its emotion to the fact, and now the fact is failing it. But for poetry the idea is everything; the rest is a world of illusion, of divine illusion. Poetry attaches its emotion to the idea; the idea *is* the fact. The strongest part of our religion today is its unconscious poetry.

Nothing could be clearer, more appealing, or as we now can see more questionable. The redemptive powers of religion were to be displaced into literature and art. Arnold, of course, had no way of knowing to what future uses these notions were to be put, but several things may be at this point noted about them. In this unprogrammatic program, still greater stress was put upon the cultivation of individuality in the form of inner self-hood.

Moreover, Arnold himself saw the disparities we have been discussing in terms of an opposition that he ascribed to fundamental impulses in human nature. Those impulses he denominated as Hebraism and Hellenism. Victorian society and culture were, he observed, dominated by the Hebraic; they needed an infusion of the Hellenic that they tended to be frightened of and deny. Here is one of Arnold's descriptions of the Hellenic:

> To get rid of one's ignorance, to see things as they are, and by seeing them as they are to see them in their beauty, is the simple

and attractive ideal which Hellenism holds out before human nature; and from the simplicity and charm of this ideal, Hellenism, and human life in the hands of Hellenism, is invested with a kind of aerial ease, clearness, and radiancy; they are full of what we call sweetness and light. Difficulties are kept out of view, and the beauty and rationalness of the ideal have all our thoughts.

In such a passage, as we move ahead in the dialectic of discourse we have been reconstructing, we can make out the first contradictory part of the hypothetical character-type giving way to a refined, attenuated and hypertrophied version (in part) of the second, although it does not quite recognize itself as such.

Arnold himself was intermittently aware of such contradictions, both in terms of the dominant character-type and of the larger social and cultural contradictions of which they were in some measure refractions. And he proposed to deal with them by a deliberate process of distancing.

It will be said that it is a very subtle and indirect action which I am thus prescribing for criticism, and that, by embracing in this manner the Indian virtue of detachment and abandoning the sphere of practical life, it condemns itself to a slow and obscure work. Slow and obscure it may be, but it is the only proper work of criticism. The mass of mankind will never have any ardent zeal for seeing things as they are; very inadequate ideas will always satisfy them. On these inadequate ideas reposes, and must repose, the general practice of the world. That is as much as saying that whoever sets himself to see things as they are will find himself one of a very small circle; but it is only by this small circle resolutely doing its own work that adequate ideas will ever get current at all. The rush and roar of practical life will always have a dizzying and attracting effect upon the most collected spectator, and tend to draw him into its vortex; most of all will this be the case where that life is so powerful as it is in England. But it is only by remaining collected, and refusing to lend himself to the point of view of the practical man, that the critic can do the practical man any service.

Arnold's contribution to the classical humanist tradition in its modern phase was decisive; there are few of us who have not in one way or another been touched by it. But it is no discredit to him to say that we can now see that it was a holding action, that it bought time and space within the prevailing social order for certain protected and privileged kinds of thought and behavior, and that it has not prevailed.

The next major figure in the tradition I shall have to address with shameful brevity. John Ruskin began as a disciple of Carlyle, a conventionally religious evangelical Christian, and a critic of painting and architecture, who believed in the redemptive power of art as well. He believed that an appropriate response to and appreciation of art and architecture were in a society inseparable from sound public behavior, morality, and justice, and he strove in his writings to amend and correct public taste in the hope of establishing social and moral deliverance in his own time. Despite his great success with a large public, he was dissatisfied, since his prophetic utterances seemed to be going unheeded. By the mid-1850s he had lost his faith in dogmatic religion, turned away from writing about art and began to write a series of brilliant critical denunciations of political economy, the industrial capitalist system as it was functioning at the time, and the styles of life and of self of the dominant middle class.[2]

Redemption and transcendance could now be achieved only by direct interventions into the social and economic order itself although Ruskin was never altogether consistent about what those interventions should be or how they might take place. I can think of no more dramatic demonstration of the contradictions that I have been referring to than this eruption and about-face. These writings of Ruskin were greeted, not surprisingly, with a storm of outrage and abuse. (As Ruskin himself rather mutedly phrased it, they "were reprobated in a violent manner, as far as I could hear, by most of the readers they met with.") But Ruskin went even further. He tried to put these two different tendencies together in a series of writings and social experiments that he sponsored and paid for in which the transcendant powers of art were to be combined with efforts at social restoration. These noble projects were not merely contradictory; they soon revealed that they were incoherent, and Ruskin himself, a member of the bourgeoisie in England (his father was a wealthy wine merchant), whose Protestant ethical side was overdeveloped to the point of deformation, and who was tormented by personal as well as cultural demons, lapsed into general incoherence and then into the silence of deranged mental powers.

An astute foreign observer had been taking note of these developments. "I have been reading the life of Thomas Carlyle," he writes,

> this unconscious and involuntary farce ... Carlyle: a man of strong
> words and attitudes ... constantly lured by the craving for a strong
> faith and the feeling of his incapacity for it ... The craving for a
> strong faith is no proof of a strong faith, but quite the contrary. If
> one has such a faith, then one can afford the beautiful luxury of

skepticism ... [In Carlyle there is] a constant passionate dishonesty against himself ... that is his *proprium*; in this respect he is and remains interesting. Of course, in England he is admired precisely for his honesty ... At bottom, Carlyle is an English atheist who makes it a point of honor not to be one.

The foreign observer continues his observations about his Victorian contemporaries:

> They are rid of the Christian God and now believe all the more firmly that they must cling to Christian morality. That is an English consistency ... In England one must rehabilitate oneself after every little emancipation from theology by showing in a veritably awe-inspiring manner what a moral fanatic one is. That is the penance they pay.
>
> We others hold otherwise. When one gives up the Christian faith, one pulls the right to Christian morality out from under one's feet. This morality is by no means self-evident ... Christianity is a system ... By breaking one main concept out of it, the faith in God, one breaks the whole: nothing necessary remains in one's hands ...
>
> When the English actually believe that they know "intuitively" what is good and evil, when they therefore suppose that they no longer require Christianity as the guarantee of morality, we merely witness the *effects* of dominion of the Christian value judgment and an expression of the strength and depth of this dominion ... For the English, morality is not yet a problem.

The inimitable ferocity, superiority, and hyperbole of tone and statement belong, of course, to Nietzsche, and the passages I have just cited come from *The Twilight of the Idols*, whose subtitle is *How one Philosophizes with a Hammer*. It was written in 1888, the last year of Nietzsche's sane life. In it Nietzsche is saying that the entire development that I have synoptically and inadequately recounted was misconceived, misbegotten, and corrupted from the very beginning; that the entire Victorian effort to find other and alternate centers of authority and value when the one supreme transcendant value had absconded was cowardly and farcical. What he, even in his genius, fails to see is that this very effort constitutes part of the abiding interest and value (as well as the limitations) of the central Victorian figures.

What he fails to see as well is the socio-cultural element, the element of class, in these intellectual goings-on. For all of these creative-critical figures were individual members of the middle class or bourgeoisie who addressed that class from *within* its social and cultural order. If their careers and writings embodied the cross-purposes of that order and the strains of what it was like to be an individual within it, those writings were also directed towards their fellow-members of the middle class. Such works were as often as not fiercely critical of the audience they were written for, and one of the singular circumstances in all of this is that these writings were actually read; they were attended to, responded to, they even may be said to have exerted an influence on the middle-class readers who were the object of their critical intentions.

What Nietzsche also fails to see is that other developments were going on. These developments represent two distinct and coherent branchings out from the mainstream of critical discourse that we have been tracing out. The first of these is to be found in the life and work of William Morris. Morris begins as a disciple of Carlyle, Ruskin, and Arnold. He starts out as a Pre-Raphaelite, moves on to restore ancient buildings, founds the Kelmscott Press, designs books, cloth and furniture of pre-industrial integrity, and becomes a leader in the effort to design a new style of civilized individual life within a vulgarized, ugly, and industrialized capitalist world. But he also does something else; he becomes a socialist, reads Marx, and goes on to become a revolutionary Communist. This succession, integral and consequent as it is, represents the first structural break in the discussion, the first stepping outside the boundaries in which the discourse had been contained. It represented a new conception of the relation of classes, offered a new group of notions of what an individual person within society might be or become, and above all held out the hope, to be realized in the revolutionary future, of a recaptured transcendance, a redeemed humanity, and an impeccable moral authority external to ourselves here on earth.

The second development had occurred some years before, and was incidentally connected with the first. In 1868 there appeared in the *Westminster Review* a review-essay of three volumes of William Morris's early poetry. It divided itself into two parts – the first was an intelligent appraisal of the works under discussion; the second was a kind of tacked-on conclusion, which does not really derive from what has come before. I should like now to quote some extended passages from that concluding section of the review.

> To regard all things and principles of things as inconstant modes or fashions has more and more become the tendency of modern thought. Let us begin with that which is without, – our physical life. Fix upon it in one of its more exquisite intervals – the moment, for instance, of delicious recoil from the flood of water in summer

heat. What is the whole physical life in that moment but a combination of natural elements to which science gives their names? ... Our physical life is a perpetual motion of them – the passage of the blood, the wasting and repairing of the lenses of the eye, the modification of the tissues of the brain by every ray of light and sound – processes which science reduces to simpler and more elementary forces. Like the elements of which we are composed, the action of these forces extends beyond us; it rusts iron and ripens corn. Far out on every side of us these elements are broadcast, driven by many forces; and birth and gesture and death and the springing of violets from the grave are but a few out of ten thousand resulting combinations. That clear, perpetual outline of face and limb is but an image of ours under which we group them – a design in a web the actual threads of which pass out beyond it. This at least of flame-like our life has, that it is but the concurrence renewed from moment to moment of forces parting sooner or later on their ways.

Or if we begin with the inward world of thought and feeling, the whirlpool is still more rapid, the flame more eager and devouring ... At first sight experience seems to bury us under a flood of external objects, pressing upon us with a sharp, importunate reality, calling us out of ourselves in a thousand forms of action. But when reflection begins to act upon those objects they are dissipated under its influence, the cohesive force is suspended like a trick of magic, each object is loosed into a group of impressions, colour, odour, texture, in the mind of the observer. And if we continue to dwell on this world, not of objects in the solidity with which language invests them, but of impressions unstable, flickering, inconsistent, which burn, and are extinguished with our consciousness of them, it contracts still further, the whole scope of observation is dwarfed to the narrow chamber of the individual mind. Experience, already reduced to a swarm of impressions, is ringed round for each one of us by that thick wall of personality through which no real voice has ever pierced on its way to us, or from us to that, which we can only conjecture to be without. Every one of those impressions is the impression of an individual in his isolation, each mind keeping as a solitary prisoner its own dream of a world.

Analysis goes a step further still, and tells us that those impressions of the individual to which, for each one of us, experience dwindles down, are in perpetual flight; that each of them is limited by time, and that as time is infinitely divisible, each of them is infinitely divisible also, all that is actual in it being a single moment, gone while we try to apprehend it, of which it may ever be more truly said that it has ceased to be than that it is. To such a tremulous wisp constantly reforming itself on the stream, to a single sharp impression, with a sense in it, a relic more or less fleeting, of such moments gone by, what is real in our life fines itself down. It is with the movement, the passage and dissolution of impressions, images, sensations, that analysis leaves off, that continual vanishing away, that strange perpetual weaving and unweaving of ourselves.

Such thoughts seem desolate at first; at times all the bitterness of life seems concentrated in them. They bring the image of one washed out beyond the bar in a sea at ebb, losing even his personality, as the elements of which he is composed pass into new combinations. Struggling, as he must, to save himself, it is himself that he loses at every moment. . . .

The service of philosophy, and of religion and culture as well, to the human spirit, is to startle it into a sharp and eager observation. Every moment some form grows perfect in hand or face; some tone on the hills or sea is choicer than the rest; some mood of passion or insight or intellectual excitement is irresistibly real and attractive for us for that moment only. Not the fruit of experience but experience itself is the end. A counted number of pulses only is given to us of a variegated, dramatic life. How may we see in them all that is to be seen in them by the finest senses?

How can we pass most swiftly from point to point, and be present always at the focus where the greatest number of vital forces unite in their purest energy?

To burn always with this hard gem-like flame, to maintain this ecstasy, is success in life. Failure is to form habits; for habit is relative to a stereotyped world; meantime it is only the roughness of the eye that makes any two things, persons, situations – seem alike. While all melts under our feet, we may well catch at any exquisite passion, or any contribution to knowledge that seems by a lifted horizon to set the spirit free for a moment, or any stirring of the sense, strange dyes, strange flowers and curious odours, or work of the artist's hands, or the face of one's friend. Not to discriminate every moment some passionate attitude in those about us and in the brilliance of their gifts some tragic dividing of forces on their ways, is on this short day of frost and sun to sleep before evening. With this sense of the splendour of our experience and of its awful brevity, gathering all we are into one desperate effort to see and touch, we shall hardly have time to make theories about the things we see and touch. What we have to do is to be for ever curiously testing opinion and courting new impressions, never acquiescing in a facile orthodoxy of Comte or of Hegel or of our own. ... The theory or idea or system which requires of us the sacrifice of any part of this experience, in consideration of some interest into which we cannot enter, or some abstract morality we have not identified with ourselves, or what is only conventional, has no real claim upon us. ...

Well, we are all *condamnés*, as Victor Hugo somewhere says: we have an interval and then we cease to be. Some spend this interval in listlessness, some in high passions, the wisest in art and song. For our one chance is in expanding that interval, in getting as many pulsations as possible into the given time. High passions give one this quickened sense of life, ecstasy and sorrow of love, political or religious enthusiasm, or the "enthusiasm of humanity." Only, be sure it is passion, that it does yield you this fruit of a quickened, multiplied consciousness. Of this wisdom, the poetic passion, the desire of beauty, the love of art for art's sake, has most; for art comes to you professing frankly to give nothing but the highest quality to your moments as they pass, and simply for those moments' sake.

These passages, with omissions, were reprinted in 1873 as the Conclusion to Pater's *The Renaissance: Studies in Art and Poetry*. Pater was, I should hasten to say, a disciple of Arnold and Ruskin. He also, it seems, did not quite realize what he had written, and as a result of the clamor these pages aroused, he dropped the section from the second (1877) edition of the work because as he said, "it might possibly mislead some of those young men into whose hands it might fall." And when he did restore the Conclusion in later editions, he progressively modified its wording so that its force was diluted and weakened. In any event, and nevertheless, the cat had been let out of the bag, and we can appropriately regard these pages as a, if not the, specimen text of modernism. The physical universe, modern science has revealed, is nothing but forces and elements in a state of flux, of combination and decomposition. Our mental existence fines down to no more than a succession of discrete, evanescent impressions. Individual identity is unstable; communication with others is an impossible illusion. And all effort and activity are without point or meaning except as they lead to sensations that are intensely pleasurable. There is no transcendence; there is nothing above or beyond us; the above or beyond have become identical with the indubitable nothing that is beneath us and upon whose edge we stand. Conventional morality, with its demands for constancy, habit, and stability, are failure and death, as is any other idea or system that requires us to sacrifice or renounce some new intensity of experience. Experience itself is the end, and there is nothing beyond it. Self-realization consists in "getting as many pulsations as possible" into the time alloted to us. If Morris's career eventuates in a break with the tradition of discourse we have been describing, Pater's statement represents its collapse upon itself and its inner evacuation.

Pater's chief inevitable disciple took this program and dramatized it in his exemplary life which culminated in exemplary disaster. In the aesthetic and decadent movements of the late 1880s and 1890s, non-conformity to middle-class expectations became fashionable, and repudiation from within of the dominant character-type became a public project. These movements were overtly anti-bourgeois, anti-philistine, anti-materialistic. They were explicitly based on snobbery and on the aping of aristocratic exclusiveness. They cultivated refinement of sensibility, floridity of individual expressiveness, and autonomy of self that chiefly appeared as insolence towards others and a worship of youth in both its beauty and its ignorance. They were explicitly narcissistic and almost explicitly homosexual. In their dandyism they were treating their physical selves as if they were works of art. In the prophetic and transitional figure of Oscar Wilde these tendencies, these early forays into the outskirts and badlands of modernity, come to a focus. As for Wilde, it may be said that almost nothing about him is memorable except himself. What one recalls is the effect of wit and paradox, the effort through ridicule to explode fire-crackers along the lines of contradiction in middle-class character and social life. Yet whenever one returns to his writing one finds there matters that one had overlooked or forgotten. Here are two passages from "The Critic as Artist."

> What is termed Sin is an essential element of progress. Without it the world would stagnate, or grow old, or become colorless. By its curiosity Sin increases the experience of the race. Through its intensified assertion of individualism, it saves us from monotony of type. In its rejection of the current notions of morality, it is one with the higher ethics ...

And again:

> The mere existence of conscience, that faculty of which people prate so much nowadays, and are so ignorantly proud, is a sign of our imperfect development. It must be merged in instinct before we become fine. Self-denial is simply a method by which man arrests his progress, and self-sacrifice a survival of the mutilation of the savage, part of that old worship of pain which is so terrible a factor in the history of the world.

Pater and Nietzsche, we see, have here joined forces. As they do in Wilde's repeated assertion that "the sphere of art and the sphere of ethics are absolutely distinct and separate." His flawed but important work *The Picture of Dorian Gray* is, of course, central to any discussion of the development we have been outlining. Dorian Gray undertakes to treat himself as a work of art – to make his life into a work of art. In the preceding historical period of Western culture, Faust made a pact with the Devil: he would sell his soul for transcendant knowledge and power. Dorian Gray's implicit pact is that he will sell his soul for eternal youth. What we see here in the domain of cultural discourse is, it seems to me, a process of devolution: from a powerful fantasy in which the autonomous ego is invested with demonic powers, to a fantasy in which autonomy is imagined beneath the sign of a narcissistic investment. But there is more to it than this. Wilde wrote of Dorian that he is "haunted all through his life by an exaggerated sense of conscience which mars his pleasures for him and warns him that youth and enjoyment are not everything in the world. It is finally to get rid of the conscience that dogged his steps from year to year that he destroys the picture; and thus in his attempt to kill conscience Dorian Gray kills himself." Wilde seems to imply that this outcome was an unfortunate accident and that in someone more happily endowed the killing of conscience might not have entailed the larger fatality. In the light of both cultural and clinical evidence, that implied assertion by Wilde seems very doubtful indeed.

It certainly was not true for Wilde, for as we now understand, he undertook unconsciously to destroy himself, largely out of feelings of guilt – and in this sense too, we can perceive him as a transitional figure. At his first trial Wilde was questioned by his old schoolmate, Edward Carson, who was counsel for the Marquess of Queensbury.

Carson: 'Is it good for the young?'

Wilde: 'Anything is good that stimulates thought in whatever age.'

Carson: 'Whether moral or immoral?'

Wilde: 'There is no such thing as morality or immorality in thought. There is immoral emotion.'

Carson: '"Pleasure is the only thing one should live for"?'

Wilde: 'I think that the realization of oneself is the prime aim of life, and to realize oneself through pleasure is finer than to do so through pain. I am, on that point, entirely on the side of the ancients – the Greeks. It is a pagan idea.'

Carson: '"A truth ceases to be true when more than one person believes in it"?'

Wilde: 'Perfectly. That would be my metaphysical definition of truth; something so personal that the same truth could never be appreciated by two minds.'

And after his release from prison, Wilde remarked in answer to a question put to him by André Gide: "Would you like to know the great drama of my life? It is that I have put my genius into my life – I have only put my talent into my work." We have arrived at the point at which Thomas Carlyle has been stood on his head; and indeed Wilde's forward-looking statements amount to an inversion of the values through which bourgeois society and culture, in the historical period under discussion, represented itself to itself, in its notions of what makes up an individual.

I propose to bring these incomplete remarks to an end. What I have been trying to demonstrate is that there occurs across a seventy-year period in English literature and culture a coherent discourse at the very highest pitch of consciousness among the most acute minds of the dominant culture. This discourse in all its ramifications amounts in uncanny ways to a prefiguration in thought and culture of what in the last thirty years or so we have begun to see being acted out in the lives of large numbers of individuals in advanced or late capitalist society and certain institutions peculiar to it. I do not know whether there are lessons to be learned here; and I do not believe that what we know historically enables us to predict what will happen next. I do think, however, that this consultation of part of the history of our culture helps clarify for us how we have come to be where we are, where we came from, and to what indeed we are not returning.

Notes

1   As it became a fundamental theoretical principle for one of the very latest of the last Victorian writers, George Orwell. In an essay on Arthur Koestler, written in the 1940s, Orwell remarks, "Few thinking people now believe in life after death. ... The real problem is how to restore the religious attitude while accepting death as final. Men can only be happy when they do not assume that the object of life is happiness."

2   For Ruskin, political economy was close to the heart of the matter, and he regarded political economy as he regarded such activities as "alchemy, astrology, witchcraft, and other popular creeds." It has "a plausible idea at the root of it." He then has a fictitious but typical political economist utter the following: "The social affections ... are accidental and disturbing elements in human nature; but avarice and the desire of progress are constant elements. Let us eliminate the inconstants, and, considering the human being merely as a covetous machine, examine by what laws of labour, purchase, and sale, the greatest accumulative result in wealth is obtainable."

What is notable in such a passage is the assumption of a culturally accepted and overt collocation between the impulses of self-seeking and the impulses towards progress and the further assumption that these are inborn or constant elements in human nature.

7 Freud and Biography

I   Freud and the Biographers

In 1936, on the occasion of Freud's eightieth birthday, Arnold Zweig sent a letter to the great old man in honor of the event. In addition to being a writer of some parts, Zweig was an ardent believer in Freud and his teachings, and an analytic patient of longstanding seniority. In the course of his celebration of Freud's achievements, Zweig remarked that he was toying "constantly with the idea of writing your biography – if you would permit me." Freud promptly replied that he was "alarmed by the threat that you want to become my biographer." There are so many better and more important things for Zweig to do and to write about, he continued:

> no, I am far too fond of you to permit such a thing. Anyone who writes a biography is committed to lies, concealments, hypocrisy, flattery and even to hiding his own lack of understanding, for biographical truth does not exist, and if it did we could not use it.
> Truth is unobtainable, mankind does not deserve it, and in any case is not our Prince Hamlet right when he asks who would escape whipping were he used after his desert?

These hyperbolically sour remarks merit thinking about. The problematics of biography, even in these advanced times, remain as unresolved as ever. And the problematics of the biographies of great men, the makers of history, the shakers and movers, the culture heroes and captains of destiny lead the way, as they have always done, in difficulties, hazards, ambushes, and traps for the unwary and the wary as well. As a rule, the great have been idealized by their followers and contemporaries. In the name of truth and reality they are subsequently, again as a rule, de-idealized. The great now seem less than great and their followers seem absurd. Something's wrong here. It has now become the turn of the de-idealization to be seen as excessive and sometimes false and hence to be itself undone. And so it goes. The great by their self-generated words and autonomous deeds have changed the course of history; every great man is the result of a convergence of cultural-historical forces and an expression of them. Who's on first, what's on second, and both have to be true. X was thought of in his own time as a greatly original mind. Generation II of scholars begins to learn that X was in fact "anticipated" in his greatly original achievements by Y, Z, A and B, pygmies of talent to a man. X is as a

consequence dissolved back into these "anticipations." His achievement it is now understood was to assemble the original work of others
and present it to the world at the right moment in culturally
appropriate and marketable form. A salesman, a promoter, not a
genius. Generation III comes along and surveys this mess of
mediocrities and leveled-down indistinction. It's not kosher; it
doesn't smell right; it looks lousy. They begin to re-examine the
anticipations and discover that not all anticipations anticipate and
some anticipate less than others. It turns out that all the minor poets
who "anticipated" Shakespeare and to whose example he owed so
much – it turns out that when they are all put together they don't add
up to a comedy of errors. It turns out that Plato is not really a
forerunner of either socialism or Adolf Hitler. Every hero has a valet
and most have a mistress. Valets and mistresses tend to have an
inflated taste for memoirs and faithful recollections of the great man
undressed. He's got a pot and wears a girdle; he scratches himself,
picks his nose and farts; he can only get it up when she wears a red wig
and makes believe she's his aunt Sadie. He weeps when he suffers a
loss. He broods over reversals. He would rather have been Jimmy
Durante than the Napoleon of theoretical physics that he is. He is the
father of his nation, but what he is really proud of is his skill at
rotation pool. All of these are true. All of them matter and don't
matter. All must be made part of the record, taken due account of,
assimilated, and appropriately discounted. And there's no end to it.
Ever.

These embroilments are part of our normal biographical
transactions with the great. The idealizings and de-idealizings are
steady elements in the continually shifting cultural weather. In this
sense even such nastinesses as Lytton Strachey have a certain value. By
exposing certain falsenesses, pretensions, and inconsistencies among
the Victorians, he and others like him forced a later generation to
begin to rediscover how truly eminent the eminent Victorians were.
The accent and tone of the recovered eminence were in the nature of
things not what they were originally asserted to be. How could they
be? But that's one of the processes through which new cultural
meanings are created. The publication of Gladstone's diaries, for
example, revealed that he was not simply a hypocrite when he
brought prostitutes home for tea and tried to reform them. They
reveal instead the terrible temptations he was tormented by, how he
struggled against them, how he punished himself for them, how he
tried in fact to live up to the impossible moral ideals and demands of
his culture and what an immense toll that effort exacted.

The life and biography of Freud represent a peculiarly acute and
perhaps unique instance of these difficulties. When it comes to him it

is not simply a matter of idealizing, de-idealizing, and then the correction of both again, although such considerations doubtless enter into our dealings with this figure. Freud created psychoanalysis, and part of that creation was the institutionalized development of a new kind of relation. It is known as transference. Freud began the work of psychoanalyzing Western culture, and he has become such a personage in that culture that almost everyone who has come into touch with his work experiences some kind of a transference relation to him. It seems to be a curiosity in the nature of this relation that it cannot be put aside, transcended, or eliminated. It is on the contrary a constitutive part of one's relation to Freud in culture, and perhaps the best means we have of dealing with it is by conscious recognition and acknowledgement that this is indeed the case. It cannot – at least for the foreseeable future – be made to disappear.

That there was much in Freud that positively promoted such a development is abundantly clear. For example, quite early in Zweig's correspondence with him, Zweig takes to opening his letters with the salutation, "Dear Father Freud." There is no evidence at my disposal which suggests that Freud ever responded with some German equivalent of "Hey, cut it out." To be sure, there were certain limits that even Freud could not help but observe. When Zweig responds to the report of a new flare-up of Freud's cancer by stating that part of Freud's endurance of his suffering is done for mankind – since his continued existence allows him to go on thinking and writing – the old man characteristically replies:

> I still have so much capacity for enjoyment that I am dissatisfied with the resignation that is forced upon me. It is a bitter winter here in Vienna and I have not been out for months. I also find it hard to adapt myself to the role of the hero suffering for mankind, which you so kindly assign me. My mood is bad, little pleases me, my self-criticism has grown much more acute. I would diagnose it as senile depression in anyone else.

The sinuosities of thought and feeling in such a passage – its dramatization of a highly complex, dry ironic consciousness – is for this reader a source of lasting pleasure. It nonetheless remains true that after a certain point in his life Freud's fundamental relation with the world was that of a transference. The primary role which he envisaged for himself was that of a father, or of some variation upon paternity. He was a paterfamilias at home; he regarded his followers as sons and grandsons, heirs and assignees. Those who broke away, in whom the transference became negative, were regarded as either disloyal sons or sons who could not fulfill (or put up with) their sonship. And the psychoanalytic movement itself was of course his essential child, his special creation.

It should therefore come as a surprise to no one that Ernest Jones's three-volume biography, *The Life and Work of Sigmund Freud*, should contain within it considerable evidence of transference. It was in the first place an official biography. And Jones himself was one of Freud's early and most loyal disciples and lieutenants. Despite its immense length, it had to be selective. Its monumental wake left behind a mass of detritus and debris. Moreover, in the interval since it was written new material has come to light. There is every reason then for a book like Paul Roazen's *Freud and His Followers*[1] to be published. Roazen's method has been to poke around in what was left behind and left out. He interviewed more than 100 people who either knew Freud personally or had some connection with or interest in the history, particularly the early history, of the psychoanalytic movement. He also gained access to Ernest Jones's papers, an archive of information in themselves. Some of the material that he has found – to which I shall turn in a moment – is of a certain pertinence.

In addition to this, however, anyone who is interested in Freud can not have felt comfortable with the manner in which those who have control over the biographical material left behind by Freud have been discharging some of their responsibilities. Until recently, the volumes of Freud's correspondence that have been published have been edited in a style that has to be described, to put it mildly, as defensive. When one has taken all questions of tact and discretion into account, there is still no way to support or condone the editorial practices that have been pursued in the various volumes of Freud's correspondence that have been published during the last twenty-odd years. Freud's letters have been bowdlerized; incomplete sets of correspondence have been put out; letters have been cut without marks of omission; sometimes when an omission has been noted, it is utterly impossible to know what principle of deletion has been followed; and sometimes (as in the important Freud-Abraham correspondence) it is impossible to make out whether any principle has been followed at all. This kind of editorial hanky-panky is altogether out of keeping with the spirit of Freud himself and with the idea of psychoanalysis, not to speak of such minor considerations as scientific and scholarly integrity. It was an absurdity and a vanity on the part of Freud (great men are entitled to both) to object to the idea of a biography of himself. It was worse when those in charge of his estate – once the Jones biography had been decided upon – started putting out volumes of laundered letters. Incidentally, one has to add, the analytic profession has not exactly covered itself with glory by its muted response to these circumstances. Only with the publication of the Freud–Jung letters in 1974 has a Freud correspondence in its integrity appeared.

What has Roazen turned up, and what do his findings amount to? On balance, and a little to my surprise, Jones stands up remarkably well. All transferences to the contrary notwithstanding, Roazen is able to make very little headway against him. He makes a few minor corrections here and there. (Jones's single major lapse, his unbalanced and misleading account of Ferenczi's last years, had been brought to public attention years ago.) And some omissions of varying degrees of importance are made good on. Roazen is quite useful in reminding us how unorthodox Freud's own practices could often be (sometimes during the summer he would have a patient stay in the same house with him), and how other analysts who knew of this could at the same time claim that such procedures, when carried out by others, were "unanalytic" in character. Moreover, what for Freud "might have been temporary or ad hoc measures became, in the hands of some devoted followers, unchangeable rituals." The orthodoxy seems to have been strongest among Americans.

Every movement of any significance brings about rivalries among its adherents. Psychoanalysis is no exception to this rule, and Roazen gives something that resembles a blow by blow account of the infighting and elbowing for place among Freud's followers. Some of these differences have meaning for the history of the movement; others are more in the way of idle gossip and chatter and do not deserve to be dwelled upon. And about the same thing holds true of the irregularity of the sexual lives and habits of the early generation of analysts. The amusing story of how it was Jung and not Freud who was awarded an honorary degree at Harvard's tercentenary celebrations deserves preservation. As does the anecdote of how on this same occasion Jung was introduced to a large audience in the amphitheatre of the Massachusetts General Hospital as "Dr Freud." It is also of interest to learn again and in some detail about Freud's undertaking to psychoanalyze his own daughter, Anna. But exactly what one is to make of this extraordinary historical oddity is something else again.

No movement can escape scandals, skeletons in the closet, secretly buried bodies, episodes and incidents in which almost no one emerges creditably. Roazen has unearthed two such incidents of some significance. The first has to do with Ruth Mack Brunswick, an American who became one of Freud's special favorites. Acting with characteristic originality, Freud had at one time Brunswick, her prospective husband and the husband's brother simultaneously in analysis with him. Brunswick lived almost exclusively in Vienna between 1922 and 1938. One particular sign of how highly she stood in Freud's regard was that he referred his famous former patient, the Wolf Man, to her. Brunswick was not, however, in good health. She suffered from a variety of ailments, some of which involved severe pain. She began to prescribe pain killers and sleeping pills for herself, and by the mid-1930s had become an addict. (She appears also to have been addicted to Freud, since she was, with some interruptions, in analysis with him from 1922 to 1938.) She returned to America where she practiced until her death at the age of 49 in 1946.

The scandal is that despite her addiction Freud continued to send her patients, and so did other analysts afterwards. Someone seems to have told Roazen that "apparently there was no overt decline in her ability to analyze until almost the end." Roazen is ordinarily skeptical and often suspicious, but this time he seems to have been taken in. In the first place, the assertion on the face of it is hardly credible. And in the second, I happen to know someone who was a patient of Brunswick's beginning in 1940. This former patient, who was then a young woman of 35, reports that Brunswick's behavior was frequently and notably aberrant. Often she would nod off in the middle of a session; on a number of occasions she conducted lengthy telephone conversations during the hour, sometimes ordering things for her household from department stores. The patient, who naturally had no way of knowing that the analyst seated behind the couch was a drug addict, would now and then summon up the courage hesitantly to ask Brunswick why she was behaving in these ways. The usual answer was the patented foolproof analytic trap. The question was turned back upon the patient, who was asked to explain why she was so anxious. In other words, Brunswick's behavior was transformed into the patient's problem. Part of the power of the classical analytic situation is that nothing that occurs within it is irrelevant to what is going on within the patient. This is one reason for the general rule of analytic abstinence, and one reason why standards for analytic candidates ought to be stringent. Misused as it was here it becomes an instrument for dissimulation and harm.

The larger scandal of this situation, however, touches upon Brunswick's analytic colleagues. They knew about her unfortunate addiction. They were in a position to blow the whistle and effectively shut her down by referring no other patients to her. They did not. Why they did not, and what and whether it had anything to do with her special relation to Freud, remains unknown. But that they behaved with professional irresponsibility seems quite beyond doubt.

The second scandal was brought to light by Roazen in 1969 when he published *Brother Animal*, which was in effect a first installment of *Freud and His Followers*. This work was an account of Victor Tausk's short and tragic life, and it was in addition an ominous sign of things to come. Tausk was a gifted and troubled man who after trying several different careers decided to become a medical doctor, psychiatrist and psychoanalyst. He enlisted himself as a disciple of Freud's, and moved to Vienna. He and Lou Andreas-Salomé were lovers for about a year. After serving in World War I, Tausk returned to Vienna and tried to enter into analysis with Freud. His request was refused – Freud was not comfortable with certain kinds of disturbed people. Instead Freud recommended that Tausk enter analysis with Helene Deutsch who was herself being analyzed by Freud. This arrangement soon became unworkable, and Tausk (who talked about almost nothing but Freud during his own sessions) began to interfere with Deutsch's own analysis with Freud. After three months Freud intervened. He told Deutsch that she had to terminate one of these relations. Deutsch chose to stay with Freud. Tausk then decided to marry (he had been married and divorced before), and chose a former patient of his own. Three months after the termination of his analysis, and on the day before he was to obtain his marriage license, he committed suicide.

These are the essential facts of the episode. Although it would not be precise to say that the psychoanalytic profession performed a cover-up of the case, it is also quite undeniably true that the profession didn't present it as a glowing incident in the history of the movement. Roazen dug around and put all the facts together. What he did with those facts is something else again, and *Brother Animal*, like *Freud and His Followers*, is both an interesting and an awful book. Sometimes Roazen literally invents things. For example, he writes that Freud "was jealous of Tausk's opportunity to have an affair with Lou." There is simply no evidence to justify such a statement. Whatever evidence there is points in the opposite direction. Years later Freud wrote that he had admired Lou immensely and had been attached to her "curiously enough without a trace of sexual attraction." (see Jones, *Life and Work of Sigmund Freud*, Vol.3, p. 213 for sources.) Roazen says things about Lou which are palpably untrue, magnifies Tausk into being a kind of genius (which he was not) and insinuates that Freud was really responsible for Tausk's suicide (which he was not). Here, in a typical sentence from *Freud and His Followers*, is the way Roazen represents the relation between the two. "Each man believed he was unique and a genius and feared being destroyed by the other." The only thing that's wrong with this sentence is that nothing in it is to the point. Whatever each may have believed, only one of them was unique and a genius; and whatever each may have feared, neither of them destroyed or could destroy the other.

Roazen's disingenuous dealings in *Brother Animal* were enough to give one the pip, and that's exactly what they gave to K. R. Eissler, who in 1971 published *Talent and Genius* in an effort to annihilate Roazen. Eissler's work of demolition was effective enough, but in the end it amounted to overkill. It was in *Brother Animal* that the circumstance of Freud's having analyzed his own daughter was first made known to a general audience. In his response to this part of Roazen's account, Eissler first states that it was widely known all along (which it was not), but then goes on to argue that if Freud decided to undertake this deviation in clinical practice then he had to be right. This is truly putting the wrong shoe on the wrong foot. As I've said earlier, one doesn't really know how to regard this piece of Freud's behavior. As I contemplate it, I find myself being struck with sentiments of dismay alloyed with some kind of horror; but along with this puzzlement and disapproval I feel a touch of jealous admiration for the audacity and *chutzpah* it involved. Freud was not beyond good and evil, but in this instance he gave it a good try.

Roazen's problem, as I've already implied, is that his ambivalence is generally out of control. One of the things Freud discovered is that there is almost no relation between human beings that is free of ambivalence. And certainly emotions of ambivalence occupy the center of the transference in a variety of both positive and negative forms. What typically happens with Roazen is that he regularly asserts that Freud is a genius, superman, and prophet while simultaneously representing him as the villain of the piece and a petty neurotic tyrant. In this sense *Freud and His Followers* picks up where *Brother Animal* left off. Now, however, Roazen has a second figure to dispose of and discredit. That figure is of course Ernest Jones. Recognizing the distinction of Jones's work on the one hand, he goes about his work of discreditation on the other as follows. In the opening pages of his first volume Jones speaks of the reluctance he felt at undertaking the huge task of the biography and then gives his reasons for having yielded to the suggestion that he nevertheless undertake it. Roazen writes that "Jones had been seeking this job for some years," and refers to a letter in the Jones archives written in 1946 by Jones to a publisher in which, according to Roazen, "he eagerly gave his qualifications as Freud's biographer." This permits Roazen to state that "in print Jones sounds reluctant," meaning that he wasn't, and the inference must inevitably be drawn that Jones was not telling the truth from the very outset and hence that what he says is suspect.

This is utterly typical of Roazen's way of going about things. Let us leave to one side the method of innuendo and the irrepressible ill will. Let us also accept the summary of the unquoted letter from the Jones archives. What is most striking about Roazen in this context is his psychoanalytical *naïveté*. It is apparently inconceivable to him that when faced with the daunting prospect of writing a life of Freud, Jones could have been ambivalent himself, that he could have badly wanted to do it and also not wanted to do it. (After all, Jones had written the classic psychoanalytical study of *Hamlet*.) Indeed one can in part understand some of Jones's idealizing remarks about Freud as an excessive response to the unconscious ambivalence he had to have *vis-à-vis* his own transference figure. But no, it's better to imply mendacity.

Roazen continues in similar style: "Despite what a reader of the biography might be led to think, Jones's own relation to Freud was relatively distant. Jones was first of all a Gentile, and Freud could be suspicious of non-Jews. ... Furthermore, Jones was in London and therefore an outsider to events in Vienna." I happen to have been a reader of Jones's biography, and what I was led to think was that Jones was one of Freud's earliest followers, the leader of the movement in England if not the English-speaking world, and a member of the original committee that was formed around Freud – after the upheavals caused by the breakings with Adler and Jung – whose members were commonly thought of as Freud's seconds-in-command. I have no way of knowing whether that is relatively close or relatively distant. There is, however, another bit of evidence that might be relevant. On the occasion of Jones's fiftieth birthday in 1929, Freud wrote him a letter which contains the following passage:

> I have always looked upon you as a member of my intimate family circle and will continue to do so, which points (beyond all disagreements that are rarely absent with a family and also have not been lacking between us) toward a fount of affection from which one can always draw again.

Is this to be read as one of Freud's Epistles to the Gentiles? Is the old man playing the Jewish Pecksniff of psychoanalysis again? (Was "always" *really* "always"?) I suppose it has to be regarded as some kind of achievement on the part of Roazen that he forces us repeatedly to commit this sort of nonsense in asking ourselves these questions.

One more example, and we are done with Jones. Roazen states that "Throughout [the biography] Jones wrote with a set of unconscious taboos." There's elegance! And he's right, absolutely right. Name one book in the history of civilization that was not written "with a set [sic] of unconscious [sic] taboos [sic]." That kind of formulation suggests again how inward Roazen is with psychoanalysis.

When Roazen moves on to Freud, things become, if possible, even worse. Sometimes he uses evidence with a nitwit's sense of significance. In a passage that discusses Freud's attitudes towards masturbation, Roazen writes that on certain occasions "Freud could seem emancipated from conventional pieties: the problem with masturbating, he is reported to have said, is that one must know how to do it well." This "report," we learn, is in a letter from Hitschmann to Jones in the Jones archives. Well, I for one couldn't care more or less if the letter was from Masters to Johnson in the Kinsey archives. What can such a statement, utterly decontextualized, mean? Its effect, however, is to make Freud seem as much a dunce as Roazen. Or there is this gem on Freud's father and his significance for history:

> In reality Jakob Freud was hardly the powerful man one might expect as the father of the discoverer of the Oedipus complex. ... The desire for a strong father may have played a role not only in Freud's formulation of the Oedipus complex but also in its acceptance by many who have been in a position parallel to Freud's, uneasy about their past and yet ashamed of repudiating it.

The slippery logic of this passage slides from an actual *discovery* to a motivated *formulation* to a compromised *acceptance* whose effect is to nullify the discovery announced at the outset. In addition, there is about as much psychological *sachel* in it as there is in a wooden Indian. Or as there is in this priceless remark about Freud's mother: "such a woman could well call forth from Freud the intense kind of emotions he would later call Oedipal." To which, one supposes, the appropriate reply might be, "I guess so. She actually seems to have been his mother."

Or there is this one: "With his family background, needing to create himself and be his own father, Freud wanted to be cared for and at the same time passionately desired to be independent." You bet. Unlike all the rest of us. Roazen's ability to reduce almost anything to platitude and twaddle is simply infallible. "Freud fostered the illusion," he writes, "that the more perfect an analyst's technique, the better the therapeutic results. An analyst can of course base his judgments only on what he sees, but the fact is that much clinical material looks different to different people." As for the first sentence, perhaps he did; and then again, perhaps not. As for the second, it is both true and feeble-minded at the same time. It was Dr Johnson who once remarked – of a poet whose work he cordially detested – that a man could write like this forever if he would but abandon his mind to it. Roazen's book amounts to a continual act of such abandonment.

Note

1   P. Roazen, *Freud and His Followers* (New York, 1975).

II Havelock Ellis: a Post-Freudian Biography of a Pre-Freudian Contemporary of Freud

Havelock Ellis is an exemplary figure in the momentous transition from Victorian culture to modernity. His life and work help us to understand in part how we have come to be what we are. Between 1897 and 1910 he published six volumes under the title *Studies in the Psychology of Sex* (a seventh supplementary volume came out belatedly in 1928). These works were the first relatively successful serious and scholarly effort in English to achieve the open-minded, liberal, tolerant, positive, and encouraging view of human sexual behavior in its many varieties that is essentially characteristic of the modern spirit. Born in 1859, Ellis represents both chronologically and in attitude a middle point between Thomas Hardy (*b*. 1840) and D. H. Lawrence (*b*. 1885) in the development of English (and Anglo-American) conscious moral culture. Ellis died in 1939. His dates, therefore, correspond almost exactly to those of Freud (1856–1939), that intellectual presence in the wider context of the evolution of modern Western civilization to whom he must inevitably be compared. For a number of quite clear reasons, Ellis compares badly, and he has been effectively eclipsed by the shadow cast by the ever-larger figure of Freud. Nevertheless, Ellis should not be forgotten. He is one of those writers in whose work the impulsions to move out of the historical past and into the light cast by science, reason, and the forces of the modern century were expressed most distinctly. Insofar as writers bear a certain responsibility for the changing climate of moral sensibility he may be assigned some genuine share for influencing the course taken by a number of our attitudes. In this valuable and fascinating biography,[1] Phyllis Grosskurth carefully demonstrates how Ellis's important work came about and suggests some of the things that it means.

Ellis's parents were an upstanding and respectable Victorian couple. His father was a merchant sea-captain, away from home for months at a time; his mother was an earnest, evangelically religious, and strong-willed woman, both slightly eccentric and entirely conventional. She was very serious and altogether literal-minded, characteristics which her son inherited – throughout his life, Ellis had no sense of humor at all and was chronically unable to appreciate it in others. From the very outset, the temperament with which he confronted the world was self-contained, intractable, reclusive, and remote. Although he was sent to school, he was like so many other outstanding individuals of his time and culture essentially an autodidact. A great reader, he was also a precocious taker of notes and keeper of notebooks. By the age of 10, he had acquired the nineteenth-century historical habit of memorializing everything: his notebooks were indexed and passages in them coordinated; whatever he read, saw and felt he treated as "data" to be compiled, sorted and set down in logical order. This "natural history method," as he described it, of accumulation and classification of material of every possible kind was the fundamental procedure he was to follow throughout his career. (He was, again characteristically, an equally prodigious writer of letters; in addition to his published correspondence, Professor Grosskurth estimates that she has read more than 20,000 letters written by Ellis.)

At school, Ellis was maltreated and miserable. The suffering that he endured, he wrote, had an "evil influence on my nervous system." At the age of 13 he began to experience "copious seminal emissions ... during sleep, once or twice a week, always without dreams or any sensations ... [which] continued whenever I was alone, for some thirty years." He was deeply bewildered by these events, since he was at the time, he reports, entirely innocent of any sexual thoughts. Yet he felt ashamed of and guilty about these emissions, and "constantly dreaded their occurrence and feared their detection." Utterly confused, ignorant and unhappy, he at the same time refused to admit that anything was bothering him or was amiss – a device of equivocation that he was to practice continually throughout his life. This defense, a kind of bland, pervasive denial, permitted him to exist with himself and to function.

In uncertain health, restless and wretched, Ellis was taken in hand at the age of 16 by his seafaring father. Captain Ellis transported his son to Australia and more or less simply deposited him there. For the next four years young Ellis was employed in a number of places as a schoolmaster. With the exception of those relations required by his pedagogical duties, he led a life of uninterrupted isolation; he occupied his solitary hours with constant reading and writing. Two other occurrences marked these years of growth and exile. Shortly after his arrival he decided one evening "to devote his life chiefly to an investigation of the problem of sex," but that project was to be pursued without succumbing to any tendencies towards what Ellis stereotypically called "morbid self-analysis" – he was permanently and successfully to resist all such impulses towards self-examination. He also experienced the loss of his religious beliefs and went through the spiritual crisis of deconversion that was as central and critical to the culture of the nineteenth century as the crisis of identity seems to be to the culture of our own era. He was delivered from his interior wasteland by the writings of one of that multitude of obscure messiahs who were left beached, as it were, along the seashore of nineteenth-century history, as the sea of faith retreated. James

Hinton was a physician and mystagogue who preached the incomprehensible revelation that man "is simply limitation of the divine spirit and can attain true life through unselfishness" (what this in fact turned out to mean, Ellis was only later to learn, was the practice of polygamy, in which man became an "artist in love" in order to "serve" women). His sense of purpose and integration with the universe reconstituted by the opaque claptrap of Hinton's *Life in Nature*, he also restored himself by reading Arnold, Herbert Spencer, and Pater and sailed back to England to make himself a career.

Ellis started out on his return as a medical student, but he devoted most of his energies in the decade of the 1880s to becoming a man of letters – a journalist, editor, literary critic, popularizer of science, and pundit-at-a-large on matters of public concern. He was by nature a rebel and a pioneer, and he joined with others of the time in London in trying to conceive of a larger personal and social life that might be guided by the ideals of empirical science, rationality, freedom of choice and experiment, decency of conduct without reference to a deity, socialism, goodness, truthfulness, and progress. Meetings at which Ibsen's *A Doll's House* was read alternated with meetings at which the future of communal organizations and sanitary reform were debated. Groups such as the Fellowship of the New Life would organize, split and give hatch to, on the one hand, crackpot grouplets that encouraged salvation through bizarre dietary regimens and the wearing of sandals, and, on the other, to such equally improbable circles as the Fabian Society. Ellis soon became a prominent advocate in print for a large number of these advanced causes. He was throughout his career an undeviating cultural radical.

The secret or trick that he shared with a number of his colleagues was the ability to write about threatening, disturbing, or less than respectable matters in the simplest, most disarming, and most apparently blameless way. This apostle to the Victorians, this virtuous adversary of the Philistines, believed that a new age of clarity and emancipation was about to dawn, that prudery and hypocrisy and double-dealing had finally had their day. Yet in order to get away in print with saying this, Ellis further cultivated his equivocating habit, as Professor Grosskurth pointedly observes, of "saying and un-saying the same thing," of putting forth a radical proposition and then at once retracting it in a qualifying remark, so that he could never be easily accused of taking a clearly defined or formulated position. At the same time high-minded talk and language had a way of consorting with less than high-minded motives and actions. Sex and spirituality kept getting confused with and mistaken for one another. Ellis and his friends talked nobly about relations that would transcend sexuality, and at the same time habitually sought out situations in which the sexuality they talked about transcending might be in some measure expressed.

Although Ellis was a natural cultural radical and strove continuously to be possessed of and to advocate the latest and most advanced views on just about anything, he was not personally a bohemian – he cannot even be said to have been genuinely adventurous. His own sexuality was too precariously secured to take such risks with it. His first sexual experiences of any adult account occurred when he was 25; they were part of the passionate friendship he formed with the South African writer Olive Schreiner, whose novel *The Story of an African Farm* is still intensely readable. Schreiner was fiercely determined to be what was thought of as the New Woman of the period; with great force of will she behaved sexually in an emancipated way and then with an equally great force of unconscious will tortured and tormented herself with guilt over her liberated conduct. Ellis was unwilling and/or unable to pay such heavy and exacting dues. He appears to have suffered from disturbances of potency all his life; he had difficulties in maintaining an erection, suffered from premature ejaculation, and it seems doubtful that he ever effected satisfactory coital union with a woman. He and Olive Schreiner caressed one another, practiced mutual masturbation when they were together and non-mutual masturbation when apart, and discussed their problems, habits, and feelings openly and at great length. It was Schreiner who first confessed to guilt and wretchedness as a result of their incompatibility and was impelled to move on – not that she ever found what she was seeking, and the remainder of her life was mostly suffering and extreme neurotic unhappiness. Ellis, who was by contrast impassive and recessive and not particularly passionate, found the relation adequate; at the same time he was certainly not devastated when Schreiner sought fulfillment elsewhere. Indeed they remained good friends for years thereafter; for another part of Ellis's peculiar, and perhaps fortunate, disposition is that he had almost no access to aggressiveness and anger; he bore no grudges and claimed, with pride, that he had never lost a friend.

He had need of all the sanguine temperament he could find to deal with his next affair with a woman. It was the most important relation of Ellis's life and had a profound effect on his intellectual career. In the late 1880s he became acquainted with Edith Lees. She too was in every sense a New Woman; she belonged to the appropriate advanced societies, gave lectures on approved radical topics, and contributed to a journal, founded by members of the Fellowship of the New Life, called *Seed-Time*. She and Ellis soon became close companions; they agreed that conventional marriage – the foundation upon which so much of the structure of Victorian life was based – had become an impossibility. At the same time both desired a permanent relationship. Edith wanted both security and complete freedom; it never becomes entirely clear what Ellis wanted. What was clear was that neither ever felt any passion for the other. Ellis described it in his high-minded way as "a union of affectionate comradeship, in which the specific emotions of sex had the smallest part." They aimed at a companionate marriage, in which both would spend time together and apart, and neither would give up separate living establishments or careers.

It was all very modern, as was the circumstance that Edith was a lesbian. Ellis knew this, but preferred to believe that it didn't matter. He seemed to be convinced that Edith's love for him would "rule out female rivals." In other words, the man who was to become the sage of sexuality in English got married knowing nothing and understanding less about sex. They also agreed that there were to be no children; instead each treated the other as a permanent baby, and they took turns at playing mother to one another. Within this relationship, which provided both connection and remoteness, Ellis could get on with the pursuit of his work, for which he required solitude. He believed that tenderness, talk, and understanding were enough to deal with whatever problems marriage might confront him with.

That belief was tested within a few months of their marriage when Ellis received, as if out of the blue, a letter from his wife telling him that she had contracted a passionate attachment to a woman. Ellis was shocked and surprised by this turn of events; somehow he had in his extraordinary ingenuousness not expected it. He was also hurt and aggrieved and felt betrayed by Edith. Yet true child of Victorian rationalism that he was, what he did not feel, what he never permitted himself to feel let alone express, was anger or outrage. He learned to accept with good nature this lover and the succession of passionate "friendships" that Edith was to develop during the course of the following decades. He also had to accept the fact that all his hifalutin and adolescent theorizings about marriage were so much eyewash. The marriage of Ellis and Edith, though it was real and enduring, was also a tragic failure. They needed each other, they supported each other (when they were together, which was rather less than half the time), but they did not find fulfillment in one another. And in due time Ellis learned to turn to other women and to find in them whatever sexual satisfaction he was capable of.

But this embroiled union had a further consequence, for it contributed to the decisive turn in Ellis's career as a writer. Reeling beneath the impact of his "discovery" of his wife's lesbian nature, and understanding nothing about homosexuality, Ellis decided to undertake an objective and "scientific" study of the subject. He was assisted in this resolve by John Addington Symonds, one of the leading English men of letters of the time, who was living in self-imposed permanent exile in Switzerland. Symonds's efforts to suppress his own homosexuality while he was still living in England had led him repeatedly to nervous collapse, and he was determined to try to affect public opinion on this matter, to mitigate some of the ferocious intolerance of British official attitudes towards homosexuality. He became Ellis's collaborator on the book; he supplied Ellis with the majority of the case histories that are central to it (while maintaining the polite fiction that they had been brought to his attention by an assortment of people largely unknown to him, when they in fact almost exclusively involved himself and his lovers), and he influenced Ellis's attitudes towards the impartiality and open-mindedness that they already tended to favor.

Finally published in 1897, *Sexual Inversion*, as the volume was called, appeared at a critical moment in the history of modern Anglo-American moral and cultural life. In 1885 the enactment of an especially punitive law had brought about the full criminalization in England of male homosexuality; Oscar Wilde was the most celebrated victim of this new act, and had just been released from prison when the volume came out. At the same time, never had the public prestige of science, medicine, and "reason" been higher, and Ellis's work purported to speak with the voice and the authority of all three. But it purported as well to speak with the voice of modernity, which is to say that although it regarded itself as advocating the values of openness, realism, and liberalism, it was regarded by the majority at the time as a deliberate incitement to vice, obscenity, degradation and degeneracy. It was indeed an apologia and a polemic. As Ellis himself wrote in a letter, "We want to obtain a sympathetic recognition for sexual inversion as a psychic abnormality which may be regarded as the highest ideal, and to clear away many vulgar errors – preparing the way, if possible, for a change in the law." In insisting that homosexuality was neither a disease nor a crime (although he did believe that it was congenital), Ellis was making revolutionary proposals. Yet he made these proposals in simple, straightforward, and decent language and with relative detachment.

The reasonability and balance of Ellis's perspective did nothing to prevent the appearance of *Sexual Inversion* from stirring up a storm. There was publicity in the form of newspaper stories, prosecution and the trial of someone who sold a copy of the volume, from all of which Ellis shrunk in fear and nervousness. After the uproar had subsided he returned to his reclusive existence, and by 1910 had completed those five other volumes of *Studies in the Psychology of Sex*, which are his best and most important works. In them Ellis continued to write as the evangel of sexual tolerance and freedom to the late Victorians. For example, after homosexuality, masturbation seemed to be the most distressing form of sexual behavior to Ellis's contemporaries; Ellis coined the neutral term "Auto-Erotism" for it, and went on to discuss the subject in his usual calm and measured way. He also was an early pioneer in his recognition of female sexuality and in his advocacy of women's right to a fulfilled sexual life. These studies helped considerably to promote the acceptance of sexuality as a topic for open and candid discussion. Written in a clear and graceful prose, they did as much as any works can be expected to do in denaturing, detoxifying, and defusing a subject that was at the time extremely sensitive and sometimes downright dangerous to discuss.

Ellis was a follower of Darwin and Spencer, a late-nineteenth-century amateur expert-on-things-in-general. His "method" was to accumulate bits of data, classify this material and then recite it descriptively back at the reader with quotation marks and long footnote-like citations. This procedure made in his mind for both scholarly sobriety and scientific reliability. In point of fact it often made for pedantic aridity and solemn foolishness. At the time he wrote the *Studies*, Ellis was a sexual innocent who had managed to remain, in Professor Grosskurth's words, "largely uncontaminated by experience." The credulousness with which he accepted some of the materials in his case histories as "facts" was equalled only by his lack of inwardness. His belief that public knowledge of sexuality was a social good has to be regarded within the qualifications created by his excessively simple notion of knowledge. In this, as in so much else, he forms a focused and instructive contrast to Freud. Ellis himself was acutely sensitive to the contrast and chafed beneath it. He resented the fact that Freud was accepted as the leading *conquistador* of the modern spirit, and he was puzzled by it as well. It is not too much to say that Ellis was unable to understand Freud at all. Freud's insights into human irrationality and his psychological and metapsychological grand conceptual schemes meant nothing to Ellis. And Freud's literary gifts – his metaphoric powers and immense expository skills – meant if possible even less. If a useful comparison to Ellis and his work is to be instituted, it is to Sir James Frazer and *The Golden Bough* that we should turn. Ellis was really an old-fashioned anthropologist of sexuality, a collector, compiler, and classifier of anecdotes, stories, accounts, and practices.

He was also the direct ancestor of Alfred Kinsey and his collaborators, and he is hence the spiritual ancestor of all those people who teach courses in sex education in our schools and courses in "human sexuality" in our colleges and universities. These activities have almost certainly been a source of good in the world. They persist as part of our legacy from the eighteenth and nineteenth centuries, part of the faith which our culture has inherited that there is nothing that cannot be rationally understood and thus taught and learned, and furthermore that there is almost nothing that cannot, if properly handled, be explained and taught to children. Our culture is probably incorrigible in this virtually dogmatic innocence, and indeed it is difficult to imagine our own existence if we try to subtract from it the conviction that it is really highly preferable to live in the light we continue to generate rather than in the darkness we have cast out and replaced.

After 1910 Ellis's important work was done. His international fame as a guru for humanity's perplexities continued to grow throughout the remainder of his long days. He learned to accommodate himself to his own sexual peculiarities – his particular quirk was a permanent fascination with women's urine – and in later life had a series of relations with women in which he found comfort, release, satisfaction, and contentment. Professor Grosskurth skillfully represents these experiences as rewards well-earned, and when one finishes her book with Ellis dead in 1939, one has a strongly renewed sense of what heroic efforts were involved in the passage of Western culture from the nineteenth century into modernity. Ellis was an important figure in this evolutionary transformation, and it is right that his work should not be forgotten.

Note

1   P. Grosskurth, *Havelock Ellis: a Biography* (New York, 1980).

III   Harry Stack Sullivan: a Non-Freudian Biography of a Post-Freudian, Pre-Freudian and Anti-Freudian American Psychiatrist

I

When Harry Stack Sullivan died in 1949, he was a powerful influence and controversial figure – not to say a notorious presence – in American psychiatry and in the intellectual disciplines of enquiry in the social sciences that psychiatry borders upon. At that time, the popular reputations of what were known as the Sullivanian, or interpersonal, schools of psychotherapy in New York and Washington, DC, were riding high in American intellectual and academic culture. According to what was then the current conventional wisdom, those schools brought together a number of praiseworthy attributes. They combined, for example, a healthy eclecticism, or pluralism, in matters of theory and therapeutic strategies, with an equally salutary hospitality to the latest findings of the new social sciencies. They were also anti-Freudian in particularly salient ways: in addition to being opposed to the orthodoxy and hierarchy of the Freudian psychoanalytic establishments in the major American metropolitan centers, they were also anti-Freudian in their refusal to accept the prepotent importance attributed by Freud and his followers to infancy and childhood experience, and in particular to the experiences of sexuality during the early years of life and even later on. They tended, instead, to stress one's current situation in life as the central point of focus in therapeutic sessions. Moreover, in sharp contrast to Freud's archaic insistence upon biology and the influence of quasi-biological and perhaps mythical forces – such as instinctual drives – upon one's personal fate, the Sullivanians were in the forefront of those who pointed to the overwhelming power of the encompassing society or culture on the life of each of us. These "culturalists" were exceptionally open to the latest data then being accumulated by such rapidly growing disciplines as anthropology, sociology, and political science, and hence they became partners in developing applications of the most up-to-the-minute forms of data-intensive and empirical scientific formulations to modern human-kind. What these formulations uniformly tended towards was an intensified awareness of the far-reaching powers of society, culture, the surrounding world – or as the dominant lingo reiterated, with what now appears to be clock-like regularity, "the environment" – over the lives of all of us. Those influences were by and large baleful, and however much our courses of personal therapy might adapt us to or free us from the deformations of "interpersonal relationships" in which we had for the most part all been trapped, it was the social world as a whole that was in chief measure reponsible for our indubitable miseries. That world was, it was often said, "sick," and the Sullivanians and their associates at large in psychiatry and allied fields tended to think of themselves as therapists of and ministers to a "sick society." In other words, their views were in general indistinguishable from the liberal orthodoxy of the time – and, *mutatis mutandis*, they are the forebears of the liberal or quasi-radical orthodoxy of the present.

Yet what such a conspectus reveals is how little of Harry Stack Sullivan there survives in public consciousness today; there remains his name, without very much attaching to it. At the same time many of his attitudes, techniques and points of view have been almost entirely assimilated to current American psychiatry in its psycho-therapeutic modes, but they are no longer specifically identified with Sullivan's career and achievements. They float about in that murky, ahistorical limbo which has long since been recognized as the natural medium of the social sciences in America, as it is indeed the indigenous habitat of contemporary cultural life as a whole. In several senses, Sullivan would have been neither surprised nor disappointed by his effective disappearance from the scene. For although on the one hand he chased after publicity and even courted notoriety during his lifetime, on the other he also sought secrecy and anonymity and tried to conduct himself in such a way as to leave as few traces as possible behind him. The recently published, "official" biography of him, *Psychiatrist of America: The Life of Harry Stack Sullivan* by Helen Swick Perry,[1] is richly suggestive in such divergent connections; for the subject of that biography was at his most perspicuous and coherent a bundle of contradictions.

Biographers are regularly beset by the problem of how closely they ought to enquire into the intimate lives of their subjects; and they are subsequently beset as well, if and when such investigations have been made, by the questions of how much of what they have found, heard, suspected, and/or inferred ought to be disclosed. There are, as it were, no "covering laws" beneath which biographers can take shelter and find secure or enduring rules for their practice. There are only historical tendencies which serve as no more than biographical rules of thumb. The typical late-nineteenth-century biographer, for example, regularly, and in good conscience, censored and suppressed (and destroyed) supposedly discreditable evidence about his subject; for the lives of "great" people – of leaders, geniuses, and other personages of note – were still held or supposed to be, at least in some substantial measure, exemplary. More recent biographical practice, however, has tended to run in the reverse direction. Understanding of and insight into how the achievements and discoveries of the greatly gifted came about are now paramount biographical goals – and nothing from private life, it is currently thought, can on principle be held back or ruled out as irrelevant to those goals. The biographer of distinguished or remarkable figures in the modern disciplines of psychiatry or psychoanalysis must face such problems in their least restricted and most acute forms. For the intellectual stock-in-trade of such figures has been their dealings with the confidential lives of others, and no reader can be blamed for his curiosity about the putative connections that may be found between such gifts at divining the inner lives and clandestine conflicts of others and the diverse configurations in the personal and private lives of the biographical figures themselves that fed such gifts and nurtured their workings-out in later life – in careers of distinction and originality. Such figures, and their biographers, cannot for very long plead the Fifth Amendment when it comes to details of private life; for them, the statute of limitations on their own least savory personal stories runs out with dismaying celerity.

Such has recently become the case of Freud himself. And even so forthright and forthcoming a biographer as Ernest Jones was thought to be at the time he wrote his three-volume *Life and Work* has come to seem more than necessarily protective and less than necessarily open about his great subject. Indeed, the publication in 1974 of *The Freud/Jung Letters* – and the disclosure through leakage of other miscellaneous bits of information since – has made it clear that as soon as enough additional uncensored material from Freud's far-flung correspondence, as well as other sources, comes to be centrally available, a new large-scale biography will be called for. If this circumstance applies to Freud, it applies in spades to Harry Stack Sullivan, who indeed had much to hide. Freud's sense of privacy and his personal reticence were integral to his identity as a late-nineteenth-century bourgeois humanist with radical intellectual powers. Moreover, he reveals himself in his works with a directness and depth that we traditionally associate with the great poets and novelists and not with men of science or scholarly pursuits. And if it is eventually revealed, as it has recently been suggested, that he had an affair with his sister-in-law, such a discovery will touch the nature and character of his achievements not much more and not much less than the discovery a few years further back that the faithful housekeeper of the family of Karl Marx bore an illegitimate son to the head of the household. But such is by no means true of Harry Stack Sullivan, who, as I have already said, had much to hide, did as much as he could to hide it during his own lifetime, was as close and cryptic about himself as he could be, laid down false trails away from his past, and was, for the largest part, as remote, impersonal, enigmatic, forbidding, off-putting, and incommunicative as anyone whose chief preoccupation in life has to do with how people deal with one another in their most fundamental relations might possibly be.

Hence his current biographer has had her work cut out for her. Helen Swick Perry has been undaunted by what almost anyone else would consider the extremely uninviting biographical prospect offered by Sullivan and has valiantly tried to make the best of an exceptionally bad bargain. She has, to be sure, been doing so since 1946, when she first went to work for Sullivan as managing editor for *Psychiatry*, the journal that was one of Sullivan's principal instruments of expression. After Sullivan's death in 1949 she became the chief editor of his posthumous papers, seeing volume after volume through the press – one of the many peculiarities of Sullivan's highly peculiar career was that he published only one book during his lifetime, and even that was something of an accident. And since sometime in the early 1960s, Perry has been loyally at work on this biography, digging through layers of myth, rumor, gossip, and invention, looking for bodies and skeletons to disinter, seeking to compose a coherent and attractive life of a man whom she holds in the highest reverence. One wishes that she had a better run of luck and a better subject to expend her labors upon, for she has fallen considerably short of her long-sustained aim. She was indeed forestalled in some measure by the publication in 1976 of an unofficial biography by an admiring psychiatrist, A. H. Chapman. Although Dr Chapman did not have access to a fraction of the material that has been put at Perry's disposal he was nonetheless more candid and less occult than she has been able to permit herself to be. For example, there is the delicate question of Sullivan's sexuality – or to be less than devious about it, his homosexuality. Sullivan was a closet homosexual, a circumstance that in the America of his time and in the profession of psychiatry both then and now requires very little explanation and certainly no justificatory maneuverings or apologetics. Dr Chapman discusses this matter in a wholly tactful and straightforward way. Helen Perry admits that there are problems with Sullivan's sexuality; but she tiptoes around the matter so studiously, and is so recessive and obfuscating in what she does discuss in this context, and how she discusses it, that we end up with what amounts to a non-account of what may well have been a largely asexual life (punctuated irregularly with episodes of homosexual activity). Perry's furtive treatment of Sullivan's own understandable furtiveness on this score only serves to incite, magnify, and deform the reader's imagination on matters that should be dealt with plainly, dryly, and with as little inflection as possible. Moreover, her biography does not contain a single reference to Dr Chapman's prior work, an act of scholarly silence that does nothing to inspire confidence in her representations of the many other problematical sides of Sullivan's life.

At least two more of these sides should be mentioned, for they too are in general omitted from Perry's lengthy account. First, Perry fails almost entirely to provide a coherent exposition of Sullivan's ideas – if that is what they were – his theories or general views of human development. In a book that lays claim to be the authoritative account of the life of a leader of a significant school of modern psychiatry, psychology and psychotherapy this is an incompleteness of the most debilitating magnitude. Second, Perry also fails to deal in any adequate sense of the term with Sullivan's relations with his students, juniors, and supervisees; and here too there is abundant evidence both published and unpublished that she has declined to take into account. Some years ago, two of Sullivan's disciples published *A*

Harry Stack Sullivan Case Seminar, which consists in large part of a printed transcript made from notes taken down by a stenographer of a seminar that met in 1947. In these discussions, which are mostly printed pages of Sullivan holding forth, we see him treating his students and younger colleagues in the most appalling manner. He is contemptuous of them; he is cruelly sadistic, personally abusive, an intellectual thug and a pretentious phony all at once. He is the psychiatric incarnation of Dickens's Mr Bounderby in *Hard Times*, a factitious self-made man whom Dickens unforgettably calls the "bully of humility." But this book too, or its substantial equivalent drawn from other sources, does not get into Perry's reconstruction of her subject. In point of fact, despite her best efforts, she has idealized Sullivan in ways that are fatally damaging to historical and biographical truth, and her book cannot be taken at anything that resembles face value. One must discount from it, add to it, fill in absences, interpret euphemistic phrases and circumlocutionary passages, and in general continually rework the material she offers. Having therefore warned the prospective reader of what he has let himself in for, I hasten to add that the book is certainly worth reading for what it tells us about America, about American psychiatry and the social sciences, and about ourselves, those latter entities whose complex fate it still remains to be shaped and to shape themselves in America.

II

Harry Stack Sullivan was born in 1892 in the small town of Norwich in Chenango County in south central New York. The nearest settlement of any size or note was Binghamton. During the nineteenth century, this now unremarkable section of the state was the center of spectacularly intense religious revivalist activities – among the multitude of millenarian and primitive Christian sects then established, one was fated to expand and prosper as a genuine native American religious movement. The Church of Jesus Christ of Latter-Day Saints, soon to become known as the Mormons, was founded in the 1830s as a result of revelations given to Joseph Smith in and around Palmyra, New York, and was destined, along with much of the rest of the country, to head west. By the time Sullivan was born the district, populated chiefly by small and indifferently successful farmers, had receded into a cultural backwater. Apart from Sullivan himself, the only person of exceptional achievement to come out of this region at about the same time was the anthropologist Ruth Benedict; and its one event of national celebrity was the murder that Theodore Dreiser was to deploy as the subject of *An American*

Tragedy. Sullivan himself was born into a family of moderately poor Irish Catholics; all four of his grandparents had emigrated from Ireland as a result of the potato famine in the middle years of the nineteenth century. The part of the country they settled in was predominantly Protestant; hence they were outsiders in an area that was itself decidedly provincial and sectarian, peripheral to the main currents of American economic and social developments. It was a region that had been culturally by-passed and defeated at a very early date and that was as a result curiously and warily sensitive to its inferior and abandoned condition. Sullivan grew up within this cultural ambiance of generalized failure and decline. The only child of parents who were themselves thwarted – his mother seems to have suffered at least one psychotic episode – from the dawn of consciousness there was borne in upon him the sense of the overwhelming and adverse power of the outside world, of "the environment," as he learned, and as all of us after him have learned, to call it. This haunted awareness of encompassing constraint, deprivation, and entrapment seems organic to our cultural soil, and different in quality and kind from what Europeans in relatively analogous circumstances appear historically to have experienced. Freud's Jewishness or D. H. Lawrence's proletarian origins did not act on them with the same irretrievably calamitous consequences as the cultural circumstances of Sullivan's childhood did on him. The two great converging truths of his early life were the ineradicable experiences of loneliness and isolation – they were to become central to his later descriptive characterizations of American social life and the personalities it tended to create, as he himself was one of the earliest, and purest, conscious precursor-members of the lonely crowd.

The solitude and emptiness of Sullivan's childhood was broken into at length by a friendship that he began when he was between 8 and 9 with a boy 5 years his senior. The relation was both formative and deforming. What one can make out from the elaborate smokescreen of Perry's text, from Sullivan's own writings and from Dr Chapman's earlier biography is something like the following. The friendship lasted for about five years and was extremely close and extremely unequal. It was also actively homosexual, in the sense, I infer, that Sullivan was persuaded/coerced to perform homosexual services for his friend's gratification while getting nothing in the way of genital satisfaction himself. The friend went on in later life to become a psychiatrist too, and like Sullivan never married. He also had nothing but foul things to say in adult life about the closest companion of his youth. As for Sullivan, he shut up like a clam and as far as is known never in his maturity even mentioned the name of his

childhood chum. But the pattern of Sullivan's sexual life, already pre-
formed in tendency by his close relation to his dominating mother
and his extreme distance from his almost entirely silent father, had
been laid down for good.

At school in the nearby village of Smyrna, Sullivan was soon
recognized as a precociously clever boy. He graduated at the top of his
class and won a scholarship to Cornell, matriculating in 1908 with the
intention of pursuing the study of physics. Immediately therafter,
however, his life enters an extended period of turbulence that is
equalled only by the dense fog of obscurity in which it still remains
cloaked, an opacity broken only intermittently by patches of fleeting
intelligence. In the spring of his freshman year at Cornell he was
suspended and never returned to college there or elsewhere.
Widespread rumor reports that he became involved in illegal if not
criminal dealings with a gang of other undergraduates, but nothing is
really known. He then disappears entirely for two years; his
whereabouts remain undetermined, but Perry persuasively suggests
on evidence gathered by her directly from Sullivan, and indirectly
from other sources, that during this period Sullivan suffered a
schizophrenic episode and incarceration in a mental institution.
When he rises to the surface again, he is almost 20 years old, and is an
entering student in the Chicago College of Medicine and Surgery,
one of the many "diploma mills" in American medical education at
the time. These pedagogical factories for mass-producing illiterate
quacks had been thoroughly denounced the year before in the epoch-
making Flexner report and were soon to be immortalized in the pages
of *Arrowsmith*, shortly after most of them had either shut their doors
or been absorbed by larger and more reputable institutions that were
themselves in a state of rapid reform. Having finished with this
educational farce in 1915, Sullivan spent the next six years working at
odd medical jobs and struggling to keep himself from going under
both psychologically and financially.

During this fitfully illuminated period, however, a pattern begins
to emerge, for the records that survive from this time clearly show
that he had begun regularly to lie and falsify about himself, his
experiences, his date of birth and even, perhaps, his name. He also
began to drink during working hours, a practice that he continued
more or less regularly to the end of his life. Everything points to a
situation of unstable equilibrium – the quasi-psychotic autodidact was
also developing into something of an impostor. These attributes were
to become permanent parts of Sullivan's character; but they were
stabilized and integrated, as it were, into a workable and less labile
identity by the great good fortune that descended upon him at the end
of 1921. While he was working for the federal government in Chicago,

he received an appointment as liaison officer for the Veterans Bureau at St Elizabeth's Hospital in Washington, DC. It was the decisive event of his adult life.

St Elizabeth's Hospital was presided over by William Alanson White, a decent, humane, and intelligent man, who kept up high morale among his staff while encouraging an eclectic assortment of relatively benign therapies for the psychotic patients who were under his care. American psychiatry was at the time in a state of rapid flux: different physical treatments such as insulin-shock coma, other drug therapies, and nutritional, hydropathic, and restraining regimens were all being widely experimented with; along with them there was also the advent of the dynamic psychological therapies that emanated from Europe, principally from Freud, his followers and his former followers. It was in this situation of experimental freedom and theoretical spaciousness that Sullivan, first at St Elizabeth's and then at the Sheppard and Enoch Pratt Hospital in Towson, Maryland, learned his profession and began to make his significant contributions to psychiatry. The first and most important of these had to do with the treatment of hospitalized young male schizophrenics, most of them already in a deteriorated state and fated for the permanent death-in-life of the back wards. Sullivan tried to create one of the first total therapeutic milieus for these by-and-large "hopeless cases." Through training lower-echelon staff, who were closer in age and experience to the population of patients, to fill key positions on the ward, he tried to create conditions of "reciprocal trust" between patients and their "keepers" and ultimately among patients themselves. Working out of his own extreme experiences, Sullivan tried to bring about an ideal "environment" in which, as he said, psychotic patients could begin to make "social recoveries." The humanity and the relative success of this plan, in the decades before the radical chemical discoveries that followed World War II, made Sullivan's work famous; and in his more prophetic moments Sullivan dreamed of an America dotted over with "socio-psychiatric communities," "convalescent camps," as he called them, for rendering effective "the great mental hygiene" that he conceived of as his pre-eminent humane mission to the sick society in which he had been bred, raised and ill-formed.

At the same time, Sullivan became acquainted with new work being done in the social sciences, in particular among the sociologists, anthropologists, and political theorists at the University of Chicago. He rapidly assimilated whatever he could from them and added it to his growing idiosyncratic armamentarium of theoretical formulations, or perhaps the older term "conceits" might be a more appropriate word. Sullivan was also quick to see that the social

sciences in America were then entering upon a phase of unprecedented exponential expansion and growth, and he determined very
early on to link together permanently the futures of psychiatry (at the
time almost exclusively medical in theoretical conceptions and
clinical procedures) and the new non-clinical disciplines. To this end,
he became closely associated with such figures as the linguist and
cultural anthropologist Edward Sapir and the young political scientist
Harold Lasswell. It was Sullivan's unswerving determination to
establish a secure place for psychiatry in academic "science" and in
the academic scientific community that led him to try at once to begin
collaborative, interdisciplinary research projects in which psychia-
trists and social scientists would work together. This determination
also led to an effort, which ultimately failed, to bring psychiatry into
membership in the newly formed Social Science Research Council
(SSRC); and after the failure of that effort, Sullivan continued until
the end of his life to work in one setting after another at the task of
institution-building. He became something of an entrepreneur or
wheeler-dealer in the world of professional organizations, foundations, training institutes, and centers for research and experimental
therapy. To be sure, he was not altogether successful in these
undertakings, for another of Sullivan's characteristics was that he was
by and large irresponsible when it came to money, both his own and
that belonging to others.

The relative failure through prematurity and opportunistic
behavior of a number of these projects led to Sullivan's decision to
move to New York City in 1930 and establish himself there in private
practice. At the height of the early phase of the Great Depression, he
also typically decided to set himself up on Park Avenue in the
grandest of styles in a top-floor of a large apartment house. He had
also by this time become a socialist, but his socialism did not extend to
his own habits of living which became steadily more extravagant. Nor
did they extend to his fees, and during the 1930s he boastfully claimed
on numerous occasions that he was one of the four or five highest paid
therapists in New York. Nevertheless, as early as 1932 the troubles on
the stock market had gotten to him, his "wealthy Jewish patients
could not pay their bills," and Sullivan had to file a petition for
bankruptcy and leave his Park Avenue address. This setback,
however, was only temporary, and throughout the 1930s Sullivan
continued to practice full-time analysis, charge high fees, live high off
the hog, and be a doctrinaire left-liberal of the period. He also
underwent some kind of unspecified psychoanalytic experience
himself with his long-time friend and colleague Clara Thompson.
Thompson had inherited wealth, and when both had become
acquainted earlier in Washington, Sullivan had prevailed upon her to

spend her summer holidays in Budapest being analyzed by Ferenczi. In New York, they undertook to transmit what she had learned in Europe to Sullivan. When Thompson tried to dissuade Sullivan from some of his more grandiose schemes for redecorating his living accommodations, he terminated his sessions with her, asserting as his reason for doing so that "he could not work with someone who had such 'bourgeois' values." Among those values were, apparently, to be included the repayment of personal debts levied on friends and colleagues – his insatiable demands for money were, it seems, equalled only by his improvidence and his eccentricities when it came to paying back what he owed. (It should be added that he could be improvidently generous as well.)

During the 1930s Sullivan continued his association with a variety of social scientists, became friendly with such disaffected Freudians as Erich Fromm and Karen Horney, worked himself up into increasingly and stridently anti-Freudian attitudes, and continued, with haphazard success, his work of institution-conjuring in both New York and Washington. This work went on amid the intense back-biting, political hair-splitting, personal incivilities, and generally detestable collective behavior that have characterized so much of the internal history of the psychoanalytic movement both in Europe and America. Sullivan found the organizational stranglehold that the Freudians had secured for themselves in the institutional arenas of prestige in America more than he could personally tolerate. He wanted his own autonomous and eclectic world of research, training, therapy, publication, and interdisciplinary inquiry. By 1939 Sullivan had had enough of New York, and returned to Washington, where he soon became the stellar attraction of the Washington School of Psychiatry – in a few years it would sprout a New York branch as well. Sullivan also had his own journal, *Psychiatry*, and from 1942 on had a post at Chestnut Lodge, a leading psychoanalytically oriented mental hospital near Washington, whose senior clinician was the highly respected Frieda Fromm-Reichmann, and where Sullivan was free to hold forth.

And hold forth he did. From 1942 onward he began a series of what were called "lecture-discussions" at Chestnut Lodge. By the time he had finished they had reached the number of 246 and they had all been stenographically or electrically recorded, as had his classes of the same period in the Washington and New York schools. A good deal of his posthumous publications have their origins in these recordings – all of which have been gone over editorially by his disciples. The style of life that Sullivan established for himself in Bethesda during these years was in accordance with the sense of importance suggested by the elaborate technology employed to preserve his spoken utterances.

And towards the end of the war he began to conceive of the need for a new kind of psychiatry; he called it, characteristically, "a psychiatry of peoples." He was at the top of his fraudulent form now and near the top of the heap in his profession as well – students and followers flocked about him and hung on his words; governments enlisted his expertise on consultantships; the world was persuaded of its need for his seasoned, humane counsel. In this connection a document of peculiar interest survives from 1948. In that year Sullivan was invited by UNESCO to meet with seven other world leaders in psychiatry and the social sciences. The meeting was held in Paris and lasted for two weeks. It was known as the "Tensions Project" and was supposed to find both causes for and solutions to the "tensions that cause wars." Among the other luminaries and very big wheels who attended this conference were Gordon Allport, Georges Gurvitch, Max Horkheimer, and John Rickman. At the end of the two-week session, the group issued a Common Statement consisting of twelve points. Eight of these are United Nations-like statements in favor of such innovative and controversial principles as motherhood and international understanding. The remaining four points have to do with the specific implementation of these noble ideals: they come down by and large to lots and lots of big bucks for Social Science on the grandest of international scales. The days of global racketeering in the academic-intellectual worlds have gone by, but this document deserves to be memorialized as a manifestation – and a manifesto – of the social sciences in their high phase of post-war megalomania. And Sullivan was in the thick of it. He was in the thick of it when he suddenly died of a stroke in Paris in 1949. His project for "a psychiatry of peoples" appears to have died with him.

III

And so did much else, including what for want of a more suitable term one is compelled to call his ideas. For Sullivan, it has to be driven home, really didn't have ideas, in any ordinary or traditional acceptation of the word. What he had were *terms* that masqueraded as ideas; and in the course of his career he would regularly redeploy these always increasing number of locutions in new and increasingly confused arrays – the tendency was almost always towards greater abstraction, and towards the appearance of systematic regularity and "scientific objectivity." As the influx of European, that is mostly Freudian, psychoanalysts continued without interruption during most of Sullivan's active career, the impulses to produce an alternate methodical diction – and thus make distinct one's nonconformity, autonomy, and originality – became impossible to resist.

Some of Sullivan's terms are little more than pointless variations, equivocal translations, vulgarizations or trivializations of words used technically by Freud. For example, Sullivan rejected Freud's notions of "consciousness" and "unconsciousness." According to him, Freud thought of the "unconscious mind" as a kind of biological thing. But the "unconscious mind," Sullivan asserts, is only a metaphor, since it cannot be seen, heard, or felt. Therefore, instead of speaking of consciousness or unconsciousness, Sullivan proposed that we substitute instead the words "awareness" and "un-awareness." To begin with, Freud never thought of the unconscious or the unconscious mind as a "thing," unless all mental events, entities, or processes are to be thought of as "things." And second, Sullivan is here proposing a difference without a distinction. The relative inconsequentiality of this piece of intellectual self-aggrandizement does not hold true for another of Sullivan's variations upon Freud. Instead of Freud's idea of "defense" or "defenses" Sullivan proposes that we substitute instead the term "security operations." Freud's term in German is *Abwehr*, a highly traditional word that carries connotations of personal combat and resistance as well as military activity. Sullivan's "security operations," however, brings with it the notion of a business, warehouse, or institution that is to be defended by watchmen or Pinkerton agents; it also anticipates the "security operations" of World War II, the Cold War, and the CIA. And it carries in its wake the epidemic "insecurity" experienced by Americans during the Great Depression.

This latter association is connected with another of Sullivan's ambitious *bouleversements*. Sullivan came to reject Freud's theory of the libido and the sub-theories based on it as too sweeping and vaguely universal to become part of a "scientific" psychology. He replaced libido as a paradigmatic theoretical concept with "anxiety," and by anxiety he meant almost every conceivable kind of emotional adversity or suffering – including guilt, shame, *angst*, dread, self-loathing, depression, feelings of worthlessness, differing degrees of inadequacy, and even the common garden variety of anxiety. In other words it takes in almost everything and therefore defines virtually nothing. And if one is to accuse Freud of loose inclusiveness and generality in his notion of the libido, one wonders what description is to be reserved for Sullivan's anxiety. One such description would have to focus upon the connection that may be said to exist in American culture between the perception of "anxiety" on the one hand and the felt need for "security" on the other – an observation which is, one suspects, entirely valid at one pitch of analysis yet entirely symptomatic of other and more fundamental disturbances at the same time. Some of those disturbances, and Sullivan's personal security operation for dealing with the anxiety brought about by them, may be suggested in the continual tippling that almost everyone observed, remarked upon and yet withheld interpretation from in Sullivan's own behavior.

Similar dilutions, distortions, and blurrings can be made out in other Sullivanian terminological inventions. Instead of Freud's painstaking efforts to describe specific neurotic afflictions and disturbances or arrestments of development, Sullivan coined the covering term "personality warp," which he used in virtually every imaginable context. Once again, this was a forward-looking innovation, for decades later the then as-yet-unborn readers of *Mad Magazine* were to tell us all about the "warped personalities" that they were both suffering and celebrating and that America had produced in them; and again too one suspects that the origins of this slightly bizarre term are to be found in some area of American technological culture. Nevertheless what "personality warp" does to the elaborate variety of psychoanalytic (and psychiatric) terms that it is intended to displace is to produce further murk and obscurity in an already uncertain region of distinctions. As does another Sullivanian coinage: Sullivan used the term "consensual validation" to describe the process by which unhealthy "interpersonal patterns" are corrected. In other words he used it to cover the experiences of insight, remembering, repeating, and working through that Freud described in elaborate detail. Or, put in more familiar terms, he used it to describe how we come to be able actively to accommodate ourselves to reality, or, to enlist Freud's conception, to permit the reality principle to have its say in guiding our behavior. But what "consensual validation" does to these notions is first to "sociologize" them in the sense that our selves now become part of a broad conceptual consensus, and second to "scientize" them in the sense that certain validation procedures that had to do with the philosophy of science current in America at the time are gone through and retraced by each of us in his personal development or therapeutic experience. In either instance something less than intellectual felicity is being wrought upon Freud's conceptions: the amendment is not an improvement; the revision does not lead to further preciseness of description or delineation. And the same may be said of Sullivan's expression, the "self-system," by which he meant the total sum of security operations which a person directs against anxiety and in search of "emotional security." In other words "self-system" is the equivalent of Freud's array of unconscious defenses; but what such a definition does, of course, is to radically impoverish an already truncated notion of the ego, since it defines that conceptual entity as a function alone of the defenses it mobilizes, rather than regarding the defenses as themselves only one part of a much more complex, aggressive, active, and many-sided psychic reality – as part, in other words, of a genuine ego, let alone the still more inclusive notion of a self.

But Sullivan did not stop there. If the unconscious had to go as a theoretical conception, the fundamental Freudian discoveries of normal infantile and childhood sexuality were not far behind: Sullivan declared them otiose and dispensed with them. And after these went the Freudian therapeutic innovations: the couch was an inconvenience, so out it went too. Free associations were impossible and a waste of time – forget about them. Dream anaylsis was useless as well; according to Sullivan, the dream images are essentially incomprehensible. Moreover, when a patient tries to interpret a dream, he experiences in the face of the enigmatic images a sudden access of anxiety, and this anxiety only serves further to distort whatever the patient may have to report about the dream. No matter that Sullivan also says that in order for psychotherapy to get anywhere the patient's anxiety must often be mobilized. Such a contradiction was no more distressing to Sullivan than was his equally self-nullifying assertion that introspection was only psychiatrically useful when it occurred in "an interpersonal setting."

Pronouncements of this order were striking because of their sweeping, headlong, unanswerable, and less than scrupulous certitude, their primitive pugnacity, their unjustified and groundless assumption of pontifical infallibility. But they also fail to convey fully the affectations of learning and scientific superiority that Sullivan pretended to, the quasi-illiterate grammar of his prose, his fatal attraction to the largest and emptiest abstractions, the pretentious polysyllabic gobbledygook that he successfully passed off as serious psychological discourse, the caricature of a man of cultivated learning and taste that he continually reveals himself to be.[2] For what his prose at almost every point reveals is a personal pathology that is at the same moment a pathology of the culture in which that person is lodged. The latter-day reader deserves to sample some of this language for himself. One of Sullivan's most "important" and widely hailed turns of phrase was what was called his "one-genus postulate." This postulate exists in both short and long forms. The short version first: "We are all much more simply human than otherwise." What this means, if it means anything at all, is: Three Cheers for the United Nations, and down with racism, prejudice, and xenophobia; and if that is what it means, then it means very little while suggesting that it implies a great deal. (That "otherwise" seems especially freighted with significance, yet yields nothing to analysis.) Now the long version: "We are all much more simply human than otherwise, be we happy and successful, contented and detached, miserable and mentally disordered, or whatever." This amplification has precisely the same puerile significance as the short form, since the effect of the "or whatever," is to reduce everything that comes after "otherwise" to nothing – anything that could come after it would have to mean the same thing.

Or there is this passage about loneliness, an experience for which Sullivan may be truly said to have qualified as an expert authority.

> Under loneliness, people seek companionship even though intensely anxious in the performance. When, because of deprivations of companionship, one does integrate a situation in spite of more or less intense anxiety, one often shows, in the situation, evidences of a serious defect of personal orientation.

The reader is invited to contemplate just how the words "performance," "integrate," and "personal orientation" work in these statements. Either they point distinctly to pathology itself – as "performance" does – or they serve to displace both meaning and anxiety through abstract, hifalutin circumlocutions. In either event, this prose is as alien to the idiom of the English language as that bewildered boy in Chenango County or the schizophrenic youth in Ithaca once was to both language and the human world to which language belongs and which it is supposed to render intelligible. Or there is this companion-piece to the last passage: "Intimacy is that type of situation involving two people which permits validation of all components of personal worth." I never would have thought it possible to find an utterance which might make "Love means never having to say you're sorry" look good, but this seems almost to have done it. Yet both statements are equally factitious, and both point to a similar circumstance of cultural pathology – namely, a disabling incapacity to describe in language what close relations between two people in our civilization have traditionally been taken to be.

Or, to change pace, there is this piece of technical profundity.

> We haven't the beginning of a clue to the scientific evolution of ethical standards, morals, and so on, to take the place of those which are being swept aside by profound social movements which we innocently at times mistake for newly discovered conditions of repression and escape from the superego.

A clinico-theoretical pronunciamento in the form of gibberish? Then try this one on for size: "Any mistakes and shortcomings in psychiatry are bound to repercuss gravely upon the social situation."

Technological jargon? Scientistic cultural fatuosity no worse than the current "Access me in the springtime"? Then how about this: "Sex is important for the twenty minutes it may occupy from time to time, but it is not necessarily behind everything else that fills the rest of time." What respect for human needs and frailties! What a sense of proportion! And what a conception of and feeling for life, "that fills the rest of time."

Even more, what is one to make of the following from Sullivan's obituary for his close friend, Edward Sapir: "His creative work ... was but moving toward its zenith in his far flung exploration of the relations of culture and personality when his heart disorganized in the Fall of 1937." Is this the Great American Psychiatrist as Mrs Malaprop, or perhaps as some semi-alive mumbler in Beckett? Or is it merely one more representation of what Sullivan called "selective inattention," in this instance inattention to the plainest matters of words and their meanings – of what language is supposed to do. In that eventuality, the "merely" will not do, as it undoubtedly does not do in the following passage about the infantile experience of suckling:

> From a syncretistic prehension of primitive hunger, the nipple, the complex kinesthetic sentience arising in oral activity, the gustatory input from the milk; out of these data vividly contrasted on a background of death-evil, the conesthesis disordered by chemical needs, there comes experience that is central in the conscious series of the individual.

This incomprehensible nonsense would be no more than good for some laughs today had Sullivan not been taken seriously by considerable numbers of highly intelligent people. If we ask what it was in this goulash of doubletalk, spiced with drivel and served up as the blue-plate special of psychobabble that they were swallowing with a straight face, answers spring readily to hand. They were, in the first instance, responding *against* the Freudians and their rabbinical, conservative, authoritarian methods of training and organization, and their relatively dim view of human possibility and social futurity. They were responding at the same time, and by the same token, to an upbeat nativist American psychiatry, with its hopes held out for the hopeless and a vision of the future in which human nature could be improved by our increased ability to control "the environment," since in this view of things human nature was itself made up of that environment and very little more.

But they were responding, I believe, to other things as well. They were responding with unconscious fascination, I speculate, to what was symptomatic in Sullivan, for he was as much a symptom of the culture he was trying to alter and cure as he was a force for improvement and mitigation. And he was a symptom of the pathology of the future as well. That portent comes into sight in the subtitle that Sullivan gave to *Psychiatry*; he called it the *Journal for the Operational Statement of Interpersonal Relations*. "Operational" represents, of course, the pathetic innocence of Sullivan's view of "science" and his trust in its thaumaturgic powers. "Interpersonal," however, is even more to the point. Sullivan called his view of the world "The Theory of Interpersonal Relations," and it was to the resonances of this piece of terminology, I suspect, that people tended to respond. It was a neologism, a tautology, and a nonsense – it was also irresistible and has become a permanent, superfluous, and useless part of the language. For what the intelligent people who listened with rapt attention to Sullivan's garrulous inanities were hearing with their imperfectly tuned third ears – but hearing however inattentively nonetheless – was the sound of the beginning of the disappearance of the person and the personal, of personhood and personal agency, of the individual self of our historical culture. They heard the sounds of this evacuation each time Sullivan uttered the word interpersonal. What they were hearing were the sounds being made by the new vacuity, by an interpersonal world without persons in it. Sullivan once gave a paper entitled "The Illusion of Personal Individuality," in which he asserted that "no such thing as the durable, unique, individual personality is ever justified. For all I know every human being has as many personalities as he has interpersonal relations." Long before recent European savants announced, to much fanfare, the philosophical disappearance of the subject, the actual social and cultural disappearance of the individual person was beginning to be effected in America.[3] The real radical change was happening here; its registration in philosophical consciousness took place later over there – the difference in time representing the interval of the Owl of Minerva's flight backwards across the Atlantic. Sullivan was a portent of the bleak future we have inherited. Those who listened to him believed that the future he was pointing towards was rosy, and they compared it favorably to the sad, stoic minimality of Freud's late-nineteenth-century humanism. Had they been able to listen more closely, or to follow Sullivan's language (as well as his behavior) with appropriate attentiveness, they would have heard the dreadful noises and anti-human clangor of much of what has become our daily cultural fare. They were listening to the right thing, but they did not really hear it. We can hear it now, but it may be too late.

Notes

1 H. S. Perry, *Psychiatrist of America: The Life of Harry Stack Sullivan* (Cambridge, Mass., and London, England, 1982).
2 There is one passage that Perry quotes in which Sullivan acutely reflects on what he and his pre-adolescent homosexual chum ultimately became. "The stresses of life," he writes, distorted them "to inferior caricatures of what they might have been."
3 The novelist Walker Percy understood what it was all about. In his novel about contemporary America, *Love in the Ruins*, one of the minor characters is an "interpersonal gynecologist." As in lesser degree did the poet Lloyd Frankenburg, an admirer of Sullivan's who nevertheless had the intuitive wit to entitle his autobiographical recollections of Sullivan "The Interperson."

IV Freud and the Biographers Again: the Internal and External Worlds

I

The relation between psychoanalysis and narrative writing is, as these things go, an ancient and venerable one. It was there, one has to recall, from the very outset. Few readers are likely to forget how in *Studies on Hysteria* Freud remarked that it struck him "as strange that the case histories I write should read like short stories and that, as one might say, they lack the serious stamp of science." And he went on to say that he had to console himself "with the reflection that the nature of the subject is evidently responsible for this, rather than any preference" of his own. That may be true, although it is at least equally true that Freud's preferences had a way of getting entangled with the "nature of the subject." In any case, psychoanalysis and narrative literary and biographical forms have been embroiled with one another steadily, as have psychoanalysis and literary criticism.

There are any number of reasons why this should be so, and there is no possibility of exhausting them upon any one occasion. Psychoanalysis has added to our understanding of literature, culture, and history in ways that are familiar to all readers. Psychoanalytic biographies of writers and other historical personages are a familiar and benignly accepted part of the academic literary scene. Psychoanalytic studies of works of literature, essays that seek to disclose the unconscious structure of particular works of art are equally familiar. As are more general psychoanalytic enquires into questions of creativity in a number of areas. In addition, literature – and in particular its narrative forms – has provided a special kind of resource for psychoanalysis.

I should like to place some stress on one area in which psychoanalysis and literary criticism seem to converge. Freud was an exceptionally literary physician and theorist. He believed that everyone has a story, but that few of us can tell his narrative history properly. Moreover, he tended to treat his patients and their productions, both verbal and other, as if they were biographical or historical texts. They were the authors of their own stories, and what they were producing were texts, their passed and vanished lives in the form of an endless running verbal account whose structure was that of a complex, biographical narrative. Since the essential medium of transaction in the psychoanalytic situation is that of language, and since from very early on psychoanalysis regarded itself as in large measure the "talking cure," the general rules or procedures that govern our dealings with verbal artifacts prevail within it. Psychoanalysis and literary criticism regard their respective objects as generators of meaning, and both disciplines assume that what they are looking for is meaning and meanings and judge the degree of their own success or failure according to the wealth of meaning they can find in the texts before them, and the degrees of intelligibility they can bring to the explanation of meaning after meaning that they can themselves generate in their transactions with the texts that they address. This concentration upon meaning, among other things, binds them together – as does their working assumption, or empirical rule, that nothing before them (in their respective situations) is ever without meaning.

Freud says somewhere that a dream cannot be completely and exhaustively analyzed. A similar assertion may be made about great works of literature and great lives. For reasons which no one really understands – but which may have to do with the way meaning is created in a text – great works and lives from the past survive by their abilities to sustain new meanings, by their uncanny abilities to masquerade as partial works and experiences of the present. In history, new perspectives continue to occur; these are trained upon the same objects, and in this transaction new meanings are created in the same objects. Psychoanalysis has been itself one of these new perspectives. When it has been trained upon great artifacts of the past, they have responded in due form. What this also implies, however, is that great works of literature or narrative accounts are probably inexhaustible; there is no final dealing with them; we will never have done with them nor they with us.

There is nothing especially alarming about any of these considerations, so long as we do not expect psychoanalysis to provide us with some ultimate or all-inclusive or most profound reading of any particular text. Great texts or lives cannot be so circumscribed or circumvented, and it is a vanity to think that any one system of reading – or of isolating and finding structured meanings – can exhaust the impacted linguistic and other densities that great poems or dramas or novels or biographical accounts represent. It seems to me informally sufficient to remind ourselves that psychoanalysis is one of several indispensable ways we have of dealing analytically with textual accounts, that it has become one of the fundamental conceptual and analytic instruments in the literary critical enterprise. There are not many areas of humanistic enquiry in which it does not find some kind of application or use.

There is, however, one loop that I should like to run back upon or retroverse. And this has to do with the literary critical analysis of psychoanalysis or of certain psychoanalytic texts. Psychoanalysis has from the outset enjoyed a mixed blessing as a prospective science, since its creator was not merely a genius, but a literary genius to boot. What this means is that Freud's writings contain within themselves the same capacity of generating, in reading, new meanings over time that other enduring works of literature and narrative structure possess. We may ask what relation exists between this capacity to produce, in reading, new meanings over time and the truth or cognitive value of a work of literature. The answer is not easy to find, and I hesitate to supply one, so to speak, light-mindedly. When it comes to the cognitive status of works of literature, we all move about cautiously. In addition, hoewever, we may also ask what value this circumstance holds for psychoanalysis itself. The answer, I think, is not very much, if formalization and systematization are uppermost on one's agenda of priorities. If one, for example, imagines a distant future in which psychoanalysis has been largely taken up into science, one fancifully sees something as follows: psychoanalytic therapy has been largely replaced by chemical agents of one kind or another or by other less inefficient therapies; psychoanalytic theory, while not abandoned, has been taken up and subsumed within some more inclusive psycho-chemical and psycho-physiological series of systems which have more or less effectively replaced it. At the same time, Freud continues to be steadily and avidly read in colleges and universities where there are courses in – Freud: the fundamental theory; Freud: before and after; Freud and his followers; Freud, instinct theory vs. ego psychology; Freud and literature; Freud and history; etc., etc. That something like this will no doubt happen, is already beginning to happen, is fairly evident. I think that one of the relevant questions at hand is who will be teaching such courses, to what effect, and to what end? What I seem to be suggesting, rather to my own surprise, is that Freud is likely to survive the institution he invented.

Moreover, I think one must regard psychoanalysis as part of the history of culture and literature itself – as well as part of the history of medicine and related activities. Let me illustrate in part what I mean.

A few years before Freud began his great work, another physician-writer made his appearance in London. The work that he began to describe as being conducted at 221b Baker Street makes for an interesting anticipation of the activities that would shortly begin in the Berggasse. The "methods" of dealing with the material which is brought before the investigator this writer represented are well known. He is first of all a master of observation. He has trained himself, he often says, "to see what others overlook." He regards behavior as "symptoms" and people as texts to be read.

> "You appeared to read a good deal upon her which was quite invisible to me," I remarked.
>
> "Not invisible but unnoticed, Watson. You did not know where to look, and so you missed all that was important. I can never bring you to realize the importance of sleeves, the suggestiveness of thumb-nails, or the great issues that may hang from a boot-lace."

His method, Holmes remarks, "is founded on the observations of trifles." From these observations he proceeds to reason by inference to conclusions which are often astonishing, more often irrefutable, and on occasion incomprehensible.

What ordinarily or typically happens in a Sherlock Holmes story is as follows. Someone comes to Holmes. This person is in trouble of some kind and seeks consultation, advice, or help. He or she is invited by Holmes to provide an account of what has happened to bring about the trouble, and the person in question then recites the narrative or story that has caused him to seek consultation with the oracle. The stories that are told seem odd, incoherent, mysterious, bizarre, and occasionally absurd. A red-headed man is paid to copy out in hand the *Encyclopedia Britannica*; a governess is hired only on condition that she cut her hair and wear a single, specific dress; a prospective husband or newly married wife unaccountably disappears. Holmes listens to these strange and often senseless narratives – "Let us have everything in its due order," he characteristically remarks – with the conviction that when everything is told in its due order a meaning will begin to emerge. "'I am glad of all details' remarked my friend, 'whether they seem to you to be relevant or not.'" Holmes believes that somehow all these stories actually and eventually make sense, and that he with his special skills can help bring overt and explicit sense to them and therefore to the reality to which they refer and whose structure they elliptically and fragmentarily represent. In other words, Holmes believes that everyone has a coherent and meaningful story to tell, although not everyone can tell it unaided. And this affirmation of the coherent nature of narrative and biographical reality is at the same time an affirmation of the coherent nature of the world itself. If the mysterious story can be made to make sense, then the world itself makes sense and has meaning. It too ceases to be incoherent, elliptical, mysterious, and apparently arbitrary. Hence the meaningful nature of existence itself is validated by rendering a puzzling and unintelligible story into causal or temporal sequences in which every odd detail fits and finds it significant place. And correlatively, the structure taken by the world – if it is to have meaning – is that of a story or biographical account. It is at its beginning a fragmentary, opaque narrative that at its end finally makes sense.

It is worth noting, however, that the secrets and puzzles and ellipses in these stories always refer to outer reality – to sleeves, thumb-nails, boot-laces, and foot-prints; to wigs and paint and cobbler's wax; to thefts, frauds, lies, plots, and murders. The world is made coherent by solving these external mysteries. When a few years later in Vienna, the physician-writer-detective with whom we are all familiar began to bring his work to the reading public he would base that work upon a strikingly similar set of assumptions and would present the world with a strikingly similar set of mysterious accounts. What the Viennese Holmes was going to do, however, was to take almost all the mysteries and secrets, and all the incoherent narratives, and place them inside. This shift from outer to inner reality marks a great historical transformation. On the one hand there seems to be something ironic in this circumstance that the detective story as a genre begins to flourish at just about the same moment in history when the locus of the mystery is in the course of dramatic change. On the other hand, the flourishing of the detective story (along with psychoanalysis, one might say) in the modern era does tell us something about the growth of a widespread and popular consciousness that the world has become an increasingly problematical place; that its structure is not immediately apprehensible; that we need help in understanding it; and that there may not be very much about the settled social or psychological order that we can take for granted. One way or another, it appears, we all need a detective. Whether he is a private eye or a third ear, we need him to help us get our lives and their stories straight.

What I have been obliquely suggesting is that there is something old-fashioned in both psychoanalysis and narrative literature. Both retain a primitive and charming belief in the sufficient authority of narrative as a means of constructing and legitimating human reality. And indeed I think it plausible to say that as long as people continue to place credence in the idea that a story, a narrative account or biographical construction or fiction is one way of accurately apprehending and representing some part of reality, including the reality of their own lives, both psychoanalysis and literature will continue to survive.

II

Yet within these circumstances of survival certain fluctuations of significance are to be made out. The courses pursued by biographical studies of Freud himself are, in this connection, much to the point. Ernest Jones's three-volume authorized biography has sustained itself with such remarkable staying power in part because it is not entirely or strictly a psychoanalytic biography. Though Jones himself was of course a psychoanalyst of originality and distinction, and although he uses psychoanalytic methods, theories, and interpretations in his study of Freud's life whenever he thinks them pertinent – he thinks them particularly pertinent to his reconstruction of Freud's childhood – his work is equally in the tradition of late-nineteenth and early-twentieth-century studies of the Life and Works of great men. It is this balance between or combination of two biographical modes that in part makes Jones's work outstanding. If one compares it with Max Schur's later *Freud: Living and Dying* (1972), one sees at once how much more highly focused on specialized psychoanalytic material the latter is, and that on these matters it is often more penetrating and insightful than Jones's work, while on others it is either silent or less adroit.

Meanwhile time has continued to pass, archives of material bearing upon the history of psychoanalysis have been growing in various depositories in Europe and America, and various discoveries about both Freud and the early history of the movement continue to be made. In addition, a variety of suppressed and distorted material in both Jones and elsewhere has been either discovered or strongly suggested. All of this leads to the inescapable inference that interest is now swinging back in the other direction – that enough new material of an external kind that has to do with the biography of Freud and the history of the movement that he founded will soon be accumulated or available so as to make another large-scale biographical effort appropriate. Such was, I believe, the general character of the thinking that was behind the publication of Ronald Clark's large volume, *Freud: The Man and the Cause.*[1] Clark is a professional biographer, and had access to some of the material collected in the major Freud archive in the Library of Congress. He also was able to consult the unused material that Jones had left behind in England, and in addition had access to an archive of family letters exchanged by Freud and his nephew Samuel that had been turned up in Manchester. Moreover, new material pertaining to Freud's early life had been discovered in both his place of birth in what is now Czechoslovakia and in Vienna. And as the older generations of psychoanalysts have gone to their just rewards, they too have left their bits of memorabilia, gossip, documents, letters and so on behind them. Clark made a thorough sweep through all of this material and produced a volume that brought the biographical reader up to date on the largest part of this store of newly available sources of information.

This material is of different orders and qualities of interest. Some of it is altogether trivial and of no conceivable account. For example, during Freud's single visit to America, in 1909, after he and his colleagues had travelled to Worcester, Massachusetts, and Clark University, where Freud received an honorary degree and delivered his famous five lectures on psychoanalysis, they went on a tour to see Niagara Falls, and after that were entertained as guests at James Putnam's camp in the Adirondacks. Before he had left Europe, Freud had declared that when faced with a difficult project, such as speaking to a foreign audience, "it was helpful to provide a lightning conductor for one's emotions by deflecting one's attention onto a subsidiary goal." Hence, he lightheartedly affirmed, his purpose in going to America was inspired by the "hope of catching sight of a wild porcupine *and* to give some lectures." When he eventually got to Putnam's mountain camp, after his exertions at Clark University and the trip to Niagara Falls, he reiterated this impulse, and his hosts indicated their willingness to help. Then comes the following passage from Clark's biography:

> Two visitors who knew the area well were assigned to accompany him. "They started the climb up a rather gentle hill," says a relative of one, "and had not gone very far before they were greeted by the stench of carrion. As they proceeded, the stench grew steadily stronger, so much so that ... [someone] suggested that they turn and go downward. Freud refused. They continued and at last came upon a bloated porcupine, long dead. Freud approached it, cautiously stuck his staff into it, then turned and announced, 'It's dead.'"

> There seems to have been no time for a further search, and Freud's ambition was therefore only half, and rather miserably, fulfilled. However, there was a minor consolation when, before he left, the Putnams presented him with a small porcupine paperweight made of metal. It was to sit on his desk for the rest of his life.

I confess to a weakness when it comes to odd or funny stories about great men. I confess even to a mild interest in knowing that in addition to writing paper, leather manuscript folders, and antiquities, Freud had an American metal porcupine on his desk. But the incident about the porcupine itself is a pure and uninflected nullity – the biographical equivalent of a brick made without straw. Clark found the material in a little article published in the *Harvard Medical Alumni Bulletin* in 1972, and the only reason for including this incident in his biography is that it actually happened. Which means that it is no reason at all.

It would be misleading to say that all, or even most, of the new material included by Clark existed at the same dead level of non-interest as the rotting porcupine; but there is enough matter of this kind so that making a point of remarking it is not irrelevant. Of greater cogency are Clark's various accounts of the different phases of the history of the psychoanalytic movement, of the bitterness, resentfulness, and epidemic uncivil behavior that has characterized so much of the inner history of this peculiar sect of modern therapists of the spirit. In a related connection, Clark has performed a very useful service in writing an original historical account of Freud's early reception in Great Britain and the subsequent ups and downs that his reputation has incurred there. He has also put together a new and highly detailed account of the efforts made by both British and American friends and officials to get Freud out of occupied Austria and the clutches of the Nazis. These pieces of narrative are entirely different in quality from the dead porcupine.

But the most interesting material of this kind has to do with things that happened in the Freud family before Sigmund was born. The evidence in question began to turn up in the late 1960s when new archival searches were made among the records kept in Freiberg, the small town in Czechoslovakia (then Moravia) that Freud was born in. It was known before this that Freud's father, Kallamon Jacob Freud, had been born in Galicia in 1815, had married a woman named Sally Kanner in about 1831, and had two sons by her, Emmanuel and Philipp, who were born in 1833 and 1836. It is not known when or where Sally Kanner Freud died, but in 1855, when the elder Freud married Amalie Nathanson, who was to bear as her first son Sigmund Freud, she was then 20, he was 40, and his two already living sons were about the same age as their stepmother. The new material concerns the year 1852, when Jacob Freud's two sons came to join their father in Freiberg, where he was running a small jobbing business. Documents, such as the local register of Jews for 1852, list a woman named Rebecca as Jacob Freud's wife – she apparently moved to Freiberg during that year along with the two sons of Jacob Freud's first marriage. Nothing more is known of her; she is never mentioned again, and no one, to anyone's present knowledge, ever spoke of her, or referred to her in any other way, including Freud's father, mother, his older brothers, and Freud himself. It is equally unknown whether the records are correct. If they are, it remains unknown what happened to her. This is everything that has been ascertained so far with any conclusiveness. Clark puts it all down carefully, says it may be important, if it is true, but under the circumstances prudently restrains himself from making too much of it.

Clark is a sensible and old-fashioned British biographer. Marie Balmary is a psychoanalyst practicing in Paris and a disciple of the late Jacques Lacan. Inspired by the material about the Freud family discovered in the late 1960s, she has written what for want of any other term has to be called a biographical study entitled *Psychoanalysis Psychoanalysed: Freud and the Hidden Fault of the Father*.[2] One is tempted at this point to remark that no more needs to be said; but intellectual conscience requires that some account of Balmary's study be rendered. I shall try to be mercifully brief.

Freud began his analyses by asking his patients to tell him their stories, or, alternatively, by asking them to tell him what was bothering them. Lacan's "decisive innovation" in this connection, according to Balmary, was to follow these questions by asking the patient an ultimately superseding question: "Who made you ill?" The answer is always "the Other," mostly Father, sometimes Mother, however the case may be. Accordingly she begins her account by retelling the Oedipus story from an alternative perspective. (Of course, she cannot go back to Sophocles' representation of the myth, which is what Freud did, but that is a minor matter.) Oedipus, she asserts, was the victim of his father's behavior; his father made him ill: this "fundamental misapprehension" of the truth of the Oedipus story is at the foundation of Freud's almost entirely misguided, if nonetheless important, project. And why did Freud read the Oedipus legend incorrectly so as to make "only Oedipus himself the source of his tragic action"? He did so because it was imperative to him, Freud, to abandon his central early theoretical formulation – "the theory of the father's fault."

In other words, the renunciation of the early "seduction theory" that Freud first constructed out of the stories told to him by his hysterical patients was the most important error of his career. What induced Freud to make such a calamitous blunder? Freud made this mistake, in 1897, in the course of his self-analysis. This self-analysis was itself in part begun in the aftermath or as a result of the death of Freud's father in 1896. According to Balmary, during that self-analysis the following crucial event or set of events took place. Freud "somehow" discovered (or had to confront) the existence of that second wife, Rebecca. He also discovered that she had disappeared, vanished without a trace, had somehow been gotten rid of (perhaps because she was childless, a ground for divorce under Orthodox Jewish law). She also, still according to Balmary, probably committed suicide as a result of her repudiation by Jacob Freud, and Sigmund may have learned of this too. But he learned even more; he "somehow" learned that his mother, Amalie, was pregnant with him when his parents were married, and that he was born in March, not May, 1856 (his parents were married at the end of July 1855). So what Sigmund Freud discovered in the course of his self-analysis is that Jacob Freud was a regular old devil, a Jewish Don Juan, a putative murderer, and the general villain of the piece, the universal paternal seducer. This view of the dead old man was unacceptable to Freud's consciousness, since he had from his infancy identified himself with his father; as a result of his discovery of his father's "fault," a fault of which we today "know nothing but its mask; the disappearance of a woman and the changing of a birth date," Freud resorted to extraordinary measures. He invented the Oedipus Complex largely as a repressive-defensive response to the truth of these discoveries and shifted the guilt on to the imaginary head of the son (himself), who became now in childhood the retroactive source of the impulses toward incest, seduction and murder which in the original reality were the actual handiwork of the father. Hence the original seduction theory was the truth, and the theory of the Oedipus complex, infantile sexuality, and everything else that flows from such conceptions are surely cover-ups for the anterior discovery of the same unsavory truth about Freud's father. Hence too, all subsequent intra-psychic theory falls under the same indictment of being a repressive defense against the truth – that truth being the infliction of sexual and psychic terror and damage by the old upon the young, and the secret conspiracies and connivances by which that damage is both transmitted and permitted to remain hidden.

What are we to make of this extraordinary set of charges – which I have presented here in extremely condensed form. To begin with, half the evidence is wrong. Examination of the records of the birth and circumcision of Freud in Freiberg make it clear beyond doubt that he was born in May and not March of 1856. (Balmary did not take the trouble to examine these records herself, copies of which are freely available in print.) But that is hardly the point. The tendency of this entire way of thinking is to push psychoanalytic enquiry back toward the situation of Sherlock Holmes; the mysteries are ultimately external acts and external facts, mediated implicitly of course by "language" which needs neither internal nor external worlds but exists autonomously, arbitrarily, and in a context that is *sui generis*. To be sure there remains much to be explained about the mysterious

Rebecca – universal silence on that score to the contrary notwithstanding. But that is not the immediate point either, which is that we are witness here to one of those swings of the historical pendulum which regularly mark or suggest large-scale changes in cultural attitudes.

What is much more to the point, of course, is that in repudiating the seduction theory, Freud did not repudiate it entirely or abandon the partial truths that remain in it. In a footnote added in 1924 to the article of 1896 in which he put forward the original seduction theory, Freud wrote:

> I attributed to the aetiological factor of seduction a significance and universality which it does not possess. When this error had been overcome, it became possible to obtain an insight into the spontaneous manifestations of sexuality of children. ... Nevertheless, we need not reject everything written in the text above. Seduction retains a certain aetiological importance, and even today I think some of these psychological comments are to the point.

Balmary cites this passage but is entirely nonplussed by it; she simply does not know what to make of it or how to deal with it.

And no wonder. Freud was one of those figures from the old culture who postulated in his theories an external world that was real and an internal world that was also real. This internal world partly depended on the external world and was partly independent of it. It had its own regularities of development and organization as well, which were different from, as well as sometimes analogous to, their counterparts in the external world. As the historical pendulum of culture swings, this kind of sustained and indeterminate complexity seems to have become increasingly intolerable to many of our contemporaries. Hence the accusation that Freud denies the responsible role played by parents in generating the neurotic and unhappy futures of their children. But how could anyone who has read the case histories, say, of Dora, or the Wolf Man, or the Rat Man possibly believe that this could be so? One can only believe it, the answer must be, if the argument one is putting forth is part of a cultural polemic. And that of course is what Balmary, who is a disciple of Michel Foucault as well as Lacan, is precisely part of. The villains are the external world, our parents, and the discourses of domination forced by both (and by language itself) upon us. To free ourselves of them, we must contrive somehow to destroy them – Freud's theoretical discourse is itself part of that apparatus of domination that must be annihilated if we are to find our way to the unimaginable freedom that such writings as Balmary's yearn for but cannot even begin to envision.

In any event, the time for a new biography of Freud is not far off. And when it does get written there is one thing we can be sure of – it will be the cause of many arguments. For the spirit of Sherlock Holmes lives on as well.

Notes

1   R. Clark, *Freud: The Man and the Cause* (New York, 1980).
2   M. Balmary, *Psychoanalysis Psychoanalysed: Freud and the Hidden Fault of the Father* (Baltimore, 1982).

8 Postscript: Notes on Psychoanalysis Today

Few people interested in the state of psychoanalysis will be able to deny the circumstance that psychoanalysis occupies today a quite different place in American society and culture from the one in which it was situated a generation ago. In the years following World War II, psychoanalysis was much closer to the centers of active, intellectual and cultural life in America than it appears to be now; psychoanalysis was a much more important, relevant, and momentous presence in the lives of those people who as groups constitute the intellectual and cultural professions in our society than it can claim to be at this moment. Intellectuals, university instructors, members of such professions as medicine and law, artists and writers, custodians of culture in museums and institutes, purveyors of culture in the arts and purveyors of entertainments and diversions in various parts of the culture industry tended to adhere in one way or another to the institution of psychoanalysis – it occupied a status and exerted an influence among them that has since visibly diminished, although it has not, to be sure, vanished altogether. And in turn the adherence and allegiance to psychoanalysis of such exceptionally visible and exemplary cultural groups gave to that institution a yet further enhanced prestige and helped its influence to diffuse and percolate into and permeate other sectors of American social and cultural life.

The attachment of such people to psychoanalysis located itself in two separate but related areas. Psychoanalysis was first looked to as a form of therapy. As is widely known, the history of the psychoanalytic movement in the United States tends to be idiosyncratic in the sense that the prestigious and orthodox Freudian organizations connected themselves virtually from the outset most closely with the profession of medicine, and made the therapeutic profession of psychoanalysis into a sub-discipline of medicine – or at least made matters appear that way. The consequences of this self-imposed prerequisite for certification were substantial. To my knowledge, in no modern Western culture does the profession of medicine enjoy a higher social esteem, reap larger economic rewards, or find itself invested with a greater diversity and weight of authority than that profession does in the United States. Primitive fantasies of magical powers, priestly privileges, and esoteric knowledge continue to cloak our physicians even as those same physicians operate increasingly as technologists, engineers, and applied chemists. There are many reasons for the essential persistence of such beliefs among Americans (although the quality of that persistence, and its periodic, partial alternation from positive to negative, should also be noted), and I cannot pause to discuss them in detail. Figuring largely among them, however, was and probably still is the poignant and apparently incorrigible American sentiment that there is nothing finally that cannot be "fixed up" – including, it sometimes seems, life and death themselves. And certainly including one's psychic, sexual, and personal life, one's career, one's difficulties with work, with mother, husband, wife, children, lover, friends, enemies, acquaintances, and pets, the pets of one's children, lover, friends, enemies, acquaintances, and so on. Many Americans were inclined to invest psychoanalytic therapy (and other therapies as well) with the power to fulfill such culturally supported aspirations, and although there is little doubt that in the course of therapy such fantasies came in, as they say, for due exploration and analysis, there is also little doubt that the profession as a whole was the direct beneficiary of this apparently ineradicable native impulse. And I must go on to say that I cannot recall, during the years in question, coming across many references in the professional literature to Freud's repeated admonitions that the major contributions that psychoanalysis had to offer would not finally be therapeutic in the accepted sense of the word. Such contributions, he held, would be found ultimately in education, in alterations of habits of child-rearing, in research and in applications of psychoanalytic theory and methods in a variety of cultural and scientific fields of endeavor.

An additional consequence of the official attachment of orthodox psychoanalysis to medicine was that it significantly limited the pool of talent from which the profession could renew and reproduce itself. Not only was this pool preselected in a particular manner; the premedical and then medical educations that psychoanalytic candidates had to undergo tended strongly to overprepare them in some skills that they would never draw upon as psychoanalytic therapists and radically to underprepare them in other intellectual skills that they would later sadly acknowledge as somehow matters of personal deficiency. The fact that many American psychoanalysts are so notoriously ill-read, a fact noted from very early on, was never an encouraging circumstance – no matter how strongly it might be urged that knowing something about books and history and society had nothing necessarily to do with the strength of an analyst's therapeutic impulse or the power of his or her therapeutic acumen.

The second area to which people outside the profession tended to attach themselves had to do with psychoanalysis as a momentous radical intellectual discipline, an instrument of modernity by means of which the world could be reinterpreted, a new and critical perspective on humankind, society, and history. It was a theory (with many subtheories), a means of research, and its applications to matters in fields beyond the immediate clinical purview promised to be rewarding. In this connection, the writings of Freud were of paramount interest and importance. It quickly became clear to those who were able to read that these writings were in the direct mainstream of the central intellectual and cultural tradition of the West. A distinct line was to be drawn from the adjuration of the oracle of Delphi to "Know thyself" to such writers of the Renaissance as Montaigne to the Romantic poets and nineteenth-century novelists to Freud. In his work a particular tradition of introspection came to culmination. The introspection as practiced in this tradition was largely secular, and its goals were those of rational understanding – in particular, a rationally governed understanding of that within us and without which was not rational. In this sense psychoanalysis was a cultural science or discipline of considerable dimensions. To be sure it could readily be vulgarized and misused, but that is the partial fate that any powerful new heuristic instrument has to undergo. Yet here too disquieting signs and tendencies were to be made out. There were, for example, the unmistakable differences between the earlier generations of mostly European analysts and their American pupils and successors; nevertheless, these cultural differences could be in some degree discounted as part of the more general difference, as far as intellectual interests and range were concerned, between Europeans and Americans, especially Europeans born in the last quarter of the nineteenth century and Americans born in the first quarter of the twentieth. Moreover, psychoanalysis as an institutional organization had established itself through a series of isolations. Some of these isolations were necessary; others may have been more questionable. I have already mentioned the location of psycho-analysis within the medical profession. In addition, as psychoanalytic institutes and societies for the training of new analysts continued to grow, there was a tendency for the work in such bodies to be isolated still further from what was going on both scientifically and culturally in the worlds outside. Hence there occurred a further professional isolation of psychoanalysis within the medical profession, as well as beyond it. The long and difficult training of new analysts tended to focus on specific clinical and therapeutic practices, on the development of certain concrete and immediate skills, while questions of wider-ranging research and intellectual interest were by and large deferred or relegated to the periphery, where they were given peripheral attention. Moreover, the institution of Freudian analysis tended to evolve as something of a closed society. Its early history supported such a tendency. Its simultaneous location in and separation from the discipline of medicine stimulated the further development of formidable and at moments forbidding hierarchical modes of organization, dispensations of authority, and allocations of reward and professional recognition. Although such problems are common to almost any professional organization, the tendency towards orthodoxy among psychoanalysts and their organizations was noted overtly, most bitterly perhaps by those who had broken with such groups and set up their own. However hyperbolic certain of these critical claims may have been, there is little question that there was some point to them, and that psychoanalysis was handling the problems of intellectual renewal, growth, and new discovery with less than perfect tact or foresight. A certain confinement of view combined with the social and cultural ambitions of a customarily respectable and uncritical order to produce a general situation that did not bode well for the future.

Finally, psychoanalysis was isolated in yet another way. In establishing itself as it did, it largely cut itself off from the intellectual life of most American universities. This was not a bad thing before World War II, but it was damaging indeed when it continued after 1945. During the years that followed, the center of gravity of American intellectual life shifted, inexorably, we now can see, towards the unversity. Psychoanalysis had put forward or founded few connections between itself and the academic-intellectual world in America. As a cultural science or discipline it seemed very odd indeed that its filiations with departments and faculties in the social sciences, the humanities, and the natural sciences were so few and far between. (Psychoanalysts are, of course, not entirely to blame for this deficiency; they were frequently unwelcome company within certain academic circles. But the question is complex and cannot be fully entered into here.) It is only in relatively recent years that such filiations have begun to play any significant role in many psychoanalytic organizations, and recent years may be a very late time indeed.

This is a very rough, abbreviated, and excessively simplified outline of certain configurations that could be made out about Freudian psychoanalysis as it appeared in the contexts of American society and culture about a generation ago. Its intellectual and social prestige among certain groups of Americans was very high; interest in it as therapy and theory was strong. It had its problems clinically, intellectually, and socially as well. But it seemed secure and, I venture to say, seemed secure to itself.

Today matters appear in a very different light. Psychoanalysis no longer commands the interest that it once did; it has lost as an institution the centrality and authority it could once lay claim to, and has suffered a general loss of self-confidence as well – the last of these may be a useful development. There is some talk in certain quarters about "the death of psychoanalysis" – but such talk, like others before it, is premature. There is also talk in other quarters that psychoanalysis is now in the phase of what Thomas Kuhn has called "normal science" – but that, I believe, is whistling in the dark. Myriad influences and events have worked their consequences, and I can only touch upon a few of them here.

To begin with, the institution has generally gone along with the inflationary character of the economy. Ten, fifteen or twenty-five dollars for a fifty-minute hour in 1950 has become fifty, seventy-five and more for a forty-five minute session. To be sure, money is not the only force at play here, but sooner or later a point of diminishing returns has to be reached. Psychoanalysts have as a rule chosen to live in a certain moderately affluent – and identifiable – style. Their fees are to some extent an expression of this choice. One of the partial results of such a determination is the diminished number of psychoanalytic patients who are embarked upon a full analysis in the older sense of the term. According to a recent survey, analysts reported that only about 20 percent of their time was now spent in classical or full-scale analysis. My impression is that this figure represents a substantial falling off from the situation that obtained for similar analysts in the past. The tendency is apparent: a large part of current analyses are conducted by the profession in order to reproduce itself. Other influences than money are at work in this connection, but we cannot overlook the economics of psychoanalysis within the context of American intellectual culture. It has traditionally been said in criticism of analysis that it could offer or afford too little to too few; today that observation applies more closely and uncomfortably than ever before.

Other circumstances have served less directly to weaken the hold of psychoanalysis in quarters where it once exerted substantial influence. Research in recent decades in the neuro-sciences – in neuro-chemistry and neuro-physiology especially – has, in conjunction with the invention of a whole new range of mood- and mind-altering drugs, led to major changes in the practice of psychiatry and psychotherapy. Freud had in the past made his prediction about "the man with the syringe," and this prediction has at least in part been fulfilled. As a corollary to this development, the movement that is rather loosely called community psychiatry made further inroads in what was for a time the analytic hegemony in the profession of psychiatry. Members of this movement contended among other things that psychoanalysis had got its priorities misordered; this movement aimed in some of its extreme manifestations at some kind of direct social change or action; its interventions were of a very different kind than those ordinarily proposed by psychoanalysts. And in the embroiled social climate of the recent past it came in – as did drug research – for substantial funding. Finally, departments of psychiatry have taken notice of the fact that their best residents tend nowadays not to apply for candidacy in analytic institutes – a distinctively altered state of affairs as compared to a generation ago.

Along with these historical changes there has developed in the inter-years an astonishing variety of new kinds of therapies. I am not referring to changes within psychoanalytically guided therapies – although such changes have also occurred. I am referring to the growth and spread of such practices as behavior-modification therapies and sex therapies, to take up only the most accessible end of a spectrum that ranges from a variety of drug therapies, encounter groups, marathon and weekend catharses to sensitivity training, touching courses and feeling games, primal screaming, aggressiveness-raising, consciousness-lifting, meditations, massages, and who knows what else. Most of these practices are overtly hostile to psychoanalysis, though many of them consist of taking one or two pieces of psychoanalytic discovery, procedure, or insight and transforming it or them into an entire therapeutic regime. From the point of view of psychoanalysis itself, these new formations have to appear as in large measure deformations of the complex theories of personality, development, and therapy that the discipline has built up in its career of three-quarters of a century.

These phenomena do not, I believe, represent the same thing as the divisions, disputes, and deviations that beset the psychoanalytic movement in its early years. It is no criticism of psychoanalysis to remark that it has always been in part something of a religion (albeit a secular one) and has been organized like a church. The early differences and splittings off – by Adler, Jung, Reich *et al.* – represented heresies and the subsequent establishment of new churches or sects. Activities like these are, according to historical sociologists of religion, characteristic of new religions in their formative periods. But many of the recent phenomena I have just referred to resemble cults more than sects or new religions, and cults, as Daniel Bell has recently observed, are ordinarily associated with religions in states of incipient or actual decline. They represent the search for immediate and authentic experience that an institution in deterioration can no longer give, especially when its organizational framework begins to fray and tatter. Cults typically claim that they have access to some special or transfiguring source of power, insight, and knowledge that the orthodoxy and its bureaucratic functionaries have hidden, suppressed, or diverted. They are frequently headed by some spellbinder or pundit who alone has the capacity to transmit the new teachings. They characteristically permit their adherents to act upon impulses that the orthodox institution had constrained, and they therefore offer the experiences of personal transcendence and liberation. They are magical, and they take effect very quickly, as magic commonly does. In turn, their magic also commonly passes away very quickly, and their initiates move on without intermission in search of new redemptions.

But these phenomena are also part of larger movements of cultural change in which psychoanalysis itself is involved. Psychoanalysis was created in particular cultural and historical sets of circumstances and bears upon it the markings of the contexts in which it originated. It came into being in the context of a liberal bourgeois culture and may in some measure be understood as an institution of late high bourgeois culture – in its strengths, weaknesses, and contradictions. (I am being very condensed here.) And what we have been witness to in the last decade and a half is the beginning of the visible and rapid destabilization and dissolution of that culture. In the progressive and rapid discreditation and decline in the legitimacy of the values and beliefs of bourgeois culture, psychoanalysis as part of that culture has inevitably been adversely affected. In this sense the Marxists were right – psychoanalysis is, I think, a bourgeois science.

There is more than adequate irony in this. American culture and society have always been, in contrast with other like entities, in a state of rapid change. Within that context of incessant change, however, psychoanalysis took its roots in America and achieved its largest influence in three overlapping periods of what can be understood as factitious or pseudo-stability. There was first the large influx of European analysts which began in the 1930s amid the false or pseudo-stability of the Great Depression (there was a widespread sense that it might never end); this was followed by the pseudo-stability of World War II, when the nation and culture were united against common enemies; and this in turn was followed by the long post-war years and the pseudo-stability of recovery, steady progress, prosperity, and even the factitious stability of the Cold War (which, it also seemed, might go on indefinitely, if not forever). In the general break-up that has since occurred we can now see how fragile and often misleading the sense of social and cultural stability and continuity within change could sometimes be.

Such larger alterations are usually accompanied by some kind of analogous alterations in personality or deeper cultural style. Although all sorts of people came as patients to the early generations of analysts, they by and large brought with them and were met by certain normative expectations and assumptions about what it meant to be an individual person. The character type referred to in such preconceptions was identifiably part of a general middle-class configuration. It valued and internalized the virtues of work, productivity, and various other kinds of disciplined behavior; it believed in rationality and in rational moral conduct; it tended to suspect pleasure and was uncommonly and ingeniously skilled at postponing gratification; it set great store by linguistic communication, both oral and written; it tended to be guilt-ridden and even in some sense to believe in the rightness and efficacy of that guilt. The neuroses it typically suffered from had to do with certain inhibitions, repressions, denials, and arrestments. The symptoms typically had to do with diminution or loss of functions in sexuality and work. The psychopathologies of these patients were in the main a consequence of certain negative social forces and values as these were transmitted to and imposed upon them through their experiences with their parents, siblings, and other kin. At the same time these persons tended largely to resent, dislike, and discredit their neuroses. They did not feel that such deformations and thwartings were worthy of what a human being should be like. They tended as well to feel that such behaviors and thoughts and fears were not really parts of themselves; often they felt invaded by their afflictions. They tended, in other words, to regard their pathologies as ego-alien. The corollary of this belief was the notion that somewhere inside them was what, for want of another term, must be called a normal human being who had gotten lost. Or, if not lost, then deposed and displaced from his central and controlling position. Their aim in seeking psychological help was to bring this person back to his center and to have him reoccupy the place that was rightfully his.

I do not have to say that this very rough model is not as dominant or prevalent today as it was in the early years of psychoanalysis – although it surely cannot have disappeared altogether. My sense is, however, that a considerable part of the psychopathology that is visible today has as much to do with the decline and weakening of those social and cultural forces whose negative power was instrumental in the formation of the classical neuroses as it does with the persistence of such forces. This is not to say that domination and repression have been simply replaced by anarchy and unmitigated license among our middle classes. It is to say that the psychopathology that seems to prevail today has part of its origins in the decomposition of those structures which made bourgeois culture and family life the complex and often highly unpleasant things they were. What they have been replaced with, we may suspect, is something with its own questionable attributes, and what the relation of psychoanalysis to these developments might be is a subject for further discussion.

I have been suggesting that the fate of psychoanalysis is to a considerable degree entailed in the fate of bourgeois culture. I have implied the stricture that psychoanalysis – particularly in its American developments – accepted its place in that culture without adequate critical regard. I believe this to be largely true. Yet one cannot in all due honesty expect a cultural discipline whose very categories are derived from a specific historical context simply to transcend that context and leave its historical origins altogether behind. That, it seems to me, is one of the dilemmas that psychoanalysis is confronted with today – as it is a dilemma of all of us who share a historical identity that we cannot put aside but that is becoming in the light of current developments increasingly problematical.

Index

aesthetic movements 206
aggression 172, 177-8
anal eroticism 109, 142
Andreas-Salome, Lou 215
Anna O. 189
anxiety 10, 103, 175-6, 178, 238-9
Arnold, Matthew 197-9

Balmary, Marie: *Psychoanalysis Psychoanalysed: Freud and the Hidden Fault of the Father* 252-5
Bentham, Jeremy 195
biography/biographers 3-4, 209, 210-12, 228-9, 249
bisexuality 28, 36
Breuer, Josef 12, 189
Brunswick, Ruth Mack 213-14

Carlyle, Thomas 193-5, 196, 197, 200
case histories 2-3, 42, 50, 62-5, 82n., 83n., 88-9, 95-6, 113, 167, 254; *see also* Dora, case of and Rat Man, case of
castration fears 174, 176
Chapman, A. H. 230
character 110, 263; c. disorder, 186; c.-traits, 107-8, 130; nineteenth century middle-class c. type, 191-3
childhood: aggression 110-11; anal-sadistic phase, 101; experiences of, 100, 108, 189; fecal incontinence, 108-9; relationship with parents, 172-3; *see also* sexuality, childhood
Church of Jesus Christ of Latter-Day Saints 231
chutzpah 76-8, 216
Clark, Raymond: *Freud: The Man and the Cause* 249-52
cleanliness 109
conscience 168, 171
conscious/unconscious 125-6, 133, 134, 166, 169, 189, 190
culture 170, 208, 219, 226; cultural change, 3, 20n., 165, 176, 262; in later nineteenth century, 9, 113, 190, 191-3, 201; sexual life and, 177

Darwin, Charles 24-6, 166
defecation 108-9, 110
determinate analysis 191
Deutsch, Helene 215
Dickens, Charles 140, 155
Dora, case of 3, 22, 42, 87, 88, 94, 122, 123, 145, 152; breaks off treatment 49, 78, 80-1; causes of illnesses, 45; change in character, 47; childhood complaints, 44; course of analysis, 48-9; crises, 46, 65-6; 'displacement upwards', 66-7; D's father, 42-3, 44, 46, 47, 69, 80, 82n., D's mother, 43, 44; dreams, 49, 62-3, 64, 69, 70-1, 74, 77-8; female sexuality in, 65-8, 72, 81; form of case history, 53-7, 62-5, 81; Frau K. and

45, 47, 69, 80; Freud as central character 76, Freud's feeling about, 81; Freud's final remarks to D., 78-9; Freud writes case history, 50-3; governesses and, 47-8; Herr K. and, 45, 46, 47, 48, 66, 67, 78, 80; history of D., 42-8; later life of D. 85n., masturbation 77; "Prefatory Remarks". 52, 57-9; reality and, 75-6, 79-80; reproachfulness of D., 69, 81; roles played by Freud 65, 71, 75; "The Clinical Picture", 52, 58, 60; time strata of history, 64
Dostoevsky, Feodor 133, 134, 140, 146
dreams 17, 49, 59, 62-3, 64, 69, 70-1, 74, 77-8

ego 98, 99-100, 103, 148, 152, 168-9; aggression and, 177-8; conscience, 168, 171; e. ideal, 168, 169-70, 172, 184-5; e. identity, 184-5; functions of e. 172; id and e. 169; introjection, 169; splitting of, 126, 134; super-ego and, 171, 172, 178
Eissler, K. R.: *Talent and Genius*, 216
Ellis, Havelock 4, 26, 219, 221-2, 225-6; cultural radical, 221-2; early life, 219-21; relationship with Edith Lees, 222-3; relationship with Olive Schreiner, 222; *Sexual Inversion*, 224; sexuality of, 222; studies homosexuality, 223-5; *Studies in the Psychology of Sex*, 219, 224-6; studies masturbation, 225
Erikson, Erik 180, 184; character disorder, 186; *Childhood and Society*, 184, 186; 'identity', 180, 184, 186; *Identity: Youth and Crisis*, 185; strengths of, 185-6; *Young Man Luther*, 184, 186

family, the 189
father-complex 89, 128, 129, 131
fathers 113, 187-8
Ferenczi, S. 213
Fliess, Wilhelm 2, 6, 12-14, 77, 85, 98; Freud's letters to, 7, 8, 9, 14-15, 50
free association 113, 240
French Revolution 197
Freud, Anna 213
Freud, Ernst 16
Freud, Jacob 251-3
Freud, Sigmund 1-2, 17-19, 20n., 38-9, 143-4, 189-90, 246, 258; analyses his daughter, 213, 216; anxiety and, 10, 103, 175-6; archaeology and, 166; Arnold Zweig and 209, 211; biography and, 3-4, 209, 210-12, 229, 249; case histories, 2-3, 42, 50, 62-5, 88-9, 95-6, 113, 167, 254; *chutzpah* and, 76-8; correspondence of, 212-13, 229; creative process, 95; development of ideas, 10-12, 14-19, 167; development of psychology, 12, 17-18, 75; D. H. Lawrence and, 158-63; early work, 7-8; family of, 251, 252-3; as a father figure,